Reflections on the Constitution

REFLECTIONS ON THE CONSTITUTION

THE AMERICAN CONSTITUTION AFTER TWO HUNDRED YEARS

edited by
RICHARD MAIDMENT *and* JOHN ZVESPER

Manchester University Press

Manchester and New York

distributed exclusively in the USA and Canada by St. Martin's Press

Published by Manchester University Press
Oxford Road, Manchester M13 9PL, UK
and Room 400, 175 Fifth Avenue, New York, NY 10010, USA

Distributed exclusively in the USA and Canada
by St. Martin's Press, Inc.,
175 Fifth Avenue, New York, NY 10010, USA

British Library cataloguing in publication data
Reflections on the constitution: the American Constitution after two hundred years.
1. United States. Constitution
I. Maidment, R A (Richard Anthony), *1944–*   II. Zvesper, John
347.302'2

Library of Congress cataloging in publication data
Reflections on the constitution: the American constitution after two hundred years / edited by Richard Maidment and John Zvesper.
p. cm.
Contents: The intellectual reference of the American constitution / Robert Garson – Redefining Federation / Richard Hodder-Williams – Congress and the constitution / James A. Thurber – Presidential autonomy in a fragmented polity / David McKay – The least dangerous branch no longer / Richard Maidment – Madison v. Madison / Douglas W. Jaenicke – Political parties and constitutional government / John Zvesper – Foreign policy and the constitution / Anthony G. McGrew – Obituary for the 'living' constitution? / Robert McKeever.
ISBN 0-7190-2818-3.
1. United States – Constitutional history.   I. Maidment, R. A. (Richard A.)
II. Zvesper, John, 1948–
KF4541.A2R44 1989
342.73'029 – dc 19
[347.30229]   88-13746

ISBN 0-7190-2818-3 *hardback*

Printed in Great Britain
by Billings of Worcester

CONTENTS

List of Contributors   vii

Preface   ix

1 **The Intellectual Reference of the American Constitution**   1

ROBERT GARSON, *University of Keele*

2 **Redefining Federalism: The Primacy of Politics over the Constitution**   22

RICHARD HODDER-WILLIAMS, *University of Bristol*

3 **Congress and the Constitution: Two Hundred Years of Stability and Change**   51

JAMES A. THURBER, *The American University*

4 **Presidential Autonomy in a Fragmented Polity**   76

DAVID McKAY, *University of Essex*

5 **The Least Dangerous Branch no longer: A Reflection on the United States Supreme Court**   97

RICHARD MAIDMENT, *The Open University*

6 **Madison v. Madison: The Party Essays v. 'The Federalist Papers'**   116

DOUGLAS W. JAENICKE, *University of Manchester*

7 **American Political Parties and Constitutional Government**   148

JOHN ZVESPER, *University of East Anglia*

8 **Foreign Policy and the Constitution: 'Invitation to a Perpetual Institutional Struggle'?**   172

ANTHONY G. McGREW, *The Open University*

9 **Obituary for the 'Living' Constitution? Policy Making and the Constitutional Framework Two Hundred Years On**   198

ROBERT J. McKEEVER, *University of Reading*

CONTRIBUTORS

RICHARD MAIDMENT Richard Maidment is author of *Politics and Democracy in the United States* and co-author of *American Politics Today* and *The American Political Process*. He is Lecturer in Politics at the Open University.

JOHN ZVESPER John Zvesper is author of *Political Philosophy and Rhetoric: A Study of the Origins of American Party Politics* and has contributed to numerous learned journals. He is Lecturer in Politics at the University of East Anglia.

ROBERT GARSON Robert Garson is Lecturer in American History at the University of Keele.

RICHARD HODDER-WILLIAMS Richard Hodder-Williams is Reader in Politics at the University of Bristol.

DOUGLAS W. JAENICKE Douglas W. Jaenicke is Lecturer in Government at the University of Manchester.

ANTHONY G. McGREW Anthony G. McGrew is Lecturer in Government at the Open University.

DAVID McKAY David McKay is Reader in Government at the University of Essex. He is the author of *Politics and Power in the U.S.A.*, *American Politics and Society* (2nd edition, 1989) and *Domestic Policy and Ideology: Presidents and the American State*.

ROBERT J. McKEEVER Robert J. McKeever is Lecturer in Politics at the University of Reading.

JAMES A. THURBER James A. Thurber is Professor of Government and Director of the Center for Congressional and Presidential Studies at the American University, Washington D.C.

PREFACE

In 1989 the Constitution of the United States will have been in operation for two hundred years. The purpose of this book is to provide readers with both a reasonably comprehensive picture of the American constitutional system at its bicentenary and some perspectives on how that picture has developed over two hundred years. We come neither to bury the Constitution nor to praise it, but to think about it – to encourage not a bicentennial celebration but (as one scholar has put it) a bicentennial cerebration. Therefore we have been less interested in 'covering' all the textbook topics on American political culture, institutions and policies, than in collecting thoughtful essays on some of those topics, which together help readers reflect on the character and the plight of the Constitution.

The reason for encouraging such reflection is practical as well as theoretical. During the last five decades, and particularly during the last twenty-five years, the American constitutional system has confronted a number of difficulties and exhibited a number of shortcomings, giving rise to widespread concern over the efficacy of the institutions of the federal government, the political parties and the policy-making process. Consequently, in whichever quarter one looks today, one can count on finding more ambivalence about the Constitution's virtues than one could see in William Gladstone's famous remark, made during the Constitution's centenary, that the Constitution is 'the most wonderful work ever struck off at a given time by the brain and purpose of man'. The confusion if not the disappearance of the federal division of powers, the fragmentation and ombudsmanisation of Congress, the institutional isolation of the Presidency, the increasing political prominence of the courts and the bureaucracy, the continuing decline of political parties, and the rise of interest group politics to an awesome level – all of these sometimes worrying developments have become hallmarks of the 'new American political system' that has emerged in the last twenty-five years. One of the most important questions that can be raised about American politics today is whether these dysfunctions (in so far as that is what they really are) can be attributed to the constitutional system itself – which therefore needs to be (not to say can be) radically amended and reformed, or whether that system is fundamentally sound and simply needs somehow to be reinvigorated and otherwise adapted to the social and technological circumstances in which it necessarily now operates. Responding to that question – even posing it in an intelligent manner – requires reflections like those that follow.

Richard Maidment
John Zvesper

1   ROBERT GARSON

The Intellectual Reference of the American Constitution

ABSTRACT

The American Constitution did not just delineate the fundamental law of the new nation; it also sought to lay guidelines for future generations. The founding fathers believed that the Constitution would only survive if it created a sense of nationality and combined it with a political ethos that encouraged ambition and industriousness. As governments could be no better than the men they governed, they had to reflect the best in their citizenry. It was believed that the Constitution could extract creativity and endeavour from Americans. By and large the Founding Fathers accepted the premises of John Locke who had argued that governments could command loyalty and compel obedience if those governments protected the values, often acquisitive ones, of their subjects. The federal Constitution combined the democratic ideals of the Revolutionary generation with the ruling elite's desire for permanence and discipline. Thus the system of checks and balances, the hallmark of the Constitution, was the means by which popular consent was encouraged and then filtered. Late-eighteenth-century thinkers were equally conversant with the ideas of the Scottish Enlightenment which taught that man was driven by passion and instinct. There was no point in changing men's selfish interests; it was better to co-opt the constructive aspects of those drives and process them for the good of society. Selfishness had its benefits, particularly economic ones. The differences of opinion that arose from men's ambitions were to be harnessed to produce energetic government and a productive economy. Thus the mixed government created under the federal Constitution was seen as a true reflection of human nature and would be obeyed for that reason.

The American Constitution was drawn up after six years of warfare with Britain and a further six years of political uncertainty. Its prime task was to forge a sense of nationhood and to foster confidence in the durability of the republic. The founders of the new nation believed they could only succeed if they recognised the existing interests, customs and aspirations of the individuals who inhabited America. The delegates who deliberated in Philadelphia in 1787 for four months on the form of the new constitution were conscious of their roles as national founders. They were presented with a unique opportunity. A new grand design would consolidate the revolutionary achievement and would also create that sense of hope, energy and anticipation that are the stuff of infant nationhood. While the immediate brief of the Founding Fathers was to write a constitution that would establish the nation's fundamental law, they also addressed themselves to the question of the quality and aspiration of the emerging nation. In many ways, the Constitution was a social blueprint. Its framers inherited the belief, so prevalent in the eighteenth century, that political systems played a decisive role in shaping the values of the societies they governed. Government existed not just to orchestrate political and social forces but to create a citizenry that was just, virtuous and morally uplifting. But the founders faced a problematic task. Most of them held that men were selfish and ambitious and that they seldom saw beyond their own horizons. But they also believed, or at least wanted to believe, that political systems could somehow guide human behaviour. Just how they intended to direct that behaviour will be the subject of this chapter.

Although the delegates in Philadelphia differed on sectional and economic issues, they shared at least one common political belief. They, or their political allies, had fought for independence from Britain, because it had flouted fundamental rights that transcended the immediate irritants of taxation, military billeting and restrictive trading. Britain was a corrupt tyranny and Americans needed to begin afresh. The new society, they believed, in part owed its existence to various philosophical premises that had carried the enthusiasm of the rebels in their war against Britain. Government was not just an instrument for ruling or disciplining a people. It had to conform to and reflect fundamental ethical and political standards. If it was not virtuous, if it did not respect and guard the basic rights of its citizenry, it had no legitimacy and forfeited the claim to obedience. Thus, however divided the delegates were on procedural matters, they were united in their desire to base the new system on a philosophical consensus.

The federal Constitution created a republic. To a man, its supporters considered themselves first and foremost republican. While some of them liked to accuse their political opponents of disloyalty to this principle, they believed that the final construction adhered to the republican ideal. The concept of republicanism dated back to classical Greek thought. Since then it had gone through various redefinitions and refinements. In late-eighteenth-century America it represented a widely understood cluster of ideas that the proposed new constitution needed to assimilate. A republic was not simply a state without monarchy, although kingship found no friends. It existed when a state was held together by an independent citizenry, united in its mission to protect civic virtue against a corrupt executive. Its leadership was skilled and trained in statecraft. This *esprit de corps*, in the version that would appear in late-eighteenth-century America, would be furthered by a sense of common economic destiny. By and large the new nation's political leaders believed a broad, but not necessarily equal, distribution of private property would create a correspondingly broad constellation of vested interests that nurtured that vital unity. The ownership of property would encourage civic participation, and civic participation would enhance political cohesion and militate against tyranny. Alexander Hamilton, for example, believed that the structure of government in the new nation had a vital role to play in the maintenance of that public spirit. Unlike Jean-Jacques Rousseau, the French political philosopher who equated virtue with poverty and selflessness, Hamilton asserted that material enrichment would create the conditions necessary for a public-spirited and motivated citizenry. The American republic was not to be an ascetic one. A republican government could only survive if the mechanisms and procedures of that government reflected the interests and aspirations of the various social and economic groupings in the state.[1] By and large the framers agreed that government had to mirror society before it could direct it. Their disagreement revolved around whether the particular powers allotted to the various departments and branches of government resulted in a distortion of that mirroring.

The federal Constitution was drawn up to impose political discipline upon a nation that was contemptuous of its central

government and teetered dangerously in its local politics. The
Revolution had shown slight regard for political authority. But
nationhood could not grow without an identifiable focus, a central
structure with clearly enumerated powers. The Founding Fathers
sought to create a political system that freed man to pursue his quest
for wealth and spiritual enrichment. But a careful balancing act was
required. Liberation for individual fulfilment and discipline for the
development of a sense of national purpose are divergent goals. They
endeavoured to establish a system of law-making that would at once
make the United States' citizens autonomous and maintain that
sense of cohesion that is so necessary for the development of
nationhood. The creation of rigorous procedures in law-making and
the encouragement of individual liberty were seen to be mutually
dependent. John Adams, in his *Defence of the Constitutions*, echoed
the general consensus that there was no conflict between liberty and
authority. 'There can be no uninterrupted enjoyment of liberty, nor
any good government in society without laws, or where standing
laws do not govern.' Individual ambition could not survive without
the protection of authority. 'The individual enjoys continually the
benefit of law,' continued Adams, 'as he does those of light and air
... If the laws were repealed all at once in any great kingdom and the
event made known suddenly to all, there would scarcely a house
remain in possession of its present inhabitant.'[2] A government had
to be devised that would ensure that law-making was careful,
deliberate and in the common interest. Above all, laws would have
to last. 'Subject that law to frequent change,' said Alexander
Hamilton, 'and the very notions of what is right and reasonable will
change frequently. So undermine respect for that law and respect
for *all* forms of authority will crumble beside it.'[3] Thus while
government was a grant made by the people in liberty, it only
possessed efficacy if it channelled that liberty and prevented social
disintegration.

The American Constitution emerged as a result of a particular
historical situation. The immediate brief of the delegates in
Philadelphia was to inject new vigour into the political system. State
governments had violated the Articles of Confederation by ignoring
the nation's treaties with other countries, by building independent
navies, and by failing to meet congressional requisitions. There were
practical problems of finance. Under the Articles the central government was almost totally dependent on the states for its income.

Yet Americans had little faith in the view that national government could work to their advantage. In creating the central government in 1781 they were more concerned with keeping it under control than with permitting it to get on with the job. State governments were believed to be closer to home and closer to the people. So the Founding Fathers had to accommodate and to some extent overcome this localism. But while such practical matters were always at the forefront of their minds, they held that a new constitution would have repercussions on political ideology. They believed that the social and moral qualities of the citizens of society was in part determined by its political procedures. Men were as good (or as bad) as their governments permitted. The debates and the polemics on the Constitution revealed a special preoccupation with the attempt to harness government to man's own ambitions and moral values. The Constitution is contextual. Like any political blueprint it reveals the underlying social, psychological and moral assumptions of the day. In the extended debates in Philadelphia the delegates constantly justified their particular advocacies by reference to their own reading of man's inner nature. Thus a recovery of the framer's diagnosis of man's condition provides a vital insight into the assumptions and strategies of the Constitution.

Opponents and proponents of the Constitution believed that government was a trust conferred by the people. The colonists had rebelled against Britain and had overthrown the Crown because that trust had been broken. In all polities there existed a contract between rulers and ruled. As the boundaries of authority changed in the 1770s and 1780s Americans particularly needed this contractual analogy to explain these rapidly changing circumstances. The flurry of constitution making in the Revolutionary period was a self-conscious exercise in the drawing up of such contracts. A constitution represented a superior law set above the entire governmental structure. The idea of a written constitution as a distinctive set of guarantees had become something of a form of legal idolatry in America. The writings of the most eminent commentator on the English constitution, William Blackstone, did not apply so neatly to the American system. Blackstone had argued that the constitution of England was indistinguishable from the array of laws that already existed. Each act of Parliament formed part of the constitution and created the truism that it was constitutional. Not so, said the Americans; a constitution had to be created in a separate exercise, originating in the people and standing above the system of law.[4] A written constitution provided supra-level guarantees against arbitrary actions from the law-makers, who could not always be trusted.

The new federal Constitution, therefore, was more than just a remedy for the political weaknesses of Confederation America. It proposed to give the new nation a fresh start. It confronted certain practical problems but sought also to lead the United States in a particular direction. Like any parent, the Founding Fathers believed that given the right beginning the fledgling nation would resist its destructive tendencies and mature into a stable and prosperous state. While they were not directly guided in their prescriptions by political and social theorists, they did employ theoretical axioms to justify positions that were taken for quite untheoretical reasons. They drew upon a variety of ideas and published sources that had permeated the political culture and provided a central reference of political thinking in the late eighteenth century. While it would be a mistake to view the framers as committed and active disciples of, say, John Locke or David Hume, they did absorb the pervasive *Weltanschaung* of the English and Scottish Enlightenment. Their deliberations reflected the values and conventions of intellectual life in the eighteenth century. Their notions of justice and the good life provided a necessary and constant filter in the apparatus of state that they eventually created. Just what the framers recovered from the Enlightenment and how they recovered it needs closer scrutiny.

The Founding Fathers were practical men who sought practical solutions to the problems of the fledgling nation. While the final outcome of the Constitution was something of a patchwork, the delegates in Philadelphia were conscious of the fact that they were designing a government that would be staffed by men of varying persuasions and temperaments. So the new government would need to embody some fundamental ideals that would be acceptable to everybody. James Madison may have overestimated their altruism, but he was not wide off the mark when he commented that the delegates were 'devoted to the object committed to them' and that they tried 'best [to] secure the permanent liberty and happiness of their country'.[5] Many historians have claimed that they sought only to defend their selfish economic interests or to soothe particular geographical or class sensitivities.[6] But this interpretation ignores a crucial reference. The debates would have made little sense without some evaluation of man's driving forces and the effect that those forces had on the shape of economic and civic life in general. While one would look in vain for a treatise on government in the Constitution, its principal defenders constantly referred to the spectrum of psychological, economic and political ideas that converged in their deliberations.

The fundamental brief was to reconcile the need for effective government with a professed belief in the full sovereignty of the people. After the Revolution Americans had become accustomed to a political order that was characterised by an unusually high degree of public involvement. The Massachusetts constitution of 1780, for example, had been drawn up by a convention elected by broad suffrage in town meetings. It had to submit for public scrutiny the draft terms of the constitution for article-by-article review. This insistence on a high degree of popular participation in government originated in the conviction that political legitimacy ultimately stemmed from popular consent. While popular judgement was not always wise or well considered, governments immunised themselves from it only at their peril. In this respect the ideas of John Locke, author of the influential and widely circulated *Two Treatises of Government* played an important role. While the text was a century old, it remained the most coherent and accessible statement of government by consent.[7]

According to Locke all men were born with reason, the ability to calculate and draw proper inferences. The Lockean individual thinks his own thoughts and can withstand the pressures of authority. His reason leads him to understand that he has certain interests and rights that are inherent and integral to his being. It is his prerogative to enforce and defend those inalienable rights. But enforcement is problematic. It is time-consuming and conducive to conflict with men who think otherwise. The individual, according to Locke, thus transfers the power to defend his individual rights to a community or civil society. Once free individuals are subject to a new juris-diction, government is created to exercise that jurisdiction. As the agent of law enforcement, government's legitimacy ultimately rests upon the decision of the majority to entrust it with that power. Thus legitimate claims to rule stem from a particular historical act of political creation. And man's reason leads him to that course and to no other.

Government, then, is an institution born of man's reason.

Sovereignty is transferred from the individual to government, but only at his pleasure. But Locke's insistence on the ultimate supremacy of the individual did not mean that he gave that individual the opportunity to change or overthrow government at whim. Locke recognised the crucial role played by political authority in the provision of stability. If governments are created by consent, then there is an obligation to obey them. 'Thus every Man,' wrote Locke, 'by consenting with others to make one Body Politick under one Government, puts himself under an Obligation to every one of that Society, to submit to the determination of the *majority*, and to be concluded by it.'[8] The framers of the Constitution agreed. They wished to reconcile the revolutionary impulse which America had recently experienced with the necessity of stable government, capable of raising a revenue, enforcing the law and defending its territory. The political ideas of Locke provided a theoretical justification for the consolidation of power. Most delegates did not want to see the new nation undermined by whim or by parochial interest. A rationale, philosophical and political, had to be found for forcing Americans to accept laws that might not be popular but were still in the interests of political harmony and survival. Locke's theory of consent provides just such a discipline. It is a means of reconciling free will and having an obligation to obey. The most important function of consent is to moralise the act of obedience to law. We obey laws, said Locke, not because obedience is morally right but because it is 'intrinsically morally right to do what one has consented to do'.[9] Locke thus found a means of reconciling the liberals' preoccupation with freedom and lack of coercion to the reality of government that necessarily has to play a coercive role. In a diverse and pluralist society men have to agree on their differences, or even if they cannot agree, accept imposed solutions.

The Constitution was designed to reflect this tenet of the Lockean credo. It sought to create a political order that reflected the broad spectrum of public opinion. This would be achieved by the method of election, direct and indirect. At the same time it had to be efficient, stable and subject to continuity. Thus its mercurial tendencies would have to be eliminated and a sense of obedience and respect nurtured. The Founding Fathers were men of means and men of the world. Almost to a man they subscribed to the idea of social hierarchy and expected men to accept the rules of an established political order. They felt that the Revolution had substituted unfamiliar and unpredictable regimes for British tyranny. State governments had fallen into the hands of those 'whose ability or situation in Life does not intitle them to it'. Policies should not be mutable, for, as Madison pointed out, mutability 'poisons the blessings of liberty itself'. No matter how popular laws are, said Madison, they would be of no avail 'if they be repealed or revised before they are promulgated, or undergo such incessant changes that no man, who knows what the law is today, can guess what it will be tomorrow'. There had to be reverence, but no such reverence would be given 'towards a political system which betrays so many marks of infirmity, and disappoints so many of their flattering hopes'.[10] So the Constitution sought to combine the democratic ideals of the Revolution with the social elite's desire for discipline and permanence. Again, the ideas of Locke provided a philosophical yardstick. Locke had insisted that majority representation in the legislature was the safest way of ensuring justice. But that majority had to be in the position to exercise authority. That authority had to rest on consent, but consent did not necessarily entail frequent elections or the possibility of sudden recall. Majorities, speaking through the legislature, had to exercise restraint themselves in the quest for political stability. The legislature, said Locke, 'cannot assume to its self a power to Rule by extemporary Arbitrary Decrees, but is bound to dispense Justice, and decide the Rights of the Subject by promulgated standing Laws, and Known Authoris'd Judges'. In short, there were some provinces and rights that were beyond the purview of legislative jurisdiction. Private property, for instance, required special respect. In Locke's words, 'if any one shall claim a Power to lay and levy Taxes on the People, by his own Authority, and without such consent of the People, he thereby invades the Fundamental Law of Property, and subverts the end of Government'.[11]

Just how the designers of the Constitution sought to harness majority will with authority will be examined below. Before discussing their solutions, however, it is necessary to trace the reference of their suspicion of majoritarian rule through the legislature. The debates in the Constitutional Convention and subsequent defences of the Constitution reiterated the fear that men could not always be trusted. As John Diggins has remarked, 'much of the reasoning behind the constitution is steeped in the psychology of temptation and the politics of suspicion'.[12] The system of checks and balances, the convoluted remoteness of the electoral college, and the indirect election of the Senate, all served to diminish the immediate control of the majority. Although authority ultimately derived from the people, the framers believed that the masses were too ignorant, too divided and too selfish to promote the national interest without intervention from other sources. The people at large did not possess natural virtue, even though they were the fountain of authority. Noah Webster, a staunch Federalist, reminded his readers that majorities are simply agents of consent. 'Public bodies, as well as individuals, are liable to the influence of sudden and violent passions, under the operation of which the voice of reason is silenced.' He welcomed the division of the legislature into two separate bodies as 'a necessary step to prevent the disorders which arise from the pride, irritability and stubborness of mankind'.[13]

Again, this guarded view of human nature was a deeply embedded belief in post-Revolutionary America. Recent scholarship has shown the debt owed by the Constitution's principal publicists, Alexander Hamilton and James Madison, to David Hume and the Scottish Enlightenment. In the middle of the eighteenth century Scotland produced a constellation of thinkers whose fame and originality could not be equalled in Europe. It revolutionised the field of political economy, and leading American educators, many of whose students were to play a formative role in the making of the Constitution, were trained there. Donald Robert, Madison's tutor for five years, was just such a product of the Scottish Enlightenment. Educated at Edinburgh and Aberdeen, he came to America and gave Madison his intellectual grounding. At Princeton University, which Madison and eight other members of the Constitutional Convention of 1787 attended, the thinkers of the Scottish Enlightenment formed the core of the moral philosophy course. The works of Francis Hutcheson, David Hume, Lord Kames, Adam Smith and Adam Ferguson informed students' thinking in history, economics, politics and psychology. In Madison's recommendations to the Confederate Congress to draw up a list for the Congressional library, the Scottish Enlightenment figured prominently. To quote Garry Wills, 'his very thinking had a Scottish accent from the start'.[14]

Probably the most profound influence was wielded by David Hume, at least in the realm of moral philosophy. The Constitution was based, as has been seen, on a theory of human behaviour that stressed man's ambitious, passionate nature. David Hume argued that there was a science of the mind and that it could be deduced from careful observation of men. Such observation showed that men's judgements were formed as much by imagination and instinct as they were by reason. Our beliefs, said Hume, cannot be justified rationally but only by an examination of human nature. We do not decide matters in an arbitrary way. Moral judgements and behaviour lend themselves to improvement, but that improvement depends upon our learning experience and the degree of personal satisfaction that emerges from revised judgements.[15] In the realm of political behaviour, said Hume, it is man's passions, ambitions and personal loyalties that motivate him. 'Reason alone can never produce any action or give rise to volition ... Reason is, and ought only to be, the slave of the passions and can never pretend to any other office than to serve and obey them.' A system of justice, which is the primary brief of government, is nothing more than a system of organising and channelling men's selfish traits. 'It is only from the selfishness and confined generosity of man, along with the scanty provision nature has made for his wants, that justice derives its origin.' Government exists, then, not to protect God-given rights but to impose discipline on man's varied and ambitious drives. Government is little more than the formal harnessing of selfish drives to a socially acceptable framework. 'Justice,' claimed Hume, 'derives its origin from human conventions ... The same self-love, therefore, which renders men so incommodious to each other, taking a new and more convenient direction, produces the rules of justice.'[16]

The framers, by and large, shared Hume's scepticism. The debates in Philadelphia revealed a healthy awareness of the role of self-interest in the style and structure of government. And it is this awareness that is the central axis of *The Federalist* written by Hamilton, Madison and John Jay, to persuade Americans that the federal Constitution offered the best prospect for stability and prosperity. *The Federalist*, a collection of eighty-five public letters under the pseudonym 'Publius' was an attempt to present a united defence of the efficacy of the Constitution by some of America's leading political figures. Although most (fifty-one) of the essays were written by Hamilton, there is a unity of theme that runs through it. This is scarcely surprising, as *The Federalist* sought to be a composite undertaking. It constituted a special collaboration and, while its authors later distanced themselves from their own advocacy, it serves as a unique explication of how the framers themselves could accept some of the provisos and compromises of the final draft.[17]

The Federalist and the debates in Philadelphia revealed a general acceptance of the view that men have selfish ambitions. It is fruitless for the state, its authors insisted, to try and create unanimity of opinion. Even the political mechanisms that sought to identify and establish a sense of national interest could not ultimately transcend the personal interests of the people who comprise the state. Speaking as a delegate from New York, Hamilton declared: 'Our prevailing passions are ambition and interest; and it will ever be the duty of a wise government to avail itself of the passions, in order to make them subservient to the public good'.[18] Thus the reconciliation of liberty and authority could be achieved by converting selfish parochial interests into a national asset. While revolutionary republicanism envisaged a sense of civic altruism, the republicanism of the Founding Fathers assumed that people have special interests and that these interests were not harmful if they were carefully monitored and balanced. Authority consisted of identifying those interests and processing them in such a way that just government resulted. It was fruitless to expect unity. Madison wrote to Jefferson in 1787 that 'those who contend for a simple Democracy, or a pure republic, actuated by the sense of the majority, and operating within narrow limits, assume or suppose a case which is altogether fictitious'. Men differ, and a simple formula for masking those differences will be counterproductive. The achievement of both Madison and Hamilton lay in their ability to turn to advantage prevailing factions and interest groups. As will be seen in the discussion of property rights, divergence was to be encouraged not only because it affirmed man's real nature but because it fostered social and economic institutions that would benefit the new nation. 'In all civilized societies,' continued Madison, 'distinctions are various and unavoidable. A distinction of property results from that very protection which a free Government gives to unequal faculties of acquiring it.'[19] In short, not only were selfish interests unerasable; they produced economic benefits, particularly property and the energy that stems from the acquisitiveness engendered by property.

The framers' principal brief, then, was to stem the corrosive effect of self-interest and convert it into a creative phenomenon. Differences of opinion and interest could be constructive; they did not necessarily doom the process of nation-building. James Madison, in his celebrated tenth *Federalist*, remarked that 'so strong is this propensity of mankind to fall into mutual animosities that where no substantial occasion presents itself the most frivolous and fanciful distinctions have been sufficient to kindle their unfriendly passions and excite their most violent conflicts'. He recognised that most organised interest groups revolved around the 'verious and unequal distribution of property'.[20] As will be seen, Madison had no wish to see any dramatic change in the distribution of property; if there was to be some redistribution it would come about by market forces, forces that were to be encouraged by the new constitution. What Madison did hope to achieve was a cementing of man's driving forces with the new mechanisms of government. 'What is government itself,' he asked, 'but the greatest of all reflections on human nature?' The formula for harnessing and co-ordinating man's selfish competitive nature was, of course, the system of checks and balances. He stated: 'You must first enable the government to control the governed; and in the next place oblige it to control itself'.[21]

The debates over the powers of the executive, legislative and judicial branches have been studied by scholars over two centuries. It is not my intention to go over such familiar ground in this short essay. What I do wish to emphasise is that in creating such provisions as a divided legislature, an executive with limited powers and varying modes of election, the architects of the Constitution believed that they had not only found a compromise that would satisfy the various economic and geographic interests in America, but also that they had created a government that genuinely reflected the nature of man as they perceived him and as they wanted him to develop. The Founding Fathers believed that passion, self-interest and ambition, if properly channelled, could provide the new nation with a creative energy unsurpassed anywhere in the world.

The solution, as is well known, was to create a political system that tolerated democracy and popular participation at the state level and in the lower house of the legislature. Representatives were to be elected every two years, but their powers would be checked by other branches and by alternative systems of election and appointment. The federal government would act as a kind of a sieve to make sure that only the safest ideas would surface in the political process. The Constitution did not relocate sovereignty: that still lay with the people. Locke's principles were reaffirmed. Rulers and people were not contending interests; government was the shield for liberty. Gordon Wood has shown that even appointive or indirectly elected offices were still viewed as hailing from the people. Every branch of government was presented as an agent of the people's will.[22] Government could command obedience as its ultimate authority still derived from the consent of the many. Even the Senate, which represented the sovereignty of the states in the first instance, owed its ultimate authority to the voters.

Bicameralism, the division of the legislature into two separate houses, provides a useful insight into the Founding Fathers' desire to exact obedience and to disguise that obedience in the wrapping of consent. Single houses, popularly elected, were regarded as the apotheosis of consent. But single houses were fickle and unstable, lending themselves to manipulation by the ambitious and enterprising men who could control elections. They might be sensitive to and conversant with opinion in the constituencies, but they would lack wisdom, foresight and a sense of national purpose. More rigorous qualifications in the form of eligibility requirements and the prospect of longer terms of office would make senatorial lawmakers less impulsive and more forward-looking. Direct representation would preserve such primary democratic concerns as the initiation of money bills. Indirect representation would provide the wisdom that was necessary in the more deliberative upper house. As Edmund Randolph, who introduced the Virginia Plan, declared, the Senate would be 'exempt from the passionate proceedings to which numerous assemblies are liable'.[23] The Senate, it was believed, unified self-interest and the common good. By keeping membership small, the prestige of an individual member would be enhanced. This would deepen his loyalty to the institution and contribute to a sense of *esprit de corps*. As Paul Eidelberg has remarked, 'the political character of the Senate is thus to compensate for defects in the personal character of men'. Hamilton hoped that the Senate would be dominated by the learned professions and that its members would have a distinct interest in society. Senators would be the very best men in government. Their civic excellence would be widely perceived and would command special admiration. Indeed, Hamilton advocated life membership of the Senate, a term of office, he believed, that would win popular approval. Madison disagreed with the idea of tenure for life, but reserved his greatest faith for the upper chamber. Government did not exist merely to further local interests. It had to discipline parochial ambition, but not to the point of extinction.[24] The Senate was an arbiter between passion and reason. Because Senators would not represent a particular social interest, as did the English House of Lords, it would command popular support. Consent did not have to be direct. We obey only because we recognise that general stability benefits everybody. Madison in *Federalist* no. 62 warned that 'no government, any more than an individual, will long be respected without being truly respectable'.[25]

In short, mixed government was established to encourage political competition and so increase the likelihood of obedience to the laws. If separate interests were represented, if there were recognisable loci of popular will, authority and wisdom, then the citizens of the new nation would feel that no laws would be passed that were contrary to the national interest. The Constitution sought to unleash a political energy through regular elections and the competitiveness that arose from the divided powers of the three branches of government. Americans believed they were an energetic people. They would only accept authority if that authority could encompass individual ambition. However much the framers may have privately distrusted democratic politics, they knew their new constitution would have to protect and encourage the burgeoning competitiveness of American life in the eighteenth century. Federalist and Antifederalist alike believed that the political arrangements in the new nation should reflect and guarantee the people's capacity for invention and the creation of wealth. St. George Tucker agreed that 'the government which possesses the most energy, and at the same time best guards its principles, is the most perfect ... Energy in such a government is the best support that freedom can desire; and freedom is more perfect in proportion to the degree of energy.[26]

When the defenders of the Constitution invoked the idea of energy they were not merely referring to the rivalry that would characterise the departments of government. They also recognised that the new Constitution had to take cognizance of that other element of man's ambition, namely his desire to acquire and hold property. Again, the framers combined their own observations of contemporary life with received political ideology. Both Locke and Hume had demonstrated the crucial role of property rights in their political theory. While the Founding Fathers did not place property rights specifically at the centre of their political cosmology, they did wish to oversee a political and economic system in which property holding would flourish and increase. In the late eighteenth century the ownership of freehold land expanded and, even more important, was changing hands rapidly. The Federalists, as the events of the 1790s were to demonstrate, hoped to encourage commerce in manufactured goods as well as in land. They intended to create a political system that did not encumber such economic growth. John Locke had taught them that the protection of private property was not simply the enactment of a basic right. It also served to make life better. Men originally held property because it represented the fruits of their own labour. Men had absolute rights over their own bodies. The product of their bodily work was represented in the ownership of property. But Locke also argued that the appropriation and subsequent protection of private property performed an additional function: it made men more acquisitive and hence more productive. The quality of life could only improve in an acquisitive society. Property rights provided men with an incentive to work and this in turn would enhance creativity and productivity.

Indeed by the late eighteenth century, the defence of property rights was not simply an exercise in the protection of vested monied and landed interests. For while the Founding Fathers did not wish to see the social order usurped – the preservation of stability was their brief – they did recognise that the pattern of property ownership was in the process of changing. The economy was becoming more specialised. The production of surplus goods for the specific purpose of exchange was not only a fact of life but also was held to be socially and morally enriching. The new political economy, inspired by Adam Smith's pioneering work, *The Wealth of Nations*, published in 1776, taught that man's self-interest and his instinctive possessiveness were constructive characteristics. The nation's wealth would grow as commercial exchange increased. A marketplace economy conformed more closely to man's psychological need for possessions and his craving for social approval. (After all, a commercial bargain is little more than an agreement by the parties involved that each is benefiting from the exchange.) The marketplace and justice were handmaidens. Even more important, Smith agreed with Hume that if people traded briskly and were easily able to own property, it would be difficult for oligarchy or concentrated wealth and power to become entrenched. Hume wrote that 'as private men receive greater security in the possession of their trade and riches from the power of the public, so the public becomes powerful in proportion to the opulence and extensive commerce of private men'. Adam Smith emphasised time and again that commerce favoured liberty as it destroyed private power and dependence. 'Nothing tends so much,' he wrote, 'to corrupt mankind as dependency, while independency still increases the honesty of the people.'[27]

Thus the Founding Fathers sought in the Constitution to preserve and encourage a competitive, property-owning society. While they did not address themselves specifically to the issue in the Constitutional Convention, they constantly revealed the importance they attached to the protection of property rights. Madison stated quite boldly in 1792 that government 'is instituted to protect property of every sort'.[28] Property was to be protected not just because its owners wished to employ the law to defend their interests but also because the distribution of property reflected the social nexus. A democratic government had to protect man's individual faculties and recognise his passions and ambitions. Social man was driven by the wish to have property. Thus the protection of property abetted the protection of other rights. 'The diversity in the faculties of men, from which the rights of property originate,' wrote Madison in *The Federalist*, is a fact of social life. 'The protection of these faculties is the first object of government. From the protection of different and unequal faculties of acquiring property, the possession of different degrees and kinds of property immediately results.'[29] The new constitution could only be effective if it accommodated men's divergent and acquisitive impulses. Men could only be free to acquire goods if they believed their goals were attainable. Thus the new political system would have to open, not foreclose, economic opportunity.

The founders of the American republic did differ in their views of *how* private property should be protected and promoted. The split in the 1790s between Federalists and Republicans revolved around this very issue. But there was a general consensus that the quest for property had to be guarded. John Adams, scarcely an economic leveller, wrote that he wanted 'to make the acquisition of land easy to very member of society'. A broad distribution of property would promote 'liberty, virtues and interest'. New constitutions had to assess the kind of economy that would promote the national welfare and permit that economy to flourish. 'The balance of dominion in land is the natural cause of empire; and this is the principle which makes politics a science undeniable throughout.'[30] While Adams advocated the creation of branches of government that corresponded to the social and landed order, men like Alexander Hamilton wanted to create a political system that encouraged the pursuit of wealth and property. The 'primary object' of statesmanship, he wrote, was 'the prosperity of commerce'. The Constitution, in his view, was to be a framework for channelling the energy of men. A flourishing and energetic market would encourage invention, commerce and innovative methods of financing. He was confident that the Constitution would promote such an economy.[31]

The defenders of the American Constitution believed that they had created a system of government that venerated property and generated creativity. Political ideas and economic stratagems were parallel exercises. The market-place had to be encouraged; this could best be done by nurturing a political system that was at once competitive and protective of property rights. Noah Webster, one of the most articulate and maskless Federalists, provided perhaps the most accurate summation of their political thinking. Like Adams and Madison he recognised that the wealthy owners of property wielded real power. But that ownership should not be static. 'To assist the struggle for liberty, commerce has interposed and in conjunction with manufacturers, thrown a vast weight into the democratic scale.' If commerce were to continue to thrive, laws would have to be passed to encourage it. 'Leave real estates to revolve from hand to hand, as time and accident may direct,' he admonished, 'and no family influence can be acquired and established for a series of generations.' If men were unencumbered in the pursuit of property, then 'the laborious and saving, who are generally the best citizens, will possess each his share of property and power'. He was confident that the diffusion of power under the Constitution would serve this end. 'The life, liberty and property of every man,' he foresaw, 'will be more fully secured under such a constitution of federal government than they will under a constitution with more limited powers.' The federal Constitution created opportunities for the successful pursuit of commerce and trade in land. Webster was as good a capitalist as he was a lexicographer. 'On the adoption of this constitution,' he predicted, 'I should value real estate twenty per cent higher than I do at this moment.'[32]

The federal Constitution, in short, was predicated on certain assumptions and goals which formed part of the philosophical and psychological inheritance of the English and Scottish Enlightenment. Its achievement lay in its ability to convert characteristics that were once thought divisive into creative forces. The Presidency, the Congress and the Supreme Court were not simply discrete branches of government that were instituted to perform certain political and procedural functions. They were part of an elaborate scheme to secure a government that embodied and fostered man's principal drives and ambitions. Furthermore, the Constitution managed to lay the foundation of a democratic system that still acknowledged the need for obedience to the new regime. The theory of consent embraced by the Founding Fathers was not a theory that encouraged or tolerated widespread popular control of or mutability in government. Locke and, to a less extent Hume, had shown that consent could not thrive without some compulsion. It was the achievement of Madison's generation to create a system of government that managed in the practical world to conjoin seemingly contrasting strands of political thought. Men's selfish propensities for power, fame and wealth were no longer regarded as threats to virtuous republicanism but were now seen as potentially creative driving forces. They compelled political institutions to deliberate, to compromise and, above all, to look energetically to the future. The American Constitution did more than reconcile warring interests. It claimed to understand political man and that such understanding would chart new futures.

NOTES

1 Further discussion of republicanism can be found in Gordon Wood, *The Creation of the American Republic, 1776–1787*, Chapel Hill, University of North Carolina Press, 1969, pp. 46–124; J. G. A. Pocock, *The Machiavellian Moment: Florentine Political Thought and the Atlantic Republican Tradition*, Princeton, Princeton University Press, 1975; Robert E. Shalhope, 'Toward a republican synthesis: the emergence of an understanding of republicanism in American historiography', *William and Mary Quarterly*, 29, January 1972, pp. 49–80.

2 John Adams, *A Defence of the Constitutions of the Government of the United States of America, I* (3 vols.), London, Dilly, 1787, p. 128.

3 Quoted in Paul Eidelberg, *The Philosophy of the American Constitution: A Reinterpretation of the Intentions of the Founding Fathers*, New York, The Free Press, 1968, pp. 230–31.

4 Wood, *The Creation of the American Republic*, pp. 260–63; Daniel Boorstin, *The Mysterious Science of the Law: An Essay on Blackstone's Commentaries, Showing How Blackstone, Employing Eighteenth Century Laws of Science, Religion, History,*

Aesthetics, and Philosophy, Made of the Law at Once a Conservative and Mysterious Doctrine, Cambridge, Mass., Harvard University Press, 1941.

5 James Madison, Journal of the Federal Convention, New York, no publisher, 1840, p. 51.

6 For example, Charles A. Beard, An Economic Interpretation of the Constitution of the United States, New York, Macmillan, 1913; Forrest McDonald, E Pluribus Unum: The Formation of the American Republic, 1776–1790, Boston, Houghton Mifflin, 1965. John P. Roche has written that the Founding Fathers 'spent little time canvassing abstractions'. John P. Roche, 'The convention as a case study in democratic politics' in Leonard W. Levy (ed.), Essays in the Making of the Constitution, New York and London, Oxford University Press, 1969, p. 199.

7 A useful review of the relationship between popular sovereignty and republicanism can be found in James T. Kloppenberg, 'The virtues of liberalism: Christianity, republicanism and ethics in early American discourse', Journal of American History, 74, June 1987, pp. 9–33. On Locke's influence, see Isaac Kramnick, 'Republican revisionism revisited', American Historical Review, 87, June 1982, pp. 629–44.

8 John Locke, Two Treatises of Government, ed. Peter Laslett, Cambridge, Cambridge University Press, 1963, p. 376.

9 Jules Steinberg, Locke, Rousseau, and the Idea of Consent: An Inquiry into the Liberal-Democratic Theory of Political Obligation, Westport, Conn., Greenwood, 1978, p. 16; Geraint Parry, John Locke, London, Greenwood, 1978, pp. 102–8.

10 Alexander Hamilton, James Madison and John Jay, The Federalist Papers, ed. Clinton Rossiter, New York, New American Library, no. 62, pp. 376–82 (hereafter cited as The Federalist).

11 Locke, Two Treatises of Government, pp. 404, 408.

12 John Patrick Diggins, The Lost Soul of American Politics: Virtue, Self-Interest and the Foundations of Liberalism, New York, Basic Books, 1984, p. 83.

13 Paul Leicester Ford (ed.), Pamphlets on the Constitution of the United States; Published During its Discussions by the People, 1787–1788, Brooklyn, New York, 1888, reprinted New York, DaCapo, 1968, p. 31.

14 Garry Wills, Explaining America: The Federalist, New York, Penguin, 1981, pp. 16–23. For a broader discussion on the intellectual origins of the Constitution see Forrest McDonald, Novus Ordo Seclorum: The Intellectual Origins of the Constitution, Lawrence, Kans., University Press of Kansas, 1985.

15 David Miller, Philosophy and Ideology in Hume's Political Thought, Oxford, Clarendon Press, 1981, pp. 24–41.

16 David Hume, A Treatise of Human Nature, II, London, Everyman's Library edn, J. M. Dent, 1911, pp. 127, 243.

17 Albert Furtwangler, The Authority of Publius: A Reading of the Federalist Papers, Ithaca and London, Cornell University Press, 1984; David F. Epstein, The Political Theory of the Federalist, Chicago, University of Chicago Press, 1984.

18 Quoted in Clinton Rossiter, Alexander Hamilton and the Constitution, New York, Harcourt Brace and World, 1964, p. 136.

19 Madison to Jefferson, 24 October 1787, in Robert A. Rutland et al. (eds.), The Papers of James Madison, vol. 10, Chicago, University of Chicago Press, 1977, pp. 212–13.

20 The Federalist, no. 10, p. 79.

21 The Federalist, no. 51, p. 322.

22 Wood, The Creation of the American Republic, pp. 534–6.

23 Madison, Journal of the Federal Convention, p. 81.

24 Eidelberg, The Philosophy of the American Constitution, pp. 144–8.

25 The Federalist, no. 62, p. 382.

26 St. George Tucker (ed.), Blackstone's Commentaries: With Notes of Reference to the Constitution and Laws of the Federal Government of the United States; and of the

Commonwealth of Virginia, Vol. I, Philadelphia, William Young Birch and Abraham Small, 1803, appendix, p. 27.

27 Both quoted in Donald Winch, *Adam Smith's Politics: An Essay in Historiographic Revision*, Cambridge, Cambridge University Press, 1978, pp. 74, 78; see also Istvan Hont and Michal Ignatieff (eds), *Wealth and Virtue: The Shaping of Political Economy in the Scottish Enlightenment*, Cambridge, Cambridge University Press, 1983; Joyce Appleby, *Capitalism and a New Social Order: The Republican Vision of the 1790s*, New York and London, 1984.

28 Marvin Meyers (ed.), *The Mind of the Founder: Sources of the Political Thought of James Madison*, Indianapolis, Bobbs-Merrill, 1973, p. 244.

29 *The Federalist*, no. 10, pp. 78–9.

30 John Howe, *The Changing Political Thought of John Adams*, Cambridge, Mass., Princeton University Press, 1964, p. 86; Adams, *A Defence of the Constitutions*, I, p. 165.

31 *The Federalist*, no. 12, p. 91.

32 Noah Webster, 'An examination into the leading principles of the federal Constitution …' in Ford (ed.), *Pamphlets on the Constitution*, pp. 46–7, 59.

Redefining Federalism: The Primacy of Politics over the Constitution

ABSTRACT

James Madison called the American Constitution a 'non-descript', meaning that it was 'sui generis' because of its unique mixture of federal and national elements. As he wrote in 'The Federalist', the Constitution 'is partly federal and partly national'. The difficulty in describing precisely the boundaries between the jurisdiction of the federal government and those of the individual state governments has provided opportunities as well as obstacles to American politicians and citizens; nevertheless, attempts to reach some precision continue, even in the late twentieth century, when the independent jurisdiction of the states sometimes seems to have been completely suppressed. This chapter traces the development of legal interpretations of federalism, especially by the Supreme Court, and shows how changes in these interpretations have related to wider political forces. These forces have recently encouraged a renewed search for the essence of federalism, but this time the search has been conducted by a more hesitant Supreme Court whose divisions reflect those of the wider political forces themselves.

I

By common consent, one of the special features of the United States is its federal structure. Indeed, Kenneth Wheare's classic book on federalism takes the original United States Constitution as the 'ideal type', noting that any 'definition of federal government which failed to include the United States would be thereby condemned as unreal'.[1] The passage of time, however, has been accompanied by considerable changes in both its formal structure (through Amendments) and its informal operations, as the environment in which the

Constitution has been applied has altered. As a consequence, the United States constitutional system does not operate at the beginning of its third century in the same ways as it did at the outset of the Republic. And yet both Americans and others remain convinced that the United States system must be a federal one.

The careful reader will have noticed by now that my language has slipped from referring to federal *structure* to talking about a federal *system*. This conscious slippage draws essential attention to the trite point that a Constitution establishes general rules but that history decides how those rules will actually affect a country's political life. As the practice of American politics has interacted with the legal rules, the nature of American federalism has changed. Inevitably, too, this tendency to adapt the 'ideal type' to contemporary needs and realities has spawned a descriptive burgeoning of adjectival glosses on the ideal; so scholars have written of 'dual federalism', 'layer-cake federalism', 'co-operative federalism', 'marble cake federalism', 'picket fence federalism', 'creative federalism', and, unimaginatively, 'New Federalism'. One observer of the scene identified 326 metaphors and models of federalism![2]

These are all variations on one single theme, which should itself, in theory, be discoverable. The central essence of any truly federal structure (and system) is that two sets of governments exist, each of which enjoys some autonomy beyond the reach of the other to *control*. Almost certainly in the twentieth century each level of government will *influence* and bring pressure to bear on the other; but, in order to remain federal, the constituent political units must retain the authority to control some matters of public concern whatever the preferences of the other level of government. This is the central concept of both a federal structure (legal federalism) and a federal system (political federalism) and it can be applied to the United States throughout its history. The difficulty, however, arises in operationalising the concept. While it is clear that the central government and the fifty state governments do each enjoy some independent authority, it is not always clear over what specific matters each *should* exercise its autonomous authority. Attempts to delineate each level of government's respective spheres of influence have taken place throughout the Republic's history but no final conclusion has yet been rendered.

In this respect the Constitution is singularly unhelpful. It does not employ the word federalism at all and hence the concept's applicability to the real world has to be inferred from the Constitution's implications, and this is not a straightforward operation. Senator Sam Ervin, some years before he presided with such avuncular authority over the Senate Watergate hearings, began his minority report objecting to the nomination of Thurgood Marshall as the first black Justice of the Supreme Court with these words: 'The good and wise men who fashioned the Constitution had earth's most magnificent dream'.[3] Perhaps. Unfortunately, like our personal dreams, the Constitution is fuzzy at the margins and fails to provide clear resolutions to its dramas. Senator Ervin, however, soon moved away from the metaphysical to claim that the Constitution 'granted enumerated powers to the Federal Government and allotted or reserved all other powers to the States or the people'.[4] Alas, this common and simplistic perception is faulty; but it does provide a convenient starting point for an examination of federalism in the United States constitutional system.

The Constitution allots virtually no powers to the states apart from delineating their contribution to the creation of the national governmental authority.[5] The reason is simple enough. The individual states were, in 1787, sovereign bodies exercising authority over the full range of day-to-day matters then thought to be within the proper provenance of government. They dealt with property law, family law, commercial law, criminal law, electoral law, the provision of education and the regulation of public health and morals, the oversight and regulation of the professions and so on. The task of the Constitutional Convention which met in Philadelphia through the summer of 1787 was to create and define a *national* government. The presumption, then, must be that, to echo the Supreme Court's 1941 formulation, 'all is retained which has not been surrendered'.[6] This is the truism of the Tenth Amendment, added to the Constitution soon after ratification, to which Senator Ervin referred.[7] A truism, however, is not meaningless or without import. For well nigh 200 years American history has, in part, been coloured by attempts to define the respective reaches of federal and state authority; or, to put it another way, what has *not* been surrendered?

The central assumption of legal federalism, with its roots firmly anchored in the Constitution, is that the states retain some independent power upon which the national government cannot encroach. We know that some autonomy exists, but we cannot seem to describe it. Just as Justice Potter Stewart could not define hard-core pornography, but knew it when he saw it,[8] so most political actors in the United States cannot define with any exactitude the specifics of state autonomy, even though they claim to recognise when it has been infringed. It is the search for the holy grail of certitude which lies at the heart of this chapter, a search conducted in the language of the Constitution (legal federalism) but often predicated on the interplay of political forces between state and national government (political federalism). The complexity of the Supreme Court's political role, both responding to and influencing political forces, is thus nicely illustrated.

II

The establishment of the Union curtailed the sovereignty of the individual states; that was its purpose. Not only did the Constitution set down specific limitations on state powers,[9] it also enumerated a range of governmental activities on which the Congress would be entitled to legislate. Two basic principles underlay the details. First, the Founding Fathers sought to establish a national government with sufficient power and authority to protect the Union from external, and internal, attack. Second, they sought to establish what we would now call a common market in order to strengthen the continental economy and encourage a freer movement of people and goods. They believed, rightly, that security and economic growth could only be achieved through a central governmental structure enjoying a superior status over the individual states in these two areas. It was not thought, however, that these twin functions would unduly infringe on the much larger number of activities for which the states were already responsible.[10]

But Article I, Section 8 of the Constitution (where most of the enumerated powers are largely to be found) contains three well-known Trojan Horses by which the national government has encroached, some would say trespassed, upon state sovereignty. With the bulwarks of the Supremacy Clause and judicial sovereignty assumed in *Marbury v Madison*,[11] the Supreme Court, under the skilful leadership of Chief Justice John Marshall, began to put political flesh onto the constitutional bones of three enumerated clauses: 'to lay and collect taxes', [to] 'provide for the common defense and general welfare of the United States' and 'to regulate commerce ... among the several states'.[12] In *McCulloch v. Maryland*, Marshall established not only constitutional support for a broad interpretation of the appropriate means to achieve goals in conformity with the specific enumerated powers but also the primacy of national laws in situations where both levels of government appeared to have constitutional rights to legislate.[13] In *Gibbons v. Ogden*, Marshall went on to define the notion of commerce in a way which led, over the years, to an extraordinarily broad conception of what constituted commerce and was therefore, in constitutional theory, potentially subject to national government regulation.[14]

Although Marshall had put in place a set of principles on which a considerable national power could be built, the opportunity was not yet taken. The first half of the nineteenth century, after all, was a period when the principle of 'he who rules least, governs best' was still the conventional wisdom. It was also, of course, the period when the indissolubility of the Union was at stake. The underlying principles of the federal Constitution itself were constantly challenged. Had the individual states merely loaned elements of their sovereignty 'to create a more perfect Union' (and were they, therefore, entitled to call in their loan when it suited), or had they surrendered their essential sovereignty and been returned by 'We, the People' those powers not granted explicitly, or by logical deduction, to the national government? The disputes over nullification or over obedience to Supreme Court judgements were merely the prelude to the Civil War, which in effect settled the issue.[15] In these crucial years, governments in Washington, responding to contemporary ideology and pragmatic political calculations, made few attempts to regulate within the states any matters which were not clearly connected to interstate commerce.

After the Civil War, however, the tensions between national power and states' rights returned to the courts. Although the jurisprudence of the Supreme Court was by no means uniform, there was sufficient consistency for scholars to characterise the period from 1895 to 1937 as the years of 'dual federalism' or 'dual sovereignty', defined by Corwin as 'two mutually exclusive reciprocally limiting fields of power'.[16] This had been hinted at in *Gibbons v. Ogden*[17] but it was not until 1895 that the court, in *US v. E C Knight Co*, introduced limitations on the commerce power (here used to constrain business combines) quite at variance with John Marshall's broad conception.[18] What a majority of the Court did thereafter was to limit the reach of the commerce power, either through a reactivated Tenth Amendment (which required some neat footwork in defining activities that were 'essentially local in character')[19] or through redefinitions of what constituted commerce or, more sinisterly, through a subjective judgement of what sorts of activity should be subject to regulation at all.[20] Some curious consequences followed. The Court, exercising its moral judgement, acquiesced in the national government's use of the commerce clause to forbid the movement across state lines, for instance, of gambling paraphernalia, coloured margarine (although it is not entirely clear why this should have disturbed the Justices' susceptibilities), liquor, and women for immoral purposes.[21] But its moral sense was not sufficiently moved to uphold the Congress's attempt to regulate the movement in interstate commerce of goods produced by children; Justice William Day summed up the Court's position in *Hammer v. Dagenhart* with these powerful words: '[If] Congress can thus regulate matters entrusted to local authority by prohibition of the movement of commodities in interstate commerce, all freedom of commerce will be at an end, and the power of the States over local matters may be eliminated, and thus our system of government be practically destroyed'.[22]

This apocalyptic vision coloured taxation matters too. It was John Marshall, after all, who had coined the familiar aphorism 'the power to tax involves the power to destroy'.[23] When he wrote those words, he feared that the states could destroy the national government, but the principle could also be applied to federal taxation of state government institutions. As with the commerce power, the initial interpretation of the taxing power accepted that it was plenary, *unless* the tax could be shown to threaten the very existence of the states and their political institutions. In 1871, however, the Court gave support to notions of dual federalism in *Collector v. Day* which established that states and nations were on a par when it came to taxing each other.[24] By the 1930s the Court had invalidated federal income taxes on state employees' federal salaries, taxes on income derived from municipal bonds and federal taxes earned on lands leased from the states.[25] Nor could Congress use the taxing power to reach social ills it sought to rectify in the states; thwarted by *Hammer v. Dagenhart* from ending the evil effects of child labour through the commerce clause, it turned to the taxing power, but this, too, was unavailing when the Court decided *Bailey v. Drexel*

Furniture Co in 1922 and argued, by 8–1 that the 'tax is a penalty to coerce people of a State to act as Congress wishes them to act in respect of a matter completely the business of the state government under the Federal Constitution'.[26]

Looking back at this period between Reconstruction and the New Deal, three important features emerge. It is probably right to notice, first of all, that the most notorious cases (*E C Knight, Dagenhart, Drexel*, and *Pollock v. Farmers' Loan and Trust Co*,[27] which outlawed the income tax) are in some ways exceptions, rather than instances of the rigid application of a theory of dual federalism.[28] They were, of course, of tremendous political significance at the time; indeed, striking down the income tax law generated the Sixteenth Amendment which in its turn permitted the national government to raise an income tax and thus, ironically, establish a powerful fiscal base for itself which allowed it to influence state social policies so thoroughly in the 1950s and 1960s. Throughout this period, many of the states, under pressure from Progressives and Populists, were involved in social engineering; the Congress, too, took hesitant steps, again under pressure from the fluctuating waves of progressive public opinion manifesting itself in representation in Washington, to regulate the worst excesses of unbridled capitalism; the Sherman Anti-Trust Act is but one example. The foundations had been laid, with simple clarity by Marshall and with more clouded reservations by later courts, for a future Court to broaden the scope of federal regulation, whether through the interstate commerce or the taxing clause.

In the second place, it is noticeable how commerce clause and taxing jurisprudence marched broadly in step. Generous interpretations of their reach were cut back in the late nineteenth century and the Justices were obviously guided in these developments by the conscious, if unarticulated, conception of the proper relationship between national and state governments. It is interesting that Chief Justice Taft, in his *Drexel* opinion, refers with approval to *Dagenhart*, even though the constitutional issues raised were actually different. This is due, surely, to the third point: the ebb and flow of national power and of regulation itself mirrors the ebb and flow of political movements. The Supreme Court may not follow the election returns precisely, but they are rarely much out of step. And, when there is no clearly dominant political force, the Court, too, will reflect the same confusion and contradictions. Although the aggressive and optimistic adherents of free-wheeling capitalism generally prevailed (and we should remember that by 1900 Republicans held control over the big cities of the United States), they did not, everywhere and at all times, have it always their own way. Progressive forces in the west and crusading moralists in many states challenged the principles of laissez-faire; after all, it was in this period that the American people made the production and sale of liquor actually *unconstitutional*.

Much, of course, has changed since those days of dual federalism. But it is important to note that, in the period before 1937, a number of cases had been decided and several powerful dissents penned which provided the intellectual foundations for a different jurisprudence; hence, when the post-1937 revolution took place, it could ground its new directions in a number of precedents and arguments drawn from the earlier era. Just as in that era, the philosophical development of commerce and taxing questions tended to go hand in hand. Just as in that era, too, the dominant political forces were reflected in those who sat upon the Court and, in most instances, provided a consistent and confident jurisprudence. In the 1970s and 1980s, this rule still applied; but, by this period, there was less of a consensus among the political elites over the proper role and jurisprudence of the Court and this was reflected in a hesitant judicial philosophy which mirrored a divided polity.

III

The Depression ushered in a revolution in American politics. Before the 1929 Crash on Wall Street, there were only fifteen grant programmes funded by the national government for expenditure within the states and these represented just two per cent of state revenues; nor did the regulatory role of the federal government much affect dual federalism.[29] President Roosevelt, however, sought through his New Deal legislation to use federal authority to make good the ravages of the Depression and introduced a host of bills to achieve this purpose. These regulatory attempts were often hastily drafted and in some cases were formulated more in terms of their worthy intentions than by careful consideration of the law.[30] A majority of the Supreme Court, if only a slender one, was in any case committed by its jurisprudence and political preferences to the reassertion of past precedents which constrained the reach of federal power; even the 'liberals' (Brandeis, Cardozo and Stone) found it impossible on most occasions to make the jurisprudential leap to endorsing the New Deal legislation, especially given the facts of the cases which actually reached them for adjudication. The inevitable result was that Roosevelt's initial legislation soon came to grief. In 1935 *Panama Refining Co v. Ryan* struck down a part of the National Industrial Recovery Act, the centrepiece of which was invalidated by *Schechter Poultry Corporation v. US* later in the year;[31] the Bituminous Coal Conservation Act was struck down in *Carter v. Carter Coal Co* and the Agricultural Adjustment Act in *US v. Butler*, both in 1936.[32] The New Deal was temporarily in shambles.

Although several of the New Deal Acts were struck down on non-federal grounds, there is no doubt that the impact was to draw attention to a conceptual dividing line between activities which the national government could constitutionally regulate (whether through the commerce clause, the general welfare clause, or the taxing powers) and activities which remained the preserve of the states and individuals. Roosevelt's response was an attempt to alter the meaning of the Constitution by altering the Justices who interpreted it; he aimed to increase the number of Justices on the Supreme Court so that there would be a majority upholding his proposed legislation.[33] He failed in this specific endeavour.[34] But, more importantly, he succeeded soon afterwards in his central purpose of ensuring constitutional blessing for his policies. Justice Owen Roberts, perhaps because the precise facts had altered,[35] perhaps because he heeded the electorate's emphatic mandate for Roosevelt's election in 1936, shifted sides; and, in 1937, Willis van Devanter retired, to be replaced by Senator Hugo Black. Thus a clear majority in favour of extensive federal power was assured and this majority grew in the following years as Roosevelt replaced retiring Justices with men whom he could reliably trust to uphold New Deal laws. Using what would now be called the 'litmus test' of commitment to New Deal laws, he created the Roosevelt Court.[36]

The new orthodoxy reached its apogee in 1941 when *United States v. Darby* was decided and a unanimous Court followed Chief Justice Harlan Fiske Stone in granting the federal government an almost limitless authority in economic matters.[37] Stone happily cited John Marshall's powerful words in *Gibbons v. Ogden*: the power of Congress over interstate commerce 'is complete in itself, may be exercised to its utmost extent, and acknowledges no limitations other than are prescribed in the Constitution'.[38] He added for good measure:

> the motive and purpose of a regulation of interstate commerce are matters for the legislative judgement upon the exercise of which the Constitution places no restriction and over which the courts are given no control. Whatever their motive or purpose, regulations of commerce which do not infringe some constitutional prohibition are within the plenary power conferred on Congress by the Commerce Clause.[39]

The Tenth Amendment, so often seen by defenders of state autonomy and critics of expansive national powers as their chief bulwark, was emasculated. It now protected only what the national government could not reach; and the new orthodoxy could find little judicial defence to the plenary use of power by a duly elected Congress.

This expansive reading of the commerce power was confirmed in the following year, once again unanimously. Farmer Filburn had grown 11.9 acres of wheat over and above the quota of 11.1 acres allotted to him under the Agricultural Adjustment Act and had consumed all 239 bushels of wheat grown on that extra land entirely within his farm. Justice Jackson, however, argued that Filburn had limited commerce because he had reduced the effective demand on the nation's wheat supply by not entering the market for those 239 bushels; he had, therefore, fallen foul of the Agricultural Adjustment Act, one of whose purposes was to control output and therefore stabilise prices.[40]

Just as the commerce power was given an expansive reading more in line with John Marshall's conception, so the taxing power also came to be seen once again as plenary, limited only if the activity taxed was 'essential to the preservation of the state government', a limitation which grew, in Felix Frankfurter's words, from 'the implications inherent in the nature of federalism'.[41] But Frankfurter forbore to elaborate on what was essential or what precisely the inherent implications might be. One part of the past was repeating itself; interstate commerce and taxing jurisprudence were marching side by side, although, of course, to a different tune.

At the same time as these developments were taking place, another set of changes occurred which had profound consequences for the autonomy of states. The seed had, in fact, been sown in 1868 when the Fourteenth Amendment to the Constitution was ratified.

The generalities of the Amendment provide some of the most fruitful material for scholarly debate, but nobody doubts that it set limitations upon what the states could do to individuals. As Justice Potter Stewart observed in 1972, '[a]s a result of the new structure of law that emerged in the post Civil War era – and especially of the Fourteenth Amendment, which was its centrepiece – the role of the Federal Government as a guarantor of basic federal rights against State power was clearly established'.[42] It may have been clearly established by 1972; it had most certainly not been one hundred years earlier.

In making appointments to the Supreme Court, Franklin Roosevelt had been concerned that his nominees would uphold his New Deal legislation. Once satisfied on this issue, Roosevelt does not seem to have thought much more about their judicial philosophies. The result was that the Roosevelt Court usually spoke with one voice on matters connected with the exercise of Congressional power but split into often bitterly opposed factions on several other issues.[43] The new central issue was this: what rights did the Fourteenth Amendment protect against state infringement? Focus shifted from structural issues about the formal distribution of power in the federal system to questions of individual rights allegedly abridged by the states. The causes of this shift remain unclear; perhaps the justification for the anti-Nazi war percolated through American society into an enhanced concern for the rights of racial and religious minorities; perhaps the accidents of history produced at this juncture the culmination of a litigation strategy spearheaded by the National Association for the Advancement of Colored People;[44] perhaps Justice Stone's now celebrated fourth footnote in the Carolene Products case really did establish a new and special agenda for the Supreme Court.[45] Whatever the reasons, the Court was now faced with a range of issues in which litigants challenged state action on Fourteenth Amendment grounds.

In 1833, the Court had seemed to assert with finality, in *Barron v. Baltimore*,[46] that the Bill of Rights (the first ten amendments) was not applicable to the states. After the Civil War, attempts were made to enforce rights through legislation based upon the Fourteenth Amendment but these were emasculated in the 1873 *Slaughterhouse* cases.[47] Although the first Justice Harlan constantly attempted to incorporate the Bill of Rights into the Fourteenth Amendment through the due process clause, he had no followers. In 1925, however, virtually out of the blue the action of incorporating at least some of the rights enumerated in the first eight amendments into the due process clause of the Fourteenth Amendment occurred. In *Gitlow v. New York* the court asserted (it did not argue): 'For present purposes we may and do assume that freedom of speech and of the press – which are now protected by the First Amendment from abridgement by Congress – are among the fundamental personal rights and "liberties" protected by the due process clause of the Fourteenth Amendment from impairment by the States'.[48] Gradually further liberties became incorporated, such as the freedom of the press from prior restraint (1931),[49] the right to counsel in capital cases (1932),[50] freedom of religion (1934),[51] and the freedom of assembly and the right to petition the government for a redress of grievances (1937).[52] Until this point, there had been little attempt to provide a sound theoretical underpinning to this selective incorporation; that came later, in 1937.

Frank Palko had been found guilty of second degree murder in a Connecticut county court and sentenced to life imprisonment; the state persuaded the Supreme Court of Errors in Connecticut that the trial contained legal errors to its disadvantage and that a new trial should be authorised. In the second trial, Palko was found guilty of first degree murder and sentenced to death. He appealed to the Supreme Court, arguing that 'whatever is forbidden by the Fifth Amendment ["nor shall any person be subject for the same offence to be twice put in jeopardy of life or limb"] is forbidden by the Fourteenth also'.[53] The Court disagreed and Palko was executed. But Justice Benjamin Cardozo's opinion for the Court set down an 'Honor Roll of Superior Rights' which were, in his words, 'of the very essence of a scheme of ordered liberty' and to be distinguished from other doubtless worthy candidates but which were not 'implicit in the concept of ordered liberty'. This assumption of fundamental, or superior, rights was augmented by an intrinsic extension of the meaning of due process to include, in Felix Frankfurter's words, actions which 'shock the conscience'.[54] This is not the place to trace the enlargement of the number of rights deemed fundamental nor to outline the arguments between the selective (and subjective) incorporators and those like Justice Hugo Black who would have incorporated all the specific rights set out in the first eight Amendments into the Fourteenth Amendment and no more.[55] The point is that, from about 1937, the Court had a rationale which enabled it to strike down state actions which shocked its conscience or were deemed fundamental to ordered liberty. The autonomy of states was about to be invaded in a major way.

From the late 1940s onwards, the Court began to outlaw many cherished state policies. It demanded a strict division between church and state, protected unloved religious minorities from state persecution, outlawed segregated school systems and subsequently all public facilities, imposed a wide range of requirements on law enforcement agencies, required state constituencies to be of roughly equal size, set stringent rules on the procedures necessary before people could be executed, supervised reform of prisons and school catchment areas, placed limitations on state attempts to outlaw abortions, and, in a myriad of other ways, challenged states to meet its requirements if they were not to be found guilty of contravening the newly discovered imperatives of the Fourteenth Amendment.[56] In many of these areas popular opinion initially sided with the Court; the outrages which the Supreme Court decisions sought to end had little generalised support. But, once the worst excesses of the worst states' actions had been ameliorated, the Court's oversight seemed less needed and more intrusive. The autonomy of the states was regularly and perceptibly being challenged.

The autonomy was under attack from another quarter at the same time. Following *Darby*, Congress's expanding role as regulator of the national economy now had full constitutional blessing. It reflected a profound and, indeed, revolutionary change in the expectations of a majority of Americans. As has already been mentioned, there had been moments in the past when progressive majorities, usually in the states, had approved the regulation of monopolies or the worst excesses of capitalist labour practices. What was new in the post World War II years was the growing transference of resources from the federal Treasury to state governments. There had, of course, been grants in the past and the New Deal years had increased such direct grants. Table 2.1 shows the extent of this growth in the 1960s and 1970s, which reflected a broad consensus that neither development in the states nor redistribution between the states could be achieved in any other way. This 'co-operative federalism' extended the national government's activities more obviously from private behaviour (which most regulatory provisions had been intended to control) to areas which traditionally had been thought of as the responsibility of state and local governments.

Table 2.1: Growth of federal grants to the states, 1950–78

Fiscal Year	Total grants (billions of dollars)	Federal grants as a per cent of		
		Total federal outlays	Domestic federal outlays[a]	State and local expenditures[b]
1950	2.3	5.3	8.8	10.4
1955	3.2	4.7	12.1	10.1
1960	7.0	7.7	15.8	14.7
1965	10.9	9.2	16.5	15.3
1970	24.0	12.2	21.1	19.4
1973	41.8	16.9	24.8	24.3
1975	49.8	15.3	21.3	22.9
1978	77.9	17.3	22.9	26.7

Notes: *a* Excludes outlays for national defence and international affairs.
b As defined in the national income and product accounts.
Source: *Special Analyses, Budget of the United States Government, Fiscal Year 1980*, p. 225.

In the 1960s Congress, urged on by President Lyndon Johnson in particular, became ever more enthusiastic about attacking what a majority of its members saw as *social* ills (rather than the economic ills at which the New Deal had been largely directed). Nowhere is this new attitude clearer than in the formulation and passage of the 1964 Civil Rights Act. Rather than using section 5 of the Fourteenth Amendment, which authorised the Congress to legislate for the rights loosely written into the Amendment, the Act's proponents cast its language and defence in terms of the commerce clause, holding that discriminatory practices limited the flow of people and goods among the states. In *Katzenbach v. McClung*, a unanimous Court upheld its constitutionality as applied to a small family restaurant in downtown Birmingham, Alabama, where interstate travellers would have been virtual aliens.[57] But Ollie McClung had bought $69,683 of beef from outside Alabama and was thus caught in the commerce clause's web.

This 'co-operative federalism', essentially broad national support for functions already being performed by states, gave way to 'creative federalism', where the national government initiated policies and negotiated directly with states and even, for the first time, sub-governments of the states. Intergovernmental relations inevitably became more salient and the impression of ever greater national involvement in state affairs more widespread.[58] Where, in the past, good arguments could sometimes be made for using government as a regulator (and thus only restraining the excesses of the market), now good arguments were being made to use governments positively to achieve societal goals. This is associated above all with Lyndon Johnson's Great Society, but it was also the driving force in the massive expansion of state governments' activities as well. In the 1960s, given the federal government's fiscal strength and policy expertise, state and local governments sought assistance from Washington. Behind a continuing rhetoric that inveighed against the federal government, in many quarters lay the reality of politicians and bureaucrats regularly flying to the capital city in order to extricate funds and preferential treatment from Capitol Hill. The ever increasing federal tentacles into the states were real enough; but they were not uninvited interventions. After all, the Washington politicians were closely tied to the states. Members of the House of Representatives, in those days often intimately tied to local parties, were deeply conscious that their political future depended on *not* alienating important sections of their constituencies. Senators were intended to represent states as states and they took this responsibility seriously. It is important, therefore, to realise that the federal government's intrusion into state matters was not only matched by state governments themselves but also authorised by politicians dependent upon state electoral support.

Interpreting the balance between state and national governments is a tricky operation. The intrusion of Washington is obvious. Even in towns of considerable prosperity, a majority of inhabitants, from both poor and middle income families, now receive a substantial part of their income from the federal government's coffers; by 1978, on average, 40 per cent of city revenue originated in Washington.[59] In a city like Middletown in Connecticut, one third of *all* income received in 1979 came from the federal government, and the city itself, which fifty years ago was funded almost entirely from local sources, got over half its income from Washington.[60] But that is only one side of the picture. There has been a resurgence of state government.[61] With greater capacity to raise revenue, with many more professional legislators and executives, with a greater degree of

popular accountability as a result of the reapportionment revolution
of the 1960s, and with constitutional and institutional reforms (the
legislatures of 'only' seven states did not meet in 1985), state government has become more innovative and more active. The two levels
feed on each other but, because they are both actively intervening in
so wide a range of policy areas, conflicts are inevitable. Complaints
are less likely to be directed against the principle of federal aid so
much as against the bureaucratisation and alleged waste that goes
with it. As Hugh Heclo has summarised the position, 'Americans
... have been learning to love their government benefits and to hate
their government'.[62]

The combined impact of close Supreme Court supervision and
Congressional action thus generated political forces which opposed
such developments. The 1980 Republican Party Platform, for
example, is replete with references to the excessive intrusion of
Washington into the states.[63] President Reagan, in his 1981 in-
augural, said: 'It is my intention to curb the size and influence of
the Federal establishment and to demand recognition of the distinction between the powers granted to the Federal government and
those reserved to the states or to the people'.[64] His dissatisfaction
with some of the Supreme Court's judgements is well known and
unashamed. His Attorney-General, Edwin Meese III, publicly
challenged the Court's jurisprudence in a widely criticised speech
to the American Bar Association in July 1985. On that occasion he
observed that nothing could be done to shore up the intellectually
shaky foundation upon which the incorporation doctrine rested.
'And nowhere else,' he went on, 'has the principle of federalism been
dealt so politically violent and constitutionally suspect a blow as
by the theory of incorporation'.[65] So, once again, the constitutionally proper relationship between national and state governments (legal federalism) was on the public agenda.

IV

It is hardly surprising, therefore, that people began to ask more
loudly whether there was *any* state activity immune from federal
intervention. All three branches of government, in their separate
ways, seemed to be emasculating that autonomy which lay at the
heart of a truly federal system. Although the Supreme Court did not
seem to be a defender of that autonomy, most of its members

admitted at one time or another that state autonomy existed; but they appeared unable to translate a theoretical area of autonomy into a real one. Although the taxing cases did admit that there were institutions 'essential to the preservation of state governments' and implied by the nature of federalism, they did not identify those institutions. The situation, then, was similar in part to the Court's judgement of the practices which were implied in the concept 'ordered liberty' or which 'shocked the conscience' or were intrinsic to an evolving sense of justice; the precise application of the concepts used in constitutional discourse was unclear. By the mid-1960s the Justices seemed incapable of defining that sacred area outside the federal authorities' reach; and, from the vantage point of states' rights advocates, this was a bleak prospect.

The possibility of help came from an unlikely quarter. Justice William Douglas had been right in the forefront of pressing uniform standards in the field of individual rights upon the states and accepting the Congress's judgement of the most appropriate economic and social policies for the nation as a whole. But he was worried by the consequences of this nationalising philosophy for federalism. In 1966, Congress amended the Fair Labor Standards Act to extend its minimum wage and overtime provisions in the private sector to state-operated schools, hospitals and similar institutions. The state of Maryland (joined by twenty-seven other states and one school district) claimed that this exceeded the powers granted to the federal government under the commerce clause and, additionally, fell foul of the Tenth Amendment.[66] Only Stewart agreed with Douglas's position at the time who felt that the legislation was 'such a serious invasion of state sovereignty protected by the Tenth Amendment that it is in my view not consistent with our constitutional federalism'.[67] He could recognise intrusion when he saw it; but he still could not categorise specifically the essential quality of that intrusion.

Despite the overwhelming 6–2 vote upholding the amendments to the Fair Labor Standards Act in *Maryland v. Wirtz*, the issue did not go away. In 1975 a very different Court (Burger, Blackmun, Rehnquist, Powell and Stevens had replaced, respectively, Warren, Fortas, Harlan, Black and Douglas) considered whether Congress had the authority, under the Economic Stabilisation Act, to fix the level of wages paid by the state of Ohio to its employees. In *Fry v. United States*, the Court upheld this exercise of power; only one Justice,

William Rehnquist, dissented.[68] Within a year, however, Rehnquist had turned his solitary dissent into a 5–4 majority striking down yet further amendments to the Fair Labor Standards Act which this time extended minimum wage and overtime provisions to those directly employed by state and local governments. For the first time in almost precisely forty years the Supreme Court thereby struck down an act of Congress fashioned upon the commerce clause; *National League of Cities v. Usery* was, indeed, a remarkable decision, testifying to the power of Rehnquist's arguments and portending significant shifts in the balance of power between federal and state governments.[69]

Rehnquist drew on Douglas's dissent in *Wirtz* and his own in *Fry* to revitalise the concept of dual federalism. Congress, he declared, could not deal with states as if they were just another individual or business enterprise subject to regulation.[70] Congress's regulations in this instance, he wrote, would 'impair the states' ability to function effectively within a federal system'.[71] Interpretations of the taxing clause and the commerce clause, it will be remembered, had traditionally gone hand in hand (expansive until the 1890s, restrictive until after the 1937 crisis); here, too, Rehnquist attempted to link the two, carrying over the immunity doctrine ('to tax may be to destroy') from taxing to commerce. *All* federal intrusions, he held, 'impermissibly interfere with the integral governmental functions of [the states]'.[72] Dual federalism may not yet have been reborn; but its philosophical underpinnings had been checked out and dusted down. The *New York Times*, the *Washington Post* and the *Wall Street Journal* all responded with an identical phrase; the decision in *National League of Cities* was 'the most far-reaching in recent memory'.[73] Its potential significance quickly percolated into academia and articles were soon being published which echoed that judgement.

But such a judgement proved misplaced. Initially, *National League of Cities* spawned a rash of litigation; but, whenever the Court chose to address the newly encouraged claims of unconstitutional federal action, it denied those claims.[74] The bold and confident phrases of Justice Rehnquist did not in the event provide adequate guidelines to distinguish activities that were properly within the national government's reach to regulate from those that were not. This is not to say that the states enjoyed *no* victories during Burger's Chiefjusticeship; the egalitarian thrust of the Fourteenth

Amendment's equal protection clause did not carry all before it, and in one very significant case, *Rodriquez v. San Antonio Independent School District*, decided two years before *National League of Cities*, the Court had upheld the state of Texas's method of financing its public schools, linking resources to the district's tax base, even though the outcome was necessarily very unequally funded schools within the state.[75] Rehnquist's concern in *National League of Cities* to assert the existence of state sovereignty was a vain attempt to define some substantive domain over which exclusive and ultimate state authority could be confidently asserted. However much one might know that such a domain existed, the descriptive tags of 'traditional', 'integral', 'typical', 'important', 'essential', or 'required' did not provide workable standards. Justice Blackmun, who had expressed his less than whole-hearted support for *National League of Cities* at the time in a concurring opinion, consistently joined the four dissenters and was frequently joined by one or two others from Rehnquist's majority. Given the extraordinary speed with which the 8–1 majority in *Fry* turned into a 5–4 majority in *National League of Cities*, it might have been sensible at the time to have questioned the commitment of all Rehnquist's supporters; Blackmun was obviously doubtful and Powell's ad hocery never fitted with the drawing of bright lines. Even so, the shift from *Fry* to *National League of Cities* is remarkable. So it was not altogether a cause of surprise, when, in 1985, the Court, now speaking through Blackmun, overruled *National League of Cities* in *Garcia v. San Antonio District Transport Corporation*.[76]

Blackmun accepted that there was a problem in demarcating the precise line which divided national and state sovereignty, but he located the solution not in the special ability of judges to fashion a guiding rule (as Frankfurter had done, for example, in his overwhelmingly subjective analysis of due process in *Rochin*),[77] but in the political process itself. 'The principal means chosen by the Framers to ensure the role of the states in the federal system,' he wrote, 'lies in the structure of the federal government itself'.[78] He thus echoed the phrase Herbert Wechsler had coined more than twenty years earlier: 'the political safeguards of federalism'.[79] Such an approach protected the Court from getting bogged down once again (as it had trapped itself in many other areas of constitutional law) in its own subjective estimation of state actions to be counted as 'fundamental' (or whatever the vogue adjective might be).

Rehnquist's certitude in asserting that 'one undoubted attribute of state sovereignty is the state's power to determine the wages which shall be paid to those whom they employ to carry out their governmental functions' has, quite simply, not been universally shared.[80] Blackmun's solution was thus pragmatically necessary in one sense at any rate and jurisprudentially restrained. It also drew useful attention to one very important, and often underemphasised, point: the national laws which were held to impinge upon state sovereignty had, after all, been passed by a majority both in the House of Representatives and also in the Senate. Conceiving of intergovernmental relations as in some way a struggle between an overweening central government divorced from the states and underprotected state governments thus betrays an ignorance of history and politics. The Great Society programme was not imposed upon the states against their wills, as though Lyndon Johnson and 'his' men on Capitol Hill rode roughshod over the complaints of the representatives of the states.

Nevertheless, there *is* a special dimension to the conflict. It is not, however, to be generalised in the easy, but misleading, form of national government against the states. The political safeguards of federalism may provide for a *generalised* oversight of the federal government by representatives drawn from the several states. But the safeguards cannot necessarily protect *individual* states from legislation of which they, perhaps uniquely, disapprove. The protagonists of state rights, when the great claims to sovereignty are shorn of their philosophical coverings, ultimately seek to defend specific practices, practices which may well find little support outside their states' boundaries. Certainly the western states felt especially aggrieved at central regulation of their environment, a disquiet which was not shown by the more populous mid-west and eastern states.[81] Just as individuals, therefore, seek to establish their rights in the courts against majorities (however properly elected), so, too, may states. Individuals, however, enjoy specific protections, which are spelled out in the Bill of Rights and other Amendments on which lawyers and judges can base contemporary applications; states do not. And that is the nub of the problem.

Although *Garcia* may seem to have reiterated the principles of *Darby* and reasserted the plenary power of the federal government, the issue of legal federalism is not dead. Two issues before the Court during the 1986 Term testified to its vitality. Each introduced important aspects of the working and justification of American federalism. In 1984 the Indiana legislature passed a law which gave shareholders of corporations registered in the state the power to approve a change in the control of those corporations. Designed to protect home-based companies from the corporate raiders of Wall Street, the law provided that, when someone sought to purchase stock that would give him (or her) at least 20 per cent of the voting power, that stock would carry *voting* rights only if a majority of existing shareholders approved. The lower courts struck the law down as an impediment to the mobility of corporate assets from state to state which the commerce clause was held to protect. In 1982, the Court had struck down earlier attempts to regulate takeovers,[82] but the Indiana law, the Court decided in 1987, merely amended corporation law, 'a traditional area of state responsibility'.[83] One special characteristic of this particular episode is that the relevant federal legislation, the 1968 Williams Act, does not attack the problem of the corporate raider although Congressional committees are currently addressing the problem. There is not, therefore, a conflict between a national and a state law. What is significant, however, is the language of Lewis Powell's opinion, with its reference to 'a traditional area of state responsibility' and its implication that Justices still hanker after the holy grail of discoverable matters uniquely the states' concern.

There is another aspect to this case which warrants comment. Indiana (and indeed, Hawaii, Ohio, Minnesota, and Missouri) had acted, as has been mentioned, in an area of considerable public concern *before* the Congress in Washington had manged to face the problem of the corporate raider. Fifty-five years ago Louis Brandeis wrote in dissent these words: '[It] is one of the happy incidents of the federal system that a single courageous state may, if its citizens choose, serve as a laboratory and try novel social and economic experiments without risk to the rest of the country.'[84] The same sentiments were expressed by Sandra O'Connor in 1982; one of the central functions of the states, she wrote (again in dissent), is as 'laboratories for the development of new social, economic and political ideas'.[85] People of very different ideological persuasions at different times in America's history have clung to this view. Sometimes these laboratory experiments may well be highly praiseworthy; the regulatory movement or the granting to women the suffrage in the late nineteenth century come to mind; in more recent years, some states have taught Washington a good deal about environmental protection and the treatment of offenders. On the other side of the balance sheet, by contrast, could be found the discriminatory practices of the southern states, limitations on freedoms of speech or intellectual teaching, and penal laws of great severity.

What the Indiana case illustrates is both the potential advantage in a continental state of subdivisions able to exercise discretionary power suited to their more parochial needs but also the irresoluble difficulty of drawing the bright lines between state and federal jurisdictions. In so many areas, both levels of government operate concurrently on the people. In its exercise of its spending power, indeed, Congress has clearly put pressure upon state governments but it is a pressure which can be resisted. Benefits can be refused as Alabama, for instance, refused in the 1950s in order to protect its segregated educational institutions. But benefits accepted become limitations accepted; as the Court has constantly made clear, the United States 'may regulate that which it subsidizes'.[86] In 1984 Congress passed a law requiring the Department of Transport to withold 5 per cent of the federal highway funds due any state that did not raise its drinking age to twenty-one by October 1986 and 10 per cent if the rise had not taken place by October 1987. Some states resisted this pressure and South Dakota, backed by an array of local government organisations, challenged its constitutionality, in part on 21st Amendment grounds and in part on general 'federalism' grounds. 'If Congress may, by the subterfuge of witholding money,' the state's brief ran, 'usurp those powers specifically delegated to the states [which is a somewhat bold reading of the repeal of prohibition amendment], the independent existence of the states as sovereigns within the federal system is threatened.'[87] Rural South Dakota just *was* different from the notorious 'blood border' problem of the eastern states, where young people crossed state borders specifically to buy and drink alcohol and where the ensuing carnage on the highways was alarmingly high.

Local dissimilarities create a variety of appropriate responses; federalism's purpose is to protect this variety. At times in the past the Supreme Court had recognised this logic, most often with words alone, but also more substantively; what counted as pornography, for example, *could* differ as between Los Angeles and New York, on the one hand, and Oklahoma City on the other.[88] More recently, the inherent conflict between *national* rights protected by the Fourteenth Amendment and *local* rights implied by federal systems has been resolved in favour of uniformity.[89] When it came to the minimum age at which alcohol could be bought, the Court decided differences were not permitted.[90] There are, therefore, no clear principles on which variety, the *sine qua non* of federalism, can be legitimated. A majority of the Court is aware of this. Blackmun's answer in *Garcia* was to return to the nineteenth century and argue that 'the principal means chosen by the Framers to ensure the role of the states in the federal system lies in the structure of the federal government itself'.[91] To the extent that the courts should get involved in adjudicating on the boundary between national and state power, he felt, courts (and here is an echo of Stone's justification for some judicial activism)[92] should only concern themselves with the openness of the political process itself. There is, therefore, something slightly peculiar in 1987 in concentrating on legal federalism rather than political federalism; it is, however, the Bicentennial of the Constitution which is being celebrated and that may be justification enough. But it would be wrong not to venture quickly into the political arena for it is there (according to *Garcia*) that the mystical boundary between the two authorities will be found.

V

The point I would make is simply that the voices which emphasise the erosion of state autonomy are misleading and perhaps also unrepresentative.[93] After the *Darby* and *Filburn* decisions, Harold Laski wrote: 'Federalism, which began by seeking to maintain variety in unity has ended by succumbing to the influence of giant capitalism, which is, by its inherent nature, unfavourable to the variety which federalism seeks to maintain ... the central result of economic development has been to emphasise the obsolescence of the federal idea'.[94] Yet, particularly to a visitor from the United Kingdom, that 'variety which federalism seeks to maintain' is tremendously in evidence. From the more bizarre variations in the imposition of the death penalty through educational policy to business law, the reality of state power is everywhere in evidence. This can be illustrated quite simply by looking at public school financing. In 1984–5, Alaska spent $6,002 on each pupil, Alabama

$1,978;[95] California raised 7.9 per cent of its funds for education in 1982–3 from local taxes, New Hampshire 89.2 per cent; Mississippi provided 53.3 per cent of its funds from state taxes, Michigan 36.1 per cent and New Hampshire only 6.9 per cent.[96] These differences represent important variations in priorities and could be replicated again and again. Just as George Sutherland was wrong when he lamented in 1937 that 'the Constitution is dead', so those who say that federalism is dead today are also wrong.

What is more, there has grown up institutional and ideological support for the current central government involvement in policy issues 'traditionally' thought of as state concerns.[97] A bevy of institutions have grown up which thrive on extensive intergovernmental relations and a new brand of politician, the topocrat, has arrived on the Washington scene, jetting importantly in from various state capitals to National Airport.[98] The networks established to continue the close collaboration between national and state capitals are buttressed by Congressmen whose functions as acquirors of resources for their districts and local ombudsmen are strengthened thereby.[99] The state and local governments have increasingly attempted to co-ordinate their activities[100] and there is now even an organisation in Washington, the State and Local Legal Centre, which is responsible for presenting cases more effectively to the Supreme Court in defence of state and local government interests. Yet there are inevitably conflicts, over economic policy and natural resources in particular, where there cannot be *the* state interest.

The *status quo* is supported also by public opinion in general. In parallel with the growth of personal support for President Reagan in the early 1980s went a broad acceptance of national government involvement in state matters; only on foreign aid and welfare did majorities in the early 1980s believe too much was being spent by the federal government while about the right amount or too little was thought to be being spent on halting crime, on drug addiction, health, education, the environment, problems of big cities, improving the conditions of blacks, and defence. The hesitant rise and dramatic fall of General Revenue Sharing, an attempt to return to the states a greater degree of policy-making, and the failure of Reagan's 'New Federalism' to establish any major structural alterations in the relationships between the states and the federal government testify to the strong roots of the current arrangements.[101] The arteries may be hardening but there are too many people who realise, once they look at the possible consequences of a radical redistribution of fiscal and administrative responsibilities, that much might be lost by change. Indeed, there is an interesting parallel between the Court's thinking and the thinking of the politically aware. In the middle 1970s we find devolution and *National League of Cities*; in the 1980s we find the failure of the New Federalism and *Garcia*. The majorities on either side may have been small, but the shifts of emphasis were reflective of shifts in articulate public opinion.

This could lead to two conclusions. First, Dahl's seminal 1957 paper, which argued that the Supreme Court essentially reflected the dominant Washington coalition of the day, remains basically sound.[102] The fractured majorities in Washington, which dealignment without realignment encourages,[103] is replicated in the fractured majorities on the Court. Analysts of the Burger Court have generally accepted Vincent Blasi's characterisation of the Court's jurisprudence as 'rootless activism' and I belong to that company.[104] But the same can be said of Washington politics. There is plenty of activism, but it lacks consistent attachment to either Great Society interventionism or New Federalism abstinence.

Second, and probably more important in the context of the Bicentennial, examining legal federalism reminds us how adaptable, flexible, yes, malleable even, the Constitution is. I am reminded of William Randolph's injunction to his fellow members on the Committee of Detail 200 years ago; they should, he advised, 'insert essential principles only, lest the operations of government should be clogged by rendering those provisions permanent and unalterable, which ought to be accommodated to times and places'.[105] I am also comforted by James Madison's 1821 reminder that 'as a guide in expounding and applying the provisions of the Constitution, the debates and incidental decisions of the Convention can have no authoritative character'.[106] I am well aware that two quotations, even from such eminent Founding Fathers, do not settle the issue. But, as I look at some members of the Court attempting to discover workable standards on which a recognisable division of powers between national and state government could be based (as the present Chief Justice likes to do and the Attorney-General encourages), I prefer Blackmun's *Garcia* escape. One cannot define the indefinable. It may be better to accept that and leave the shifting line to be drawn by the political process. The loser, of course, is the individual state whose representatives cannot operate the log-rolling, coalition politics of Capitol Hill. But I do not think that is the Constitution's fault nor yet the fault of the Justices of the Supreme Court.

The future is as yet unseen. The New Right's 'litmus test' will surely prove as incomplete as Roosevelt's did; the precedents are there for a different jurisprudence; the paradox of knowing intuitively that something called state sovereignty exists without being able to define it will still trouble Americans. My guess is that in fifty years time a review of legal federalism will not differ much from my own; there will be different cases to cite, different shifting majorities in Washington and on the Court to chronicle; Sam Ervin's successors will still hold simplistic views of the federal principle; and they will still be wrong.

NOTES

1 K. C. Wheare, *Federal Government*, Oxford, Oxford University Press, 4th edn, 1963, p. 1.
2 W. H. Stewart, 'Metaphors, models and the development of federal theory', *Publius*, XII, 1982, pp. 5–24.
3 *Nomination of Thurgood Marshall: report with minority views*, Senate Executive Report No. 13, 90th Congress, 1st Session (1967), p. 5.
4 *Nomination of Thurgood Marshall*, p. 6.
5 Article I, ss 2,3,4 (elections to Congress); Article II, s 1 (elections to the presidency).
6 *United States v. Darby*, 312 US 100 (1941), at 124.
7 'The powers not delegated to the United States by the Constitution, nor prohibited by it to the States, are reserved to the States respectively, or to the people.'
8 *Jacobellis v. Ohio*, 378 US 184 (1964), at 197. See also his dissenting opinion in *Ginzberg v. United States*, 383 US 463 (1966), at 499.
9 See particularly Article I, s 10.
10 At least, those who drew up the Constitution in Philadelphia probably felt this. The attack on the Constitution during the ratification process (which only narrowly failed) certainly imagined a more interventionist role for the national government. Prescient though it may have been, this view had to wait a century or more before it was vindicated. For such fears, see Herbert Storing, *The Abridged Anti-Federalist*, Chicago, University of Chicago Press, 1985.
11 *Marbury v. Madison*, 1 Cranch 137 (1803).
12 Article I, s 8.
13 *McCulloch v. Maryland*, 4 Wheaton 316 (1819).
14 *Gibbons v. Ogden*, 9 Wheaton 1 (1824).
15 The best short account of this 'nationalising period' is still Robert G. McCloskey, *The American Supreme Court*, Chicago, University of Chicago Press, 1960.
16 E. S. Corwin, *The Commerce Power versus States' Rights*, Princeton NJ, Princeton University Press, 1936.
17 *Gibbons v. Ogden*, 9 Wheaton 1 (1824), *passim*.
18 *United States v. E. C. Knight*, 156 US 1 (1895).
19 A good exposition of the reach of federal power, as interpreted by the Court in the 1930s, can be read in *Schechter Poultry Corp. v. United States*, 295 US 519 (1935), at 542–50.

20 *Hammer v. Dagenhart* (the child labour case), 247 US 251 (1918) and *Bailey v. Drexel. Furniture Corporation* (the child labour tax case), 259 US 20 (1922) are the classic instances.
21 *Champion v. Ames*, 188 US 321 (1903), 'lottery tickets across state boundaries'; *Hippolite Egg Co. v. United States*, 220 US 45 (1911), 'colouring in margarine'; *Hoke v. United States*, 227 US (1913), 'transportation of women across state boundaries for prostitution'; *Clark Distilling Co. v. Western Maryland R. Co.*, 242 US 311 (1916), 'intoxicating liquors'.
22 *Hammer v. Dagenhart*, 247 US 251 (1918), at 276.
23 *McCulloch v. Maryland*, 4 Wheaton 316 (1819).
24 *Collector v. Day*, 11 Wallace 113 (1871).
25 Richard E. Johnston and John T. Thompson, 'The Burger Court and federalism: a revolution in 1976?', *Western Political Quarterly*, XXXIII, 1980, p. 201.
26 *Bailey v. Drexel Furniture Co.*, 259 US 20 (1922), at 39.
27 *Pollock v. Farmers' Loan and Trust Co.*, 156 US 601 (1895).
28 John E. Semonche, *Charting the Future: the Supreme Court responds to a changing society*, Westport Conn., Greenwood Press, 1978.
29 David B. Walker, 'A perspective on intergovernmental relations' in Richard H. Leach (ed.), *Intergovernmental Relations in the 1980s*, New York, Marcel Dekker, 1983, p. 1.
30 Peter Irons, *The New Deal Lawyers*, Princeton NJ, Princeton University Press, 1983.
31 *Panama Refining Co. v. Ryan*, 293 US 388 (1935); *Schechter Poultry Corp. v. United States*, 295 US 495 (1935).
32 *Carter v. Carter Coal Co.*, 298 US 238 (1936); *United States v. Butler*, 297 US 1 (1936).
33 William E. Leuchtenberg, 'The origins of Franklin D. Roosevelt's "court-packing plan"', *Supreme Court Review*, 1966, Chicago, Chicago University Press.
34 Leonard Baker, *Back to Back: the duel between FDR and the Supreme Court*, New York, Macmillan, 1967.
35 This was Felix Frankfurter's defence of Roberts. See his 'Mr. Justice Roberts', *University of Pennsylvania Law Review*, CIV, 1955–6, pp. 313–17.
36 Herman C. Pritchett, *The Roosevelt Court: a study in judicial politics and values 1937–1947*, New York, Macmillan, 1948.
37 *United States v. Darby*, 312 US 100 (1941).
38 *Ibid.*, at 114.
39 *Ibid.*, at 115.
40 *Wickard v. Filburn*, 317 US 111 (1942).
41 *Helvering v. Gerhardt*, 304 US 405 (1938).
42 *Mitchum v. Foster*, 407 US 225 (1972), at 238–9.
43 Pritchett, *The Roosevelt Court*.
44 Richard Kluger, *Simple Justice*, New York, Knopf, 1976.
45 *United States v. Carolene Products*, 304 US 144 (1938), fn. 4.
46 *Barron v. Baltimore*, 7 Peters 243 (1833).
47 16 Wallace 36 (1873).
48 *Gitlow v. New York*, 268 US 652 (1925).
49 *Near v. Minnesota*, 283 US 697 (1931).
50 *Powell v. Alabama*, 287 US 45 (1932).
51 *Hamilton v. Regents of the University of California*, 293 US 245 (1934).
52 *De Jonge v. Oregon*, 299 US 353 (1937).
53 *Palko v. Connecticut*, 302 US 319 (1937).
54 *Rochin v. California*, 342 US 165 (1952), at 173. This always horrified Justice Hugo Black because of its innate subjectivity; see *Mr Justice and Mrs Black: the memoirs of Hugo L. Black and Elizabeth Black*, New York, Random House, 1986, *passim*.
55 *Adamson v. California*, 332 US 46 (1947); Hugo Black, *A Constitutional Faith*, New York, Knopf, 1968; Hugo Black, 'The Bill of Rights', *New York University Law Review*, XXXV, 1959–60, pp. 865–81.

56 Henry Abraham, *Freedom and the Court: civil rights and liberties in the United States*, New York, Oxford University Press, 2nd edn, 1972.
57 *Katzenbach v. McClung*, 379 US 294 (1964).
58 In this area, see generally: Deil S. Wright, *Understanding Intergovernmental Relations*, North Scituate, Ma., Duxbury Press, 2nd edn, 1982.
59 Wright, *Understanding Intergovernmental Relations*, p. 89.
60 Theodore Caplow *et al.*, *Middletown Families: fifty years of change and continuity*, Minneapolis, University of Minnesota Press, 1982, pp. 26–9.
61 Ann O'M. Bowman and Richard C. Kearney, *The Resurgence of the States*, New York, Prentice-Hall, 1986.
62 Hugh Heclo, 'Two traditions of general welfare', *Political Science Quarterly*, CI, 1986, p. 193.
63 *Congressional Quarterly Weekly*, XXXVIII, 1980, pp. 2034, 2035, 2046.
64 *Congressional Quarterly Weekly*, XXXIX, 1981, p. 187.
65 Edwin Meese III, 'The Attorney-General's view of the Supreme Court: towards a jurisprudence of original intention', *Public Administration Review*, XLV, 1985, p. 704.
66 *Maryland v. Wirtz*, 392 US 183 (1968).
67 *Maryland v. Wirtz*, 392 US 183 (1968), at 201.
68 *Fry v. United States*, 421 US 542 (1975).
69 *National League of Cities v. Usery*, 426 US 833 (1976). For a general positive discussion of this case, see Sotrios A. Barber, '*National League of Cities v. Usery*: new meaning for the Tenth Amendment', *Supreme Court Review*, 1977, pp. 161–82.
70 *National League of Cities v. Usery*, 426 US 833 (1976), at 845.
71 Citing *Fry v. United States*, 421 US 542 (1976), at 547.
72 *National League of Cities v. Usery*, 426 US 833 (1976), at 851.
73 See generally Johnston and Thompson, 'The Burger Court and federalism', pp. 197–216.
74 For example, *Hodel v. Virginia Surface Mining and Reclamation Ass.*, 452 US 264 (1981); *Hodel v. Indiana*, 452 US 314 (1981); *United Transportation Union v. Long Island Co.*, 455 US 742 (1982); *FERC v. Mississippi*, 456 US 742 (1982); *EEOC v. Wyoming*, 460 US 226 (1983).
75 *San Antonio School District v. Rodriguez*, 411 US 1 (1973).
76 469 US 528 (1985). See Andrzej Rapaczynski, 'From sovereignty to process: the jurisprudence of federalism after *Garcia*', *Supreme Court Review*, 1986, pp. 341–419.
77 *Rochin v. California*, 342 US 165 (1952).
78 469 US 528 (1985) at 550–51.
79 Herbert Wechsler, 'The political safeguards of federalism: the role of the states in the composition and selection of the national government', *Columbia Law Review*, LIV, 1954, p. 543.
80 *National League of Cities v. Usery*, 426 US 833 (1976), at 845.
81 R. D. Lamm and Michael McCarthy, *The Angry West*, Boston, Houghton Mifflin, 1982.
82 *Edgar v. MITE Corp.*, 457 US 624 (1982).
83 *CTS Corp. v. Dynamics of Corp. of America*, 107 S. Ct. 1637 (1987). See Donald C. Langevoort, 'The Supreme Court and the politics of corporate take-overs', *Harvard Law Review*, CI, 1987–8, pp. 96–118.
84 *FERC v. Mississippi*, 456 US 742 (1982), at 788.
85 Dissenting in *FERC v. Mississippi*, 456 US 742 (1982) at 788.
86 *Ivanhoe Irrigation District v. McCracken*, 357 US 275 (1958), at 296, citing *Wickard v. Filburn*, 317 US 111 (1942) at 131.
87 *Congressional Quarterly Weekly*, XLV, 1987, p. 727.
88 *Miller v. California*, 413 US 15 (1973).
89 *Pope v. Illinois*, 107 S. Ct. 1918 (1987).
90 *South Dakota v. Dole*, 1075. Ct. 2793 (1987).

91 469 US 528 (1985) at 551.

92 *United States v. Carolene Products*, 304 US 144 (1938), fn. 4.

93 See Bowman and Kearney, *The Resurgence of the States*; compare with Terry Sanford, *Storm over the States*, New York, McGraw-Hill, 1967.

94 Harold Laski, *The American Democracy: a commentary and an interpretation*, London, Allen and Unwin, 1949, p. 50.

95 Murray S. Stedman, Jr., *State and Local Governments*, Boston, Little Brown, 3rd edn, 1982, p. 432.

96 J. Richard Aronson and John L. Hilley, *Financing State and Local Governments*, Washington, DC, Brookings Institution, 1986, p. 253.

97 See, generally, Marylin Gittell (ed.), *State Politics and the New Federalism*, London, Longman, 1986.

98 Samuel H. Beer, 'Federalism, nationalism and democracy in America', *American Political Science Review*, LXXII, 1978, pp. 9–21; David H. McKay, 'The rise of the topocratic state', in D. Ashford (ed.), *Financing Urban Government in the Welfare State*, London, Croom Helm and New York, St. Martin's, 1980, pp. 50–70.

99 See several of the chapters in John E. Chubb and Paul E. Peterson (eds), *The New Direction in American Politics*, Washington, DC, Brookings Institution, 1985.

100 Alfred R. Light, 'Intergovernmental sources of information in state administration', *American Politics Quarterly*, VI, 1978, pp. 147–65.

101 On General Revenue Sharing, see, among others, Paul R. Dommel, *The Politics of Revenue Sharing*, Bloomington, Indiana University Press, 1974; Richard Nathan and Charles Adams jnr (eds), *Revenue Sharing: the second round*, Washington, DC, Brookings Institution, 1977; G. Ross Stephens, 'The great reform in federal grant policy or whatever happened to general revenue sharing?', in L. Kenneth Hubbell (ed.), *Fiscal Crisis in American Cities: the federal response*, Cambridge, Mass., Ballinger, 1979.

102 Robert A. Dahl, 'Decision-making in a democracy: the role of the Supreme Court as a national policy-maker', *Journal of Public Law*, VI, 1967, pp. 279–95.

103 Byron Shafer, *The Changing Structure of American Politics*, Oxford, Clarendon Press, 1986.

104 Vincent Blasi (ed.), *The Burger Court: the counter-revolution that wasn't*, New Haven, Yale University Press, 1983, esp. pp. 198–217.

105 Cited in Clinton Rossiter, *1787: the grand Convention*, New York, Macmillan, 1966, pp. 201–2.

106 James Madison to Thomas Ritchie, 15 September 1821, cited in H. Jefferson Powell, 'The original understanding of original intent', *Harvard Law Review*, XCVIII, 1984–5, p. 936.

Congress and the Constitution: Two Hundred Years of Stability and Change

ABSTRACT

The first article of the Constitution establishes the American Congress, which remains today one of the most powerful legislatures in the world, but which also remains part of the system of separated powers, requiring it to co-operate with or at least to relate to the other branches of government. This chapter looks at the changing ways in which Congress has organised itself for the constant requirement of relating both to the rest of the government and to the voters and interest groups. The contemporary Congress of the 1970s and 1980s exhibits some important differences both from the pre-modern Congress of the first century of American government and from the modern Congress that developed from the 1880s, but certain bedrock constants are shown to remain. The tension between the requirements of efficient legislation and oversight of the executive on the one hand, and representation of and accountability to constituents on the other, is shown to be a constant theme of Congressional experience. These constitutional constants need to be reckoned with in any reforms aimed at Congressional activity.

'If men were angels, no government would be necessary. If angels were to govern men, neither external nor internal controls on government would be necessary. In framing a government which is to be administered by men over men, the great difficulty lies in this: you must first enable the government to control the governed; and in the next place oblige it to control itself. A dependence on the people is, no doubt, the primary control on the government; but experience has taught mankind the necessity of auxiliary precautions.'

James Madison, *The Federalist*, no. 51

INTRODUCTION

The United States Congress has existed in its present constitutional form for two centuries. Although its original design establishing a powerful and decentralised representative legislative assembly persists, Congress continues to change, to adapt to a dynamic political environment. To understand Congress, it is useful to describe its historical and constitutional roots and to explain why certain aspects of Congress remain the same and others have changed. To achieve these purposes the chapter is organised around three topics: (1) the historical roots of Congress, (2) decisions of the Constitutional Convention establishing Congress, and (3) stability and change in Congress.

HISTORICAL ROOTS OF THE CONGRESS

The constitutional design of Congress grew out of 500 years' experience with legislatures in Western Europe and England. The drafters of the Constitution were especially influenced by the British experience with Parliament. The framers designed a Congress that followed the long struggle toward representative and powerful legislatures in Great Britain and later in the colonies. James Madison, a major author of the Constitution, put the primary focus on Congress succinctly: 'In republican government, the legislative authority necessarily predominates'.[1]

The importance of Congress in the Constitution came directly from the development of the British Parliament which was well known by the framers. The evolution of Parliament occurred in several stages and had a direct impact on the design of Congress. In the late thirteenth century, British monarchs established Parliaments consisting of nobility and landed gentry primarily to conserve peace, to administer justice and especially to levy taxes to provide revenue for the King's needs. Parliaments gradually acquired other legislative powers beyond responding to the King's call for a vote on taxes. By the late seventeenth century Parliament put limits on the King's power in lawmaking and raising money for his purposes. It took the beheading of Charles I in 1649 and the dethroning of James II in 1688 to assure parliamentary ascendancy over the Crown. *The Declaration of Rights* (1689) codified the rights won through the puritan revolution and glorious revolution of 1688, further extending representation and limits on the monarchy by stating that no laws and no armies would be established without the consent of Parliament.[2]

The philosopher John Locke was an important intellectual influence on the drafters of the constitutional design of Congress.[3] The Constitution expresses Locke's philosophy that a contract must exist between 'We the People' and government to protect the rights of citizens.[4] Locke further argued that 'the legislative is not only the supreme power, but is sacred and unalterable in the hands where the community have placed it'.[5] It was also Locke who best described the popular concept of separation of legislative and executive power that is a central element of the Constitution. These concepts are reflected directly in the Constitution.

The delegates to the Constitutional Convention also brought their experience of colonial and early state legislative assemblies to Philadelphia. Colonial and later state legislatures started from the state of Parliament in the early seventeenth century. The legislative power in the colonial assemblies grew quickly. Most lower houses in the American colonies had popularly elected members that were distrustful of executive power, the British governors. During the colonial period, the executive was represented by British governors appointed by the monarchy and the legislatures were considered to be American. These legislative assemblies had some control over their own colonial affairs and often confronted the governors over unpopular policies. By 1787 the Constitutional Convention delegates drew upon eleven years of independence and working models of strong legislatures in the states. A natural fear of the executive was a central element of the debates at Philadelphia; thus, the new Congress would be strong, independent, representative of diverse interests, and would check the power of the President.

The American Revolution overthrew the British governors and their linkage to George III when the Continental Congress issued the Declaration of Independence on July 4, 1776. The first US Constitution (from 1781 to 1787) established a weak one-house Continental Congress with strong bicameral legislatures within each of the states. The Articles of Confederation and Perpetual Union of 1776 established no executive or judicial branch.[6] The single-chambered Congress was a weak assembly of 'ambassadors' from sovereign states. Its members were elected for one-year terms and were only allowed to serve a maximum of three out of every six years. The Continental Congress had no independent revenue; it could not pay debts; and it had no effective direction of national defence or foreign policy. The Congress under the confederation could make treaties with foreign nations, but the states could refuse to honour them. It had no enforcement power, no way to cope with trade barriers among the states or even rebellion. States had autonomy and power over the Congress. This weak central government under a loose confederation of thirteen states could not even establish a common currency; each state had its own money which might be considered worthless in another. State protectionist trade barriers which obstructed the free flow of interstate commerce, rebellions, concern about national security, all eventually doomed the Articles of Confederation. Shays' rebellion in 1786 dramatically revealed the weakness of the Articles of Confederation and gave rise to the governmental reform movement resulting in the Philadelphia Constitutional Convention the next year. Although the delegates to the Convention had experienced the failure of a weak central government under the Articles of Confederation, they remembered the evils of an overly strong central government under the British monarchy. The authors of the Constitution tried to check the power of a strong national executive, preserve the primacy of the states, but correct the weak national legislative assembly under the Articles. It was difficult to avoid the dangers of each extreme. The founding fathers faced a major challenge: how could they design a government that would bind the thirteen sovereign and rival states into one union *without* undermining the traditional freedoms for which they fought? Several key decisions were made by the farmers protecting these freedoms, giving Congress a shared base of power, and establishing the concept of government by consent of the governed. The rights of the people were to be protected by diffusing power among rival interests: the President and Executive Branch, the US House of Representatives, and the US Senate.

DECISIONS OF THE CONSTITUTIONAL CONVENTION

The fifty-five delegates who gathered in Philadelphia in 1787 devoted most of their time at the Constitutional Convention to the provisions in Article I of the Constitution, the article establishing the Congress and setting forth its powers.[7] Article I of the Constitution vests 'legislative powers herein granted' to a Congress consisting of two chambers, a Senate and a House of Representatives, and requires bills be passed in identical form by both bodies and signed by the President before it can become law. Many of the basic principles establishing Congress come directly from the experience with legislatures in Europe, England, the Colonies, and the failure of the Articles of Confederation. These principles include limited government, separation of powers, checks and balances, and federalism.

Congress is designed with the intention to function in at least three ways: to legislate or to make national laws, to represent the people of the United States, and to check and help control the power of the President. The framers created a powerful and democratic Congress. Most of the controversial compromises at the Constitutional Convention were about the powers Congress would hold; however, the general agreement that the United States would have a powerful national legislature was never seriously questioned. The framers' decisions resulted in a powerful but restrained legislature that has forced the US government to struggle with the problem of disintegration for two hundred years. As James Madison argued in the *Federalist* papers nos. 10 and 51, Congress is designed to be powerful but limited.[8] Its power is limited by the judicial and the executive branches of the federal government, by the states, and by the power of the people to organise and to put popular political pressure on the institution.

The framers authored a Constitution that deliberately fragments power between the national government and the states, and among the executive, legislative, and judicial branches. They also divided legislative powers by creating two coequal houses, a bicameral Congress. Although divided, Congress was designed to be independent and powerful, checking the power of the executive and directly linking the people to government through popular, free periodic elections. The framers wanted an effective and powerful federal government, but they wanted to limit its power in order to protect personal and property rights. They were wary of excessive authority in an executive, for they had experienced the abuses of English monarchs and their colonial royal governors. They were also concerned with 'elective despotism' or excessive legislative power which they had experienced with their own state legislatures under the Articles of Confederation.

The framers created three branches of government, the executive, the legislative, and the judicial, with none having a monopoly. This separation of powers restricted the power of any one branch and it required co-operation among the three in order to govern effectively. Thus, the history of Congress and the Constitution is one of pressure between integration and disintegration, representativeness and efficiency, co-operation and conflict, stability and change. Political action requires co-operation among the branches, within Congress, among the levels of government, and with non-governmental institutions, to overcome the constitutionally and politically-based disintegration of the American government system.

However, the Constitution created an open invitation for conflict and struggles for power by the President and Congress. The framers called for the executive and legislature to share powers; however, each is independent and able to check the other. The principle of separation of powers and this system of checks and balances allows each branch to limit the power of the other. Congress was further checked by being divided into two independently elected bodies, each requiring consent to pass a law. This bicameral design drew from the working models of strong legislatures in the states under the Articles of Confederation during the years leading up to the Constitutional Convention. The network of checks and balances creates conflict and requires co-operation, accommodation, and a tempered presidential and congressional power. Despite the limits placed on Congress, the primary mission of government lies upon the broad policy decisions of Congress.

Congressional power is also limited by the power of the states. Political power is divided among the three branches and further between the levels of government. The Tenth Amendment limits Congressional power by stating that 'powers not delegated to the United States by the Constitution, nor prohibited by it to the states, are reserved to the states respectively, or to the people'. Although state powers are 'residual' rather than simply listed, the jurisdiction of state government is nonetheless broad and puts limits on Congress. However, states are required, of course, to pass laws that are constitutional. Congressional power and authority is further limited by the Bill of Rights which contains several prohibitions concerning civil rights. For example, Congress may not pass laws abridging freedom of speech, press, or assembly. It may not deprive people of 'life, liberty, or property without due process of law'. Congress may not require excessive bail or deny a trial by jury. It also may not adopt laws respecting an establishment of religion. Article I, Section 9 also specifically prohibits Congress from adopting *ex post facto* laws or passing bills of attainder.

The framers avoided a parliamentary design for the US government. The President and members of Congress are elected independently, unlike parliamentary systems throughout the world. Cabinet members are not drawn from Members of Congress nor is the President given the power to dissolve Congress. Congress and the President, each with different terms of office, times of election, and constituencies have different priorities in lawmaking. Although they often disagree, national policy must reflect the judgement of both the President and Congress.

Article I of the Constitution provides for a Congress of two chambers each with a different constituency, and was adopted by the Convention with little opposition. The bicameral design followed the precedent set by the British Parliament and ten of the thirteen colonies. There was extensive debate over representation, the question of how members would be elected, who votes and under what conditions. Originally members of the House of Representatives were given short terms and direct elections while US Senators were given long terms with provisions for election through respective state legislatures. The framers designed the House of Representatives to be the 'popular' House. However, 'popular' election in eighteenth-century United States did not include blacks, women, many non-property-owners, Indians, and many others. The design for Senate elections caused lengthy debate at the Convention. The indirect selection of Senators in state legislatures was intended to be a check on the radical democratic views expressed in the House. The Senate was expected to be representative of the more privileged interests. Every state was given two Senators as the only acceptable method of checking the radical views of the masses.

The framers left to the states the question of who could vote in the election of House members. The Constitution states that all persons who were eligible in each state to vote for members of that state's most numerous legislative house could also vote in the election of a member of the US House of Representatives from that state. Later laws and constitutional amendments established federal standards for voting and appointment of votes so that House districts are of approximately equal size. A person must be twenty-five years of age and a US citizen to be elected a member of the House of Representatives. There is no limit on how many times a person can be elected to the House of Representatives, and many now make it a career. To ensure that the House of Representatives would represent the 'popular will', the framers limited the term of office for members to two years, which forces members to go back frequently to the people for approval.

The framers intended to insulate the Senate from control by a popular majority. Thus, the Constitution guarantees every state two Senators, regardless of the state's population; the present Senate has one hundred members. All Senators must be at least thirty years old and citizens, and are elected for six-year terms. One-third of the Senate is elected every two years. There is no limit on how long a Senator may serve in Congress. Senators must be residents of their states and represent whole states while House members must be residents of their districts and they represent districts of approximately 500,000 citizens. Although members of the Senate were originally elected by state legislatures, in 1913 the seventeenth Amendment to the Constitution changed the mode of election to provide for direct election by the voters of the state.

The Congress is given a variety of specific formal powers in Article I, Section 8 of the Constitution. The list of powers ranges widely, but the greatest power of Congress is its authority to pass laws directly binding upon all citizens. Section 8 of Article I gives Congress the power of the purse, the power to appropriate government funds. Presidents may proposed budgets for the federal government but Congress has the final decision on spending. Congress also has the power to levy and collect taxes, to borrow and coin money and to regulate foreign and interstate commerce. It has power to establish the Supreme Court and federal judicial system. Congress has the power to declare war, to create an army and navy, to provide for a militia, and to adopt laws concerning bankruptcy, naturalisation, patents, and copyrights. The list also includes the authority to regulate standards and measures, to establish post offices, and to set up a government for the capital district.

In addition to these specified powers (also known as *delegated powers* because they represent a delegation of authority by the people to the national government), the final clause of Article I, Section 8 gives Congress the power 'to make all laws which shall be necessary and proper for carrying into execution the foregoing powers, and all other powers vested by this Constitution in the government of the United States, or in any department or officer thereof'. The doctrine of *implied powers* allows Congress broad authorisation to carry into execution its delegated powers. The Constitution and court cases further reinforce Congressional power in the 'supremacy clause' which states that Congressional laws 'made in pursuance' of the Constitution 'shall be the supreme law of the land' (Article VI, Section 2). This 'supremacy clause' has come to mean that state laws and constitutions in conflict with the Constitution or acts of Congress are unconstitutional, null and void, in effect giving Congress substantial power over the states.[9] This clause makes federal enactments superior to those of the states and requires state and federal judges to enforce their provisions.

Any measure having to do with taxes must originate in the House, not the Senate. All other bills may be originated in either house. This power to originate 'revenue raising measures', which was a part of the so-called Connecticut Compromise, was a concession to those who opposed the idea of each state having the same number of members in the Senate. It allowed the house representing the 'popular will' to decide first about taxes. This provision has been customarily interpreted by the House and Senate as applying to any tax bill, whether it raises or lowers taxes, and also as a norm to appropriations bills, which deal with spending. Thus, traditionally appropriations bills are introduced in the House first. A bill going to the Senate after passage by the House may be amended in the Senate. So, a Senator who wants to change tax or budget law can simply wait until a tax or spening bill comes to the Senate from the House and if a majority of the Senate agrees, can attach the measure to the House bill as an amendment. The amended bill must then go back to the House for approval of the change, but in effect, a revenue-raising or spending measure can be originated in the Senate by this method.

Congress puts limits on the power of the executive and judicial branches through 'checks and balances'. Congress has the authority to establish executive branch agencies and departments. It has the power of oversight of the executive, which may take several forms. Congress provides budgets and salaries for justices, judges, and executive branch personnel. Funds must be authorised and appropriated by Congress for the executive. The Senate must approve nominees for the President's cabinet, ambassadors, and Supreme

Court and federal judicial appointees before they can take office. Principal executive officers of the federal government cannot be appointed by the President without the consent of the Senate. A President can not enter into a binding treaty with a foreign government without a two-thirds vote of the Senate, nor can he 'declare war', a power the Constitution purposely gives Congress.

Another more dramatic but rare check on the executive branch is impeachment. Officials can be impeached (formally accused) by a majority vote in the House of Representatives and tried in the Senate. If two-thirds of the Senators present and voting vote to convict, the official is removed from office. Only President Andrew Johnson has been tried on impeachment charges. The vote on that occasion fell one short of the number required for conviction. The House Judiciary Committee recommended that President Richard M. Nixon be impeached for transgressions in connection with the Watergate burglary of the offices of the Democratic National Committee and the ensuing cover-up. President Nixon resigned the Presidency before a full session of the House could vote on the impeachment issue.

Congressional power is extensive but not unlimited. Congress may not delegate its powers to any other body or authority. For example, the Congress may not delegate its power to the people in the form of a national referendum. Separating Congress and the President with checks and balances on each other forces both to work closely together in legislating and administering. This interdependence and necessity to co-operate checks the power of both branches of government. Congress is further checked by federalism, the powers of state governments. Finally, the 'tyranny of the majority' is checked by allowing Congress to represent a diverse set of 'factions' or interests. Congress, the President, the judiciary, interests outside government and the electorate are all mutually interdependent in governing US national policy. The Constitution created a unique legislative assembly that has the power to compete with the executive branch and to exert a major impact on public policy. How Congress uses its constitutional power to legislate, oversee the executive, and represent interests often brings it into conflict with the President. The design of the Constitution forces Congress to represent different interests than the President. Members of Congress are chosen by states and local constituencies that vary widely in their social, economic and political conditions.

The President is elected by the entire nation and has a national constituency. Thus, members representing specific interests often come into conflict with the President who represents the nation as a whole. The federal system of state-based political party organisations also provides members of Congress with even more independence from the President. The President must work with weak decentralised political parties with little discipline and even less leverage with members of Congress. In modern times Senators and Representatives usually run their own races with their own financing, responding to local conditions with little reference to nationally or Presidentially established party platforms or policies. Members are free to pursue their own interests without fear of discipline from the President.

In sum, the US Constitution makes clear that the principal functions of government are entrusted to Congress (for example, to declare war, to authorise and appropriate funds for programmes, to tax, to oversee the executive), but these powers are limited by the principles of checks and balances, separation of powers, and federalism. Consequently, in pursuing its constitutional functions of lawmaking, representation, and oversight, Congress is ensured to clash with the President and other political actors. However, Keefe and Ogul conclude that Congress in the end is supreme:

> In the catalogue of government functions, it is Congress which determines the broad policies and creates the administrative organizations to execute them, which fashions standards for administrative action and for the appointment and removal of administrative officials, which appropriates funds for the support of governmental functions, and which, in varying degrees, supervises and reviews the work of administrative establishments.[10]

SOURCES OF CONGRESSIONAL STABILITY

How has the original constitutional design of Congress been maintained and how has it changed over time? Three key characteristics in the constitutional structure of Congress help to explain the stability of the institution and the differences between the House and Senate: size, terms of office, and constituency.

The first Congress (1789–91) served a population of four million in thirteen Atlantic Coast states and consisted of twenty-six Senators and sixty-five Representatives. Congressional activities were limited to the passage of 108 laws which dealt with the creation of the new government and its relations with the states and with matters of defence and foreign affairs. Because of the size of both chambers, deliberations were guided by a few simple rules on the floors of the Senate and House. They conducted most of their deliberations on the floor of both chambers but that soon shifted to temporary select committees and later to permanent standing committees, a stable feature of Congress.

The US House of Representatives has always been larger than the Senate; today the House has 435 members and the Senate 100. House members have shorter terms of office (two years) compared to their counterparts in the Senate (six years). The constituencies of House members are much narrower and more focused than the broad and more varied state-wide constituencies of Senators. These characteristics have not changed significantly over time and they have generated several important differences that have remained constant between the House and Senate (see Table 3.1). Because of the large size of the House there is a need for more structure and formality in the rules than in the smaller Senate. The House is more hierarchically organised with less evenly distributed power than the

Table 3.1: Major differences between the House and Senate

House	Senate
Larger (435)	Smaller (100)
Shorter term of office (2 years)	Longer term of office (6 years)
Narrower constituency	Broader, more varied, constituency
Less flexible rules	More flexible rules
Policy specialists	Policy generalists
Less press and media coverage	More press and media coverage
Power less evenly distributed	Power more evenly distributed
Less prestige	More prestige
More expeditious in floor debate	Less expeditious in floor debate
Less reliance on staff	More reliance on staff

Source: Adapted from Walter J. Oleszek, *Congressional Procedures and the Policy Process*, Washington, D.C., Congressional Quarterly Press, 1989, p. 24.

Senate. The House uses a Rules Committee to control the flow of legislation to the floor. The Senate has no counterpart. Debate, amendments, and voting in the House is tightly controlled and designed to expedite legislative business. The Senate has much more informal control over legislation coming to the floor. The Senate is more individualistic and personal than the House. Much of the Senate's business is handled by unanimous consent agreements between the majority and minority parties and by informal norms, by contrast with the elaborate and more tightly controlled floor action seen in the House. The House uses a strict rule of germaneness and the Senate does not. All House amendments must pertain to the subject matter of the legislation under consideration on the floor. Senate rules rarely call for debate or amendments to be germane to the bill being considered. The Senate is allowed unlimited debate (the filibuster) which cannot be employed by the House. Senate Rule 22 protects minority rights by allowing an individual to speak without being stopped unless an extraordinary majority of sixty members votes to close debate. The Senate operates in a spirit of comity, respecting the prerogatives of all its members. Consequently, floor debate is more expeditious in the House than in the Senate. The flexibility of the Senate allows delay and even deadlock. Generally, House members fulfil the role of technical experts and the Senators are less concerned with technical perfection of legislation and more involved in gaining general public support for policies. The House has a larger work force and their division of labour allows for policy specialisation by its members. The Senate is smaller with the same amount of work, thus Senators do not usually specialise. They are compelled to become policy generalists. As a result of size and the policy generalist tendency, the Senate relies on personal and committee staff to a greater degree than the House.

Another difference between the House and the Senate is that power is distributed more evenly among the 100 Senators than among the 435 House members. Senators are more visible, have their floor amendments adopted more easily, have more immediate influence in committees, are more successful in scheduling their bills for consideration, and in general participate more widely than do House members. Although the House and the Senate are covered by live television in recent years, there is less interest by the media in the House than the Senate. The Senate is more prestigious and visible than the House. Generally these characteristics have remained relatively constant between the House and the Senate although there have been significant changes within both bodies since passage of the Constitution.

Two other facts have helped to establish the stability of the two houses over the last one hundred and fifty years. First, there have been only two major parties controlling the House and Senate since 1828. The Democrats have had primary control of both houses since 1932 (except in the Senate from 1947 to 1948; 1953 to 1954; and 1981 to 1986). The second major source of stability is the committee system. Committees and subcommittees are where the work of Congress gets done and that has been the way the institution has worked for well over one hundred years. As the United States grew and new states were established the size of Congress reflected these changes. The volume and complexity of legislative activities also increased which led to the establishment of permanent standing committees. Committees were such a stable and important characteristic of Congress that in 1885, Woodrow Wilson wrote: 'It is now, though a wide departure from the form of things, no great departure from the fact to describe ours as a government by the standing committees of Congress'.[11] Over the years the most distinguishing characteristic of Congress is the predominant role played by the committee system. Since the early 1800s most of the business of Congress is done in committees (see Table 3.2). The number of committees and their jurisdiction has been relatively stable until the 1970s. Until the major reforms of the 1970s (discussed below) committees were powers unto themselves. Most committees and their chairmen had power to operate pretty much as they wished. The most important committees in the Senate are Appropriations and Finance. The most powerful committees in the House are Rules, Appropriations, and Ways and Means. The committees play a determining life-or-death role over legislation at every stage of the legislative process.

The modern Congress (post-1880s) has evolved into an institution with low turnover of members, few contested elections, and long sessions with a heavy workload (see Table 3.2). The floor proceedings are guided by more complex rules and are generally more orderly than they were before the 1880s. There is a low turnover of committee members with stable criteria for assignment to the committees. Committees generally have a fixed and predictable

Table 3.2: Primary differences between pre-modern Congress and modern Congress

Pre-modern Congress	Modern Congress (post-1880s)
High turnover of membership	Low turnover of membership
Many contested elections	Few contested elections
Short sessions, light workload	Long sessions, heavy workload
Chaotic floor proceedings	Orderly floor proceedings
High turnover of committee members; shifting criteria for assignment	Low turnover of committee members; stable criteria for assignment
Numerous criteria for appointment of committee chairs	Seniority the dominant criterion for appointment of committee chairs
Undeveloped political party structures	Well developed political party structures

Source: Adapted from Randall B. Ripley, *Congress: Process and Policy*, New York, W. W. Norton and Company, 1983, p. 53.

set of responsibilities with well defined jurisdictions. Seniority and political party are the dominant criteria for appointment of committee chairs. The political party structure and leadership hierarchy (although weak and decentralised) is much more well developed than it was in the pre-modern Congress of the pre-1880s. House and Senate party leaders have often worked closely and co-operated to co-ordinate legislative action and to confront the executive. Party leadership has always been crucial in the smooth functioning of the legislative process.

In sum, three important underlying factors that influence the operation of the House and Senate are their size difference, their differing bases of representation (states versus districts) and their different terms of office. The larger House is more formal and hierarchical, it acts more quickly and with more rigid rules. Power is unevenly distributed in the House. It is more impersonal and less prestigious than the Senate. Since the Senate has only one hundred members, it is less formal, less hierarchical, it moves more slowly, the rules are more flexible, and power is distributed more evenly. It is more personal and has greater prestige. Senators serve longer terms than Representatives which gives Senators more freedom from constant campaigning. These characteristics have not changed significantly since the first Congress. Both institutions have the same responsibilities: legislating, oversight of the executive, and representation. Historically these responsibilities have not changed, but the way Congress has done its work has varied according to the political and economic environment of the times. Both the House and Senate have always used political parties to organise legislative work. Political parties have always been a feature of the congressional landscape, but they only emerged as a central feature of Congress in the late nineteenth century. The role of party has waxed and waned. Both bodies have always conducted their business through a decentralised committee system. The committee system is at the heart of congressional work. Both the Senate and House have equal workloads and in modern times this workload has been especially heavy.

SOURCES OF CONGRESSIONAL CHANGE

Although Congress is a relatively stable institution, as its size grew in the nineteenth and early twentieth centuries and as the volume and complexity of problems facing it multiplied, it underwent several important changes. The structure of Congress is decentralised through its committee and subcommittee system. The modern Congress is marked by a diffusion of power, a weak central core of authority and little unity of command. Leadership is weak and divided among committee chairman, subcommittee chairmen, and the party leaders.

Congress changed dramatically especially as a result of major reform in the 1970s. The changes of the 1970s have had a significant impact on many things, including the legislative workload, rules and procedures, committees and subcommittees, staff bureaucracies, the seniority system, the budget process, leadership style, the role of party organisation, constituency demands, oversight of the executive, the nature of decision-making, and ethics. What are the major recent changes in Congress?[12]

Change in membership

Over 90 per cent of the members of the House and Senate are new since 1968. For the first time since 1954, the Republicans controlled the Senate from 1981 to 1986. Members are younger and more conservative on fiscal policy and social issues (for example, abortion and school prayer). They are well-informed, activist, and unwilling to wait to be heard. There are slightly more women and more minority members. Districts are safer for incumbents, but at the same time the turnover of members in the Congress as a whole has increased (primarily due to voluntary retirements). The 1970s and 1980s saw a reversal in the long-time trend of increased tenure of office. The number and proportion of veterans in Congress dropped steadily in the 1970s and 1980s, while the number and proportion of junior members increased. If seniority characterised Congress in the 1960s and early 1970s, 'juniority' is a more appropriate term in the late 1970s and 1980s. This change in membership helped to bring the impressive reforms in committees and subcommittees, in leadership, staff and analytic capabilities, in the Congressional budget process, open decision making, in campaign finance, and the ethics of members.

Committee reform and 'democratisation' of power

The 1970s brought a 'democratisation' of decision making to the House of Representatives. In January 1969, the House Democratic Caucus re-established control over committee assignments by requiring that the Committee on Committees receive Caucus approval of committee assignments before taking them to the House floor for *pro forma* approval. In 1973 further inroads on the seniority system occurred in the House, by requiring an automatic secret ballot vote on committee chairmen at the start of each Congress (this is also now the case in the Senate). At the beginning of the 94th Congress, three chairmen were defeated through this process. Also in 1985 the Democratic Caucus removed the sitting Armed Services Committee chair from his post and Les Aspin (D–Wis.) was selected to replace him, although Representative Aspin was well down the list of senior Democrats. The power of committee chairmen was also limited through the election of subcommittee chairmen by the Democratic members of each committee in the House. Committee majority caucuses were also given the right to organise each committee and the subcommittee 'bill of rights' was adopted in the House that allows subcommittees and subcommittee chairmen to have staff and budget and thus more power. These reforms helped to take power away from the 'barons' (committee chairmen) and give it to the 'baronets' (subcommittee chairmen), thus decentralising influence in the House. Congressional government has become 'subcommittee government'. The Senate has always adhered to seniority in selecting committee chairs although they have cut down on the total number of committee leadership positions any individual could hold.

The House also limited subcommittee chairmanships to one and committee memberships to two. Representatives were guaranteed a major committee assignment, including freshmen, for the first time in 1973. All Democratic members of a committee were given an opportunity, also during 1973, to bid in order of seniority for subcommittee vacancies on committees in the House. The House also brought 'sunshine' to committee meetings (as did the Senate) by requiring a separate rollcall vote to close a committee meeting or hearing (first passed in 1973 and strengthened in 1975).

Each House committee was required to establish at least four subcommittees (except Rules and Budget), which had the consequence of spreading the power of the Ways and Means Committee (that had no subcommittees before this reform in 1973). In 1975, a 'revolution' in Committee rules and procedures came to the House, which included giving the responsibilities of the Committee on Committees of the Ways and Means Committee to the Steering and Policy Committee, requiring a caucus vote on Appropriation subcommittee chairmen, establishing additional limitations on committee service of full committee chairmen, opening conference committees and expanding minority staffing for each committee (one-third of the committee staff on each committee). This was a major move to 'democratise' the House.

The unsuccessful attempt of the Bolling-Hansen committees to reorganise the sizes, numbers and jurisdictions of committees in the House in 1973–74 was not repeated in the Senate in late 1976 and early 1977. Table 3.3 lists the reform efforts of the late 1960s and 1970s. Passage of Stevenson's committee reorganisation brought new committee and subcommittee assignment limitations to the Senate, it modernised and realigned committee jurisdictions (especially energy, environment, and governmental affairs), it eliminated several committees, and it gave the leadership more power to refer bills and to monitor the health of the Senate committee system more effectively.

The changes of the 1970s modified the House seniority system for selecting committee chairs, limited the number of chairmanships

Table 3.3: Major reform and study efforts, House and Senate: 1965–80

House
- Joint Committee on the Organization of Congress
  11 March 1965–21 July 1966
- Committee on Organization, Study, and Review
  'Hansen Committee'
  March 1970–8 October 1974
- Joint Study Committee on Budget Control
  27 October 1972–18 April 1973
- Select Committee on Committees
  'Bolling Committee'
  31 January 1973–8 October 1974
- Committee on Administrative Review
  'Obey Commission'
  1 July 1976–12 October 1977
- Select Committee on Committees
  'Patterson Committee'
  20 March 1979–30 April 1980

Senate
- Joint Committee on the Organization of Congress
  11 March 1965–21 July 1966*
- Joint Study Committee on Budget Control
  27 October 1972–18 April 1973
- Temporary Select Committee to Study the Senate Committee System
  'Stevenson Committee'
  31 March 1976–4 February 1977
- Commission on the Operation of the Senate
  'Culver Commission'
  29 July 1975–31 December 1976

Note: *Senate members of the Joint Committee continued their work as
an intrachamber committee and filed an additional report on 21
September 1966.

an individual could hold, devolved power to subcommittees, and
revised the committee assignment process. The reforms democra-
tised the House and made it more responsive; however, members
are still profoundly dissatisfied with the existing committee system
and are pushing for new committee realignment in the 1980s. For
both the Senate and House the arguments of the 1970s still exist:

reduce the number of committees and subcommittees, reduce the number of committee assignments, and reduce the overlap of jurisdictions among committees.

Leadership reform

Until the 1970s committee chairmen held power through the seniority system (that is, length of tenure on each committee rather than election) and therefore were not subject to party control. The committee assignment reforms and secret ballot selection of committee chairmen established in the 1970s led to an anomalous situation for party leaders. Today's leaders are stronger on paper, but still need more power to lead because in practice there are no disciplined parties to be led.

The last decade brought new leaders and personalities to all of the party positions in the House and the Senate. Party leadership in the Senate changed from Democratic to Republican in 1981 and back to Democratic in 1987. Change in leaders and their style was also accompanied by several major changes in the formal powers of the leadership (especially in the House). These include giving the Speaker the chairmanship of the House Democratic Steering and Policy Committee which has the authority to nominate committee chairmen and make committee assignment nominations. The reforms also give the Speaker sole power to nominate the Democratic members and the chairman of the Rules Committee so that they would be more responsive to the leadership. The Speaker was also given authority to nominate several members to the Steering and Policy Committee. On paper these reforms give the Speaker much more power than before the 1970s. In reality he is much weaker than Speakers Rayburn, Cannon, and others.

The Democratic Caucus in the House has also been given more power to co-ordinate the legislative process. In January 1969, the rules of the Caucus were changed requiring monthly meetings and giving individual members the right to place matters before the Caucus for debate and action. This reform, more than any other, set the ground work for the major changes in the 1970s: the use of the Caucus to pass reform measures.

The Senate has been cautious in giving more power to the Majority Leaders, although through the style of leadership under Senators Byrd, Baker and Dole, power and influence has increased for Senate Majority Leaders. However, central party leadership in both the House and Senate is still suspect by most members in the 1980s, and decentralising forces still predominate. Critics argue that there is still a need for stronger central leadership to orchestrate the activities of the scattered committees and subcommittees, to schedule consideration of bills, and provide better central services.

Staff and analytic capabilities

During the reform years of the 1970s, Congress improved its staffing and information gathering capabilities. Congress gave its members and committees more staff and better access to information. In the late 1980s Congress employs well over 40,000 staff for committees, members' offices, and support agencies. Some 23,500 staff work for the four support agencies and 17,000 work for members and committees. Personal staff has grown enormously. Senators now are entitled to a staff aide for each committee assignment beyond their basic personal staff (which is based upon the population of each state). Congress now has an expanded Congressional Research Service and an improved General Accounting Office. Congress created the Office of Technology Assessment in 1972 and the Congressional Budget Office in 1974 which improves its analytic support capabilities. There have also been recent impressive improvements in computing capacity and utilisation by both the House (House Information System) and the Senate. These reforms expanded the capacity of Congress to do policy analysis and to carry out evaluation of presidential initiatives and department requests. However, Congress has grown not one bureaucracy but many, clustered around centres of power. This growth has presumably improved the responsiveness and accountability of Congress but others argue that it has reduced its efficiency. Efforts to impose a common framework on staff and the new Congressional bureaucracy have generally failed. Efforts to reduce the size and power of staff is a common theme of Congress in the 1980s.

Congressional budget reform

The budget reforms of 1974 were passed to recapture fiscal power from the President and to pursue both liberal and conservative policy objectives. The Budget and Impoundment Control Act of 1974 established two budget committees, a budget timetable, the Congressional Budget Office, and a tough procedure for controlling Presidential impoundments (recissions and deferrals). The 1974 budget reform, the 1985 Gramm-Rudman-Hollings (G-R-H) Balanced Budget Act and its 1987 amendments call for Congress to establish a budget with firm expenditure levels, to project revenues, and to estimate surplus or deficit (which has existed for the last two decades), pass budgets on time, and express fiscal discipline. Congress has failed to meet these objectives.

It requires Congress to do something that it has never done before: account for expenditures, revenues and deficits in a single resolution rather than figuring out what has happened to the budget at the end of actions by the Appropriation Committees. The budget and impoundment control procedures give Congress new capabilities to counter the President's budget with its own analysis and priorities. However, the 1980s have seen ever-increasing budget deficits and an inability to pass budget and appropriation bills on time. Congress is still dominated by special interests and difficult money decisions and the Budget and Impoundment Control Act and G-R-H have not given them enough new courage to deal with those decisions.

'Sunshine' reforms

'Sunshine' or openness, less secrecy and more accountability, was pushed upon Congress by 'good government' organisations like Common Cause in the 1970s and supported internally by those concerned about the poor public image of the institution. In response Congress passed several major reforms from the 1970s to the 1980s that changed its visibility, efficiency and public image. Television and radio coverage of House committee hearings was authorised in 1970. House and Senate committee votes were recorded and made available to the public during the same year. In 1973, all House committee sessions were open to the public unless a separate roll call vote was taken to close the sessions. All Senate committee sessions were opened to the public in 1975. This had the effect of opening almost all committee sessions in both the House and Senate. In 1977 the House voted to require a full House recorded roll call vote to close conference committee hearings. In 1978 continuous television coverage of the House floor sessions was permitted and the Senate did the same in 1985. This openness brought more accountability and permeability, and less efficiency in the way Congress makes laws and oversees the executive.

Ethics and management

The American electorate's traditional distrust and boredom toward politicians turned into overt cynicism in the 1970s and it has not changed much in the 1980s. Politicians felt a backlash following Watergate, the Vietnam War, the corruption of Adam Clayton Powell and ABSCAM, and the way members collected money for election campaigns. Congress became keenly aware of the low esteem in which it was held in the public eye, especially after Wilbur Mills' aquatic exhibitionism, the Wayne Hays affair with a non-typing typist, the questions about contributions made to Congressmen by the Korean government, and the rapid growth of special interest campaign money. In response, Congress passed the campaign finance reforms of 1974 which limited individual and organisation contributions to Congressional campaigns and required candidates to report the sources and use of campaign funds. Members also must report earned income, dividends and interest, gifts, holdings in property and securities, and total debt. Congress addressed the issue of public cynicism with a new vigour, by passing stricter codes of conduct (in 1977 and 1978), by establishing two new Ethics Committees, and by limiting outside incomes (1985). They also studied their problems through a Commission on the Operation of the Senate, a Temporary Selection Committee to Study the Senate Committee System, and a Commission on Administrative Review of the House. Although the intent of these reforms and study groups was to inhibit unethical behaviour and restore public confidence in Congress, members are still concerned about the lack of public trust in their institution.

CONCLUSION AND RECOMMENDATION FOR REFORM

Congress has maintained its three essential functions: lawmaking, oversight, and representation over the past two hundred years. It still firmly holds the power of the purse; it oversees the executive and checks the power of the President; it legislates new programmes (although slowly) and reviews old ones. Most importantly Congress is still responsive (some think too much so) to political preferences and public pressure. It is representative. This is the stable core of Congress; however, the institution has also changed dramatically. The reforms of the past two decades have made Congress more representative and accountable; given it more tools to do better oversight, and changed the way it makes laws and passes budgets. Pressure to check the power of the President (for example, the 1973 War Powers Act and the Budget and Impoundment Control Act of 1974) brought reforms that helped Congress reclaim some of the power it had lost to the President during the previous decades. Internal pressure for more democratisation brought decentralised power in Congress and helped to make the institution more inefficient and permeable. With openness came more accountability and responsiveness at the price of efficiency and effectiveness as a lawmaking body. Presidents find Congress harder to influence; it is more independent. Congressional party leaders have more difficulty in co-ordinating the legislative process as Congress becomes more democratic. The struggles between representativeness and efficiency, openness and accountability, Congress and the President, specific interests and the 'public good', continue today as they did two hundred years ago during the debates in Philadelphia. Many observers have argued that the changes of the 1970s have pushed Congress into a state of paralysis which was not the intent of the authors of the Constitution two hundred years ago.[13] They argue that Congress is so inefficient that it can no longer legislate and oversee as it was intended. Several major problems have been identified by those who would reform Congress:

- the budget process is overly complex and inhibits timely action on the federal budget;
- the demands for campaign funds prevent members from devoting adequate time for the business of Congress;
- there are too many committees and committee assignments and too many overlapping jurisdictions among the committees; and
- there are too many staff members who cause members to be more responsive to staff than to constituents and unnecessarily delay the legislative process.

Congress does seem to have difficulty passing budgets on time; it seems closely tied to special interests because of the need to fund ever-more-expensive campaigns; it seems overly complex with its 'three ring circus' approach to legislation (authorisation, appropriations and budget committees); and the growth of the Congressional bureaucracy (almost 40,000 employees) does seem to cause delay and over-reliance on staff by members of Congress. The pendulum of change seems to be moving to correct these problems;

however, the major sources of stability – size, terms of office, constituency, party, and the committee system – remain the predictable bedrock of the institution. The Congress of the future will be distinct from that of the 1780s, 1880s, and 1980s, but it is not clear in what ways. Unless there is a major constitutional crisis, which is unlikely, the constitutional design of Congress will remain relatively stable but it will continue to change with the political environment as it has during its first two hundred years.

NOTES

1 Benjamin F. Wright (ed.), *The Federalist by Alexander Hamilton, James Madison and John Jay*, Cambridge, Harvard University Press, 1961, (Federalist no. 51), p. 356.
2 Blackstone's *Commentaries* (1765) were also well known to the framers and were an important influence on the constitutional design of the Congress. See William Blackstone, adapted by Robert Malcolm Kerr, *Commentaries on the Laws of England of Public Wrongs*, Boston, Beacon Press, 1962.
3 See John Locke, in Peter Laslett (ed.), *Two Treatises of Government*, New York, New American Library, 1965.
4 *Ibid.*
5 *Ibid.*
6 For an excellent analysis of the Articles of Confederation, see Merrill Jensen, *The Articles of Confederation*, Madison, University of Wisconsin Press, 1940.
7 For an excellent record of the Convention, see Max Farrand (ed.), *The Records of the Federal Convention of 1787* (4 vols), New Haven, Yale University Press, 1966. See also Michael J. Malbin, 'Congress during the Convention and Ratification' in Leonard W. Levy and Dennis J. Mahoney (eds), *The Constitution: A History of its Framing and Ratification*, New York, Macmillan, 1988.
8 See *The Federalist*, no. 10 and no. 51.
9 See the reasoning of Chief Justice Marshall in *McCulloch v. Maryland*, 4 Wheaton 316 (1819).
10 William J. Keefe and Morris S. Ogul, *The American Legislative Process: Congress and the States*, Englewood Cliffs, NJ, Prentice-Hall, Inc., 6th edn, 1985, p. 38.
11 Woodrow Wilson, *Congressional Government*, Boston, Houghton Mifflin, Co., 1885, p. 55.
12 See Leroy N. Rieselbach, *Congressional Reform*, Washington, D.C., Congressional Quarterly Press, 1986 for an analysis of the reforms of the 1970s.
13 See James L. Sundquist, *Constitutional Reform and Effective Government*, Washington, D.C., Brookings, 1986.

Presidential Autonomy in a Fragmented Polity

ABSTRACT

The second article of the Constitution, establishing the executive power, was one of its most innovative features. The Presidency was expected to be second to Congress in political prominence, but nevertheless to add to the new government an effective force for unity, energy and public purpose. The history of the Presidency is a history of Presidents, some of whom have lived up to that original expectation and some of whom have not. In the twentieth century, particularly since the Second World War, greater demands on Presidents have been accompanied by greater realisation that Presidential power may be inappropriately designed to meet those demands; modern Presidents, irretrievably immersed in the chaotic pressures and bargaining of domestic and international politics, seem doomed to oscillate between ill-disguised impotence and half-covert assertiveness. However, this chapter argues that contemporary conditions actually leave greater space for Presidential political autonomy than is generally recognised. Nevertheless, crucial differences remain between this modern Presidential autonomy and a more authentically constitutional Presidential power. The new strength of the Presidency is personal, plebiscitary and shifting, rather than constitutional, partisan and stable.

There is little doubt that the Founding Fathers considered the President the embodiment of the US state. Chosen by an electoral college and specifically designated as chief executive and head of state, the Presidency was designed to operate as an institution above both the self-interested machinations of factions or special interests, and the sometimes unthinking instincts of the mass population.[1] As we all know, the institution evolved into something far removed from this, so that today most commentators consider the Presidency to be just one more component – albeit a crucial one – in the pluralistic confusion characteristic of American politics. Hence in modern America, Presidents are obliged to bargain and negotiate with a wide range of political actors, and especially with what is now a decentralised and highly independent Congress. In addition, Presidents are now cited as the examples *par excellence* of the increasingly intimate link between the mass public and political authority.[2] They must please a vast and varied national constituency through constant public appeals on television and radio. The clear implication is that Presidents, rather than in any way being above society, are very much influenced by it. It follows that they can rarely act autonomously. Instead, they are obliged constantly to bargain, negotiate and compromise with Congress, the federal bureaucracy, courts, organised interests, and ultimately with the broad mass of the American public.

Moreover, scholars seem agreed that with the decline of party and the increasing fragmentation characteristic of American politics and society, the position of Presidents is getting weaker rather than stronger. Indeed the office is now usually described in terms of its failure to live up to expectations. So Theodore Lowi calls his recent and influential book on the institution *The personal presidency: power invested promise unfulfilled*, and Godfrey Hodgson describes Presidents as having to be *All things to all men: the false promise of the American presidency*.[3] It is also increasingly recognised that the impossible nature of the office has led some recent incumbents to by-pass normal constitutional processes and indulge in secret and often illegal acts.[4]

The purpose of this essay is to argue that the near-universal tendency to portray the institution in this way derives at least in part from a theoretical perspective which has led scholarship away from asking certain questions about the presidency and its relationship to American society. In particular, what is called *the bargaining model* of the Presidency has discouraged work which attempts to measure the relative autonomy of the office, and how the power of Presidents to shape the policy agenda may have changed over time. In this context, this paper has three objectives: first, to demonstrate the limited utility of the bargaining model by examining its explanatory power when applied to recent changes in federal government expenditures; second, to show how alternative approaches using state-centred and developmental perspectives also fail to provide a convincing explanation of recent trends; and third, to present a further alternative based on the assumption that the United States is now experiencing what is called regime fragmentation. It will be tentatively argued that in this new environment, Presidents have much greater scope for autonomous action than is commonly supposed.

THE BARGAINING MODEL

At first sight, the theme that unites most Presidential scholarship is leadership. The subtitle to Richard Neustadt's *Presidential Power* is 'The politics of leadership from FDR to Carter'.[5] That leadership must be central to any study of the Presidency is axiomatic, however. More important is the context in which leadership is exercised. Until the publication of Neustadt's seminal work, it was assumed that the most important of the President's power resources were those relating to constitutionally mandated commands. While such instruments as the veto and the President's status as Commander-in-Chief remain important in some contexts (indeed they may be more relevant than in the past, of which more later), few could doubt that in order to get budgets approved, bills passed, Supreme Court nominations confirmed and generally to run the day-to-day business of government, Presidents need to use all the bargaining resources they can muster. As Neustadt puts it: 'It is the need to bargain that keeps presidential power as uncertain as in most respects I find it. And the need to bargain is the product of a constitutional system that shares formal powers among separate institutions.'[6] As earlier suggested, however, increasingly presidents can do little to influence Congress, and members of Congress have little to benefit from association with the President and his policies. So Morris Fiorina laments:

> The situation of the contemporary presidency is not a happy one. The occupant of that office must expect to be judged by his success in maintaining peace, high employment, low inflation, adequate and inexpensive energy, harmonious racial relations, an acceptable moral climate, and a generally contented nation. Meanwhile, his co-partisans on the Hill are relatively insulated from such concerns. No longer expecting to gain much from the president's successes or suffer much from his failures, they have little incentive to bear any risk on his behalf.[7]

The result is a decline in 'responsible government' in the United States, and the erosion of the policy-making capacity of the President. The assumption is, of course, that without Congress Presidents can do very little. And given the particularistic nature of the legislature, the national interest has to be championed by what has become an emasculated chief executive. In one variant or another, this perspective now dominates Presidential scholarship. Presidents are almost always characterised as strategic actors involved in a complex bargaining game dominated by the legislative/executive impasse.[8] Short of constitutional change, there is apparently very little that Presidents can do about this. As Samuel Kernell has shown, it is rational for them to appeal to a wider constituency by 'Going Public', but this too can hold perils and pitfalls at every turn.[9] Public opinion can shift against presidents very quickly, as it did during the Iranian hostage crisis, the 1981/2 recession and the Iran–Contra affair.

The major problem with the bargaining model lies in its failure to focus on what Presidents achieve as opposed to what they cannot achieve. Little attention is payed to Presidential ideology or to the ways in which Presidents can change the nature of the political agenda. Put another way, the bargaining model assumes that Presidents essentially *react* to a hostile environment, rather than themselves help mould or create that environment. Of course in reality, Presidents do both, but it is assumed that increasingly American chief executives are in the business of reacting to events beyond their control, or are engaged in damage limitation, rather than actually providing the sort of moral and policy leadership that most commentators agree is needed in the United States. Testing to what extent Presidents have made a genuinely independent contribution to policy is, of course, highly problematical. But this is true of executive power in all democratic systems. In an interdependent world the agenda is often shaped by uncontrollable external events. And in all systems, constraints on executive power come from organised interests, legislatures, public opinion and the courts. In some respects, the American Presidency has more power resources than other chief executives. The President is almost completely unconstrained by political party pressures, he has a formidable veto sanction, and is unambiguously designated as chief executive.[10]

One way of assessing executive power is to identify those changes in public policy which have occurred over the last few decades and then attempt to judge whether they have resulted from Presidential policies and priorities as opposed to Congressional initiative, pressure from public opinion, or some other source. While we cannot do this in any systematic fashion, we can make informed judgements which suggest that Presidents remain the primary shapers of major areas of public policy.

Public policy does change substantially in the United Staes over time. For example, an examination of the federal budget over the last thirty years reveals sometimes dramatic shifts in spending priorities. As Table 4.1 shows, as a proportion of total federal outlays, defence spending has fluctuated sharply since 1959. Presidential priorities are a major explanation of some of these changes – most notably the defence build-up during the 1960s and the more recent increases under Reagan.

Almost as impressive are the fluctuations in domestic spending. As a proportion of total spending, payments for individuals (mainly social security, welfare, Medicare and Medicaid benefits) rose sharply from the 1960s through the late 1970s, but have since levelled off. Distinguishing cause from effect in this policy area is difficult, but considerable evidence exists to suggest that the impetus provided by Lyndon Johnson's highly personalised Great Society agenda helped increase political support for a range of income security measures.[11] As far as Ronald Reagan is concerned, the evidence is less ambiguous. Most of the cuts in income maintenance of the 1980s were a direct result of the 1981 Budget Reconciliation Act and subsequent budgets.[12] Moreover, if some of the data in Table 4.1 are disaggregated, the direct effects of Presidential initiative are even more obvious. For example, if welfare spending as opposed to social security is examined on its own, then the decreases characteristic of the Reagan years are marked. During the 1970s, the maximum monthly AFDC (Aid for Families with Dependent Children) and Food Stamp benefits for a family of four in the median state fluctuated between $659 and $769. The lower figure applied during 1979 after the Carter-inspired budget cuts. By 1984, benefits had been reduced to $542.[13] Similarly, grants to state and local governments for a wide variety of purposes have declined very sharply both as a proportion of total federal spending and by most other measures (Table 4.2). The reasons for this relate almost exclusively to the Reagan Administration's priorities, notably budget cutting and an ideological commitment to the decentralisation and defunding of a wide range of programmes.[14]

The bargaining model of American politics fails to explain these sometimes sharp variations in the federal role. For it assumes that the policy process is dominated by Congress, the bureaucracy and organised interests in ways which should prevent significant decreases or even sharp increases in spending. Instead, public goods provision should slowly creep upwards in incremental fashion. Or at worst, problems associated with coalition building in the new decentralised Congress should distort spending in ways not compatible with the public interest.[15] Neither scenario allows for sudden shifts in spending upwards or downwards. The bargaining model of the bureaucracy also fails to explain these changes. According to most students of the subject, bureaucrats are budget maximisers, not budget cutters.[16] If they were able to exercise a really independent influence on policy, then they should somehow have been able to resist the swingeing cuts in military spending in the 1970s and in domestic spending in the 1980s. Of course, if some higher political authority was able to replace key bureaucrats in line with a new public ideology, then permanent officials may well have accepted major policy changes. But such a sequence would be evidence more of bureaucratic weakness then strength.

The data on aid to state and local governments presented in Tables 4.1 and 4.2 are particularly relevant to those theories which assign pride of place to organised interests in the American system. According to such perspectives, Congressional 'pork barrel' projects should be especially well protected during periods of retrenchment.[17] If anything, however, public works, housing and community development programmes have suffered greater reductions than almost any other area.[18] Neither the organisations representing state and local governments which were identified as so powerful during the 1970s,[19] nor more conventional organised interests were able to exploit the 'electoral connection', 'iron triangles', or 'policy networks'[20] to any effect during the early- and mid-1980s. If this is so, perhaps we should question whether, as so many have claimed, such interests were the prime movers in producing the rapid increases in expenditure typical of the 1970s.[21]

None of this is to deny that the Reagan Administration and previous governments have been constrained by Congress, public opinion and other political forces. Clearly they have. Reagan was,

Table 4.1: Percentage distribution of federal budget outlays, 1959–87

Year	Amount (billions of dollars)	Constant prices (1982 $)	Defence	Total Non-defence	Payments for individuals	Grants[a]	Other	Net interest
1959	92.1	*	49.1	50.9	20.6	19.7		10.7
1960	92.2	*	48.9	51.9	21.9	18.3		10.8
1965	118.4	*	40.1	59.9	24.6	25.7		9.7
1969	184.5	*	43.9	56.1	28.6	20.6		6.9
1971	211.4	509.4	39.8	61.2	35.5	8.5	14.9	6.7
1975	326.2	586.0	27.3	72.7	45.4	10.0	14.5	6.9
1979	493.6	660.0	24.1	75.9	45.7	10.9	14.5	8.3
1980	579.6	699.1	23.5	76.5	46.5	9.8	14.8	8.9
1982	617.8	745.7	24.9	75.1	47.8	6.7	12.7	11.4
1984	666.5	789.9	26.8	73.2	46.7	6.2	11.2	13.0
1985	734.1	848.0	27.0	73.0	44.7	6.0	12.2	13.6
1986	769.1	866.2	28.0	72.0	45.0	6.0	10.9	13.6
1987e	842.4	862.3	28.1	71.9	45.5	5.3	11.4	13.4

Notes: e estimated
* not available
a Grants to state and local governments
Source: *US Budget in Brief 1982 and 1988*, Washington, D.C., US Government Printing Office, Table 2, p. 77 (1982) and p. 99 (1988).

for example, intent on cutting social security and medical benefits. He failed to make significant inroads into either, largely because public opinion, often expressed through Congress, was highly resistant to such cuts. However, neither was public and Congressional opinion in any way committed to the cuts in welfare and aid to state and local governments – cuts which were nevertheless approved, as a result of great administrative pressure. On the contrary, public opinion shifted in favour of increased federal welfare provision during the Reagan years. This is a point we will return to later.

In sum, the bargaining model of the Presidency – and of American politics generally – although clearly relevant and useful in some contexts, is of limited utility when applied to some areas

Table 4.2: Federal Grants in Aid to state and local government: selected
            years, 1955–87

	Federal grants in aid		
	Amount (1972 $ billions)	As % of state/local receipts from own source	As % of total federal outlays
1955	5.6	11.8	4.7
1960	10.8	16.8	7.6
1965	15.5	17.7	9.2
1970	27.0	22.9	12.3
1972	34.4	26.1	14.9
1975	39.2	29.1	15.0
1978	49.4	31.7	17.0
1979	48.1	31.3	16.5
1980	48.2	31.7	15.5
1981	46.1	30.1	14.0
1982	40.4	25.6	11.8
1983	40.7	24.7	11.4
1984	41.3	23.7	11.5
1985	43.1	23.7	11.2
1986e	40.1	21.4	10.7
1987e	37.7	19.5	10.1

Note: *e* estimated
Source: Advisory Commission on Intergovernmental Relations, *Significant
        Features of Fiscal Federalism*, 1985/6 Edition, Washington, D.C.,
        US Government Printing Office, 1986, adapted from Table 8.
        For qualifying notes, see original.

of public policy. In particular, in spite of the fact that what may be
called the policy environment has grown more hostile over the last
few decades, Presidents can still exercise considerable influence independent of Congressional, special interest and bureaucratic power.

ALTERNATIVE APPROACHES

A growing literature on the role of the state in American politics and
society points to those instances where state actors have played a

relatively autonomous role in policy making.[22] Such a perspective is of obvious relevance in foreign policy, which is generally recognised as being more insulated from societal influence than most domestic policy areas. Hence, Stephen Krasner asserts that: 'The American state: the president and those bureaus relatively insulated from societal pressures, which are the only institutions capable of formulating the national interest ... must always struggle against an inherent tendency for power and control to be dissipated and dispersed'.[23] In other words, there is a structural problem of control in the American system relating to a high level of institutional fragmentation. In foreign policy this manifests itself as battles between the White House and various departments and bureaus responsible for foreign and foreign economic policy. Unfortunately, in his empirical analysis, Krasner has difficulty distinguishing between actions that emanate from the President as opposed to other actors in the policy process. Shifts in policy (the protection of US raw materials sources overseas) do occur, but it is not altogether obvious who is responsible for them.[24] Of course, in other contexts Presidents do make a difference in foreign policy, even if their freedom of choice is limited by a range of societal influences. It is in domestic policy that the greatest limitations on Presidential freedom apply. State-centred theorists have argued to the contrary, pointing in particular to the independent role played by officials. In the New Deal, for example, Skocpol and Finegold argue that Department of Agriculture bureaucrats were responsible for helping create a new policy agenda.[25] That officials can play a relatively autonomous role seems indisputable. Unfortunately, scholars have been less eager to assess the extent to which officials are acting on their own as opposed to following Presidential or White House directives.

A more interesting approach is taken by students of American political development, and in particualr in the study of the interaction between Presidential leadership and the structural constraints imposed by political regimes. Here the focus is less on the President as strategic actor and more on what Presidents can achieve given prevailing institutional dynamics and elite values. So Stephen Skowronek distinguishes between the politics of reconstruction, articulation and disjunction which correspond to the rise and decline of political regimes.[26] Franklin Roosevelt was fortunate to be incumbent when elite values were changing rapidly as a result of the

Great Depression. Popular political forces were also re-aligning rapidly, giving the Democrats a solid majority in Congress thus enabling the President to exercise effective leadership. In the strictly programmatic sense, FDR failed – his policies did not rescue the US from the Great Depression. But he was able to repudiate the old order and shift the political agenda sharply to the left. Lyndon Johnson was able to exercise leadership in a different sense. For according to Skowronek he was relatively free to indulge in a politics of articulation, or to pursue policies much in tune with the ongoing regime. As a result, the Great Society programmes were effectively launched. Eisenhower and Nixon were obliged to confront a hostile regime, while Jimmy Carter was unfortunate to find himself presiding over a decaying regime.[27] By implication, at least, Ronald Reagan could exploit a rapidly changing environment and lead the country into a new era of reconstruction. While at first sight attractive, this perspective does little to solve the problem of distinguishing between the capacities of individual Presidents and the constraints imposed by the regime. To be fair to Skowronek, he does focus on leadership and therefore on the talents of individual Presidents, but the reader is left with the impression that should an incumbent find himself in the 'wrong' regime, there is little he can do about it. In other words, by focusing on regimes, it is the regime constraints and possibilities rather than individuals' capacities that are assigned the greatest explanatory power. Yet if both Kennedy and Johnson were incumbent during the same regime, why was Johnson so successful in changing the domestic agenda (effectively in just two years) compared with Kennedy? No new social movement emerged in 1964 to provoke Johnson into action (the Civil Rights movement constituted an ongoing campaign). Poverty was simply not a national issue in 1963.[28] The answer lies at least in part in the different style, policy priorities and ideologies of the two presidents. Kennedy gave higher priority to foreign policy, while Johnson initially gave highest priority to domestic affairs.[29] Random events also played a part. Johnson was aided by the traumatising effect on the public of the assassination of Kennedy, and eventually by the disarray among the Republicans in 1964.

The experience of the Reagan Administration is also difficult to reconcile with the political development approach. As suggested, Reagan was able to change the style and substance of domestic policy, but there is little evidence to suggest that he did this with the support of the sort of re-alignment of values and voters typical of other realigning periods, such as the early 1930s. Democratic support in the House and in state government remained strong, and even the Republicans' slim majority in the Senate was to last just six years. Moreover there was little shift in public opinion either in favour of decentralisation, or, more specifically, against welfare provision during the 1980s. One 1987 report was able to conclude that:'[While] we cannot make exact comparisons, ... our judgement is that the public is more liberal on these issues than it was when Jimmy Carter left office. It has reacted against the Reagan Administration's social welfare policies and especially the spending reductions, some of which, as is often forgotten, began under Carter (ie., slowing the rate of increase).'[30] The Reagan measures, rather than reinforcing existing trends and shifting the policy agenda further to the right, led if anything to a reappraisal in the opposite direction. In contrast, Franklin Roosevelt was able effectively to repudiate the old order, and move the agenda to the left. The fact that he was not successful in curing the Great Depression is not strictly relevant. The point is that after 1933 the nature of political discourse changed in a number of fundamental ways. Hands-off, non-interventionist strategies were not to be considered realistic alternatives to New Deal-type measures for many years. Moreover, as the 1930s progressed, social movements supporting intervention were brought together in an unbeatable electoral coalition represented by the Democratic Party.

Ronald Reagan did, of course, manage to modify the agenda, but, as suggested, he was unable to transform it. By 1988, none of the Democratic candidates and possibly only two of the Republican candidates (Kemp and Robertson) were presenting a range of policies to the American people closely resembling the original Reagan agenda of 1980.[31] Neither were to come close to winning the nomination.

THE PRESIDENCY DURING PERIODS OF REGIME FRAGMENTATION

While most of the forces accounting for the New Deal regime have declined, no new regime has emerged to take its place. Claims that the Republican right constituted a new social movement which would eventually underpin a new regime, were premature. By 1988, the Democrats remained in control of both houses of Congress, and of most of the Governors' mansions and state legislatures. As is well documented, however, the great majority of politicians today owe their incumbency not to national, regional or state party support, but to personal party organisations specifically created to elect them. In spite of various attempts at reform, there is no sign of any move away from this highly individualised form of politics. On the contrary, an increasingly fragmented Congress and a polity which in most respects is becoming more accessible to interest group representation, indicate an accelerating dispersal of power.

In such a context, it is highly unlikely that political parties will produce coherent and ideologically consistent programmes of social and economic change. And while it could be argued that compared with most European countries this has never been a function of political parties in the United States, there certainly have been times (such as the 1930s) when parties came close to a programmatic (as opposed to individualised or instrumental) politics.

Today, therefore, we are in the midst of what might be called *regime fragmentation*. As mentioned, the response of most scholars to this new environment has been hostile. Public accountability has, according to the critics, been damaged by the absence of clear lines of responsibility from the voters to Congress and thence to the Presidency. While this may be true, it does not necessarily follow that such changes have weakened the Presidency. Indeed, in some respects, the institution may even have been strengthened – at least in relation to other sources of political authority. Let us look at the relationship between regime fragmentation and the Presidency in more detail.

THE PRESIDENCY AND PARTY DECLINE

Since the introduction of popular elections for Presidents, they have been in a position to appeal to national constituencies. The Vice-President apart, no other elected official in the system can do this. For members of Congress who are now caught up in the sometimes extreme particularism characteristic of the electoral connection and policy networks, any clear conception of the national interest is difficult to articulate. Arguably, it was not always so. When parties were stronger, Senators and Representatives depended to some extent on the fortunes of Presidents. Presidential coattails were often long, and close association with the White House usually brought rewards. As the last few elections have shown coattails have all but disappeared, and the link between Congressional and Presidential elections is tenuous at best.[32]

If, as a result, Presidents are more insulated from Congress, they also stand almost alone as the champions of the national interest. They remain subject to election and re-election, of course, but as Theodore Lowi has pointed out, this more resembles a national plebiscite on Presidential performance, than an ongoing system of accountability whereby party organisations provide the connective tissue between political authority and the broader society.[33] Put another way, the social and political changes of recent years have served to help sever one of the major links between the chief executive and American society. In Eric Nordlinger's terms,[34] the relative autonomy of the institution has increased – at least in the sense that networks of party influence often based on regional political alliances centrally placed to influence Presidential nominations have declined. A number of institutional and policy consequences have followed:

1. Presidents today are freer to appoint immediate aides and (especially) cabinet members according to their own personal priorities and preferences. Repaying old electoral debts incurred earlier in their careers and during the nomination process, is largely no longer necessary. A Franklin Roosevelt or John Kennedy was obliged to pay such debts and therefore appoint some officials with whom they were politically or ideologically out of tune. In contrast, Jimmy Carter and Ronald Reagan were able to gather around them men and women whose first allegiance was to the President as an individual, rather than to state and local parties and constituents.[35]

2. Presidents are also less constrained by past political obligations when making appointments to the federal bureaucracy and to the courts. Evidence demonstrating how Ronald Reagan used this power to place loyal ideologues in top judicial and civil service positions is considerable.[36] Of his appointments to the US Courts of Appeal through 1986, 90.4 per cent have been categorised as conservative compared with only 48.4 per cent of the Nixon appointees.[37] Similarly, Congressional hearings into Reagan administration appointments to the newly created (in 1978) Senior Executive

Service, reveal a pattern of predominantly conservative appointments and promotions.[38]

3. The increasing isolation of the President from Congress has accelerated those changes in the administrative or institutional Presidency which have been centralising power in the White House for over thirty years. So a rational response by Presidents to what they see as increasing Congressional and bureaucratic intransigence has been to elevate the Office of Management and Budget (OMB) to central administrative gatekeeper within the White House. Agency and departmental rule-making powers have been subject to stricter controls via the implementation of two executive orders, EO 12291 (February 1981) and EO 12498 (January 1985). As a result, agencies are now required to submit plans and proposals to OMB for review. This effective veto power over agency rule making has caused a minor storm of protest among Congressional oversight committees – largely because the administration has used these new orders to further the conservative agenda in such areas as civil rights enforcement and environmental protection.[39]

As a number of commentators have noted, even together with other administrative devices, these changes cannot on their own transform the policy making environment.[40] Congress can legislate to remove or reduce executive discretion over such areas as legislative clearance and the number and rank of officials subject to Presidential appointment. Court action is also always possible, and administrative powers are almost certainly a poor substitute for legislation. This is especially so if Presidents are intent on large increases or decreases in expenditure. As was indicated earlier, recent incumbents have, in fact, had a considerable, if not always precisely measurable, impact on public expenditure patterns. How, in such a fragmented and generally problematic policy context, have Presidents managed to achieve so much?

AGENDA SETTING AND REGIME FRAGMENTATION

When measuring Presidential success, most scholars look to the specifics of the Congressional/Presidential contest. Hence the centrality of such indicators as Presidential success and party support scores in Congress.[41] While interesting and of clear relevance in some contexts, such indicators do not capture the essence of

Presidential power. In particular, they fail to measure in full the agenda setting capacity of the President. As E. E. Schattschneider noted some years ago:

> Political conflict is not like an intercollegiate debate in which the opponents agree in advance on a definition of the issues. As a matter of fact, *the definition of the alternatives is the supreme instrument of power*, the antagonists can rarely agree on what the issues are because power is involved in the definition. He who determines what politics is about runs the country, because the definition of alternatives is the choice of conflicts, and the choice of conflicts allocates power.[42] [emphasis in the original]

No one is better placed than Presidents to define the political alternatives in the American system. This applies *tout force* during the first two years of first term Presidents. At such times Presidents have a unique opportunity to present a new agenda to Congress and the American people. They have always enjoyed a honeymoon period during their first year, but today they have the additional advantages of freedom over appointments and the absence of anything resembling a party mandate for social and economic change. Again, the Reagan experience is apposite. Although public and Congressional opinion did move to the right during the 1970s, nothing resembling a social movement emerged which heralded the beginning of a new era. Nonetheless, Reagan was able to mould the terms of public debate at least during his first term. Considerable increases in defence spending and reductions in social spending were accepted as necessary by most sources of political authority. Controversy over the details persisted, but few disputed the need for the changes championed by the administration. As a result, Congress acquiesced in the radical reordering of priorities which the 1981 Budget Reconciliation Act represented. Although these initial successes were never to be repeated, the terms of debate were fundamentally different after 1981. And this in spite of what many observers agree was a less than efficient policy making process in the White House.[43] Ronald Reagan may have lost his hold on the office after 1983, or more likely, after 1984, but the agenda did not revert to the pre-Reagan era. Congress was simply incapable of providing an alternative agenda. It could pick away at Reagan's programmes, but not replace them with anything that resembled a coherent alternative.

Reagan was able to do this – and in theory so could any new

president – because no other political authority exists which can focus public attention on national issues in a relatively unambiguous manner. Reagan's own ideological determination – if not consistency – no doubt helped win some success.

As earlier noted, the key weapon available to Presidents, and generally unavailable to other politicians, is the capacity to make appeals to the mass public through television and radio.[44] Increasingly, therefore, Presidents are able to design their policies in the secrecy of the White House relying on personally selected aides, and then sell these policies to Congress by way of public appeals. Such efforts will not always be successful, in part because innovative policies are today not underpinned by a dominant social movement for change. Indeed, Presidents must use all their moral authority and political skills to mobilise opinion for each item of legislation or policy initiative. To repeat the point, by so doing they help determine the terms of debate or shape the policy agenda. On many issues – most recently, aid to the Contras, school prayers, and the welfare cuts – a majority of voters may be against the President's position. But the shape of political discourse will have been set by the President. And once established, Congress, the courts and state and local governments have great difficulty providing an alternative agenda.

Such a strategy seems a long way indeed from the bargaining model of the institution along with its implied negotiation, dealing, compromise and persuasion. Of course these continue to go on, but Presidents are clearly more confrontational or plebiscitary than they used to be. This shows itself not only in numerous public appeals by Presidents designed to put constituent pressure on members, or in the sort of by-pass measures outlined earlier, but also in the tendency for Presidents to fall back on their command resources. In response to an unprecedented use of the Commander-in-Chief power in peacetime by Presidents Johnson and Nixon, Congress produced a number of executive curbing measures, but there is little it can do to prevent a legitimate exercise of the veto power by Presidents. The usual way to characterise the use of the veto is as an indicator of some sort of breakdown in executive legislative relations. Hence both Nixon and Ford used the veto extensively during periods of serious conflict between the two branches. On closer examination, however, we discover that there is a secular trend in favour of increased veto use, and in particular the application of the veto to foreign policy and appropriations bills – areas which were never subject to the veto until recently (Table 4.3). In Reagan's case, the data in Table 4.3 are of especial interest, because throughout this period the Senate was controlled by the Republicans. In fact, the size of the Senate majorities against Reagan's vetoes was actually higher than those against Nixon's and Ford's vetoes.[45] Party ties between the two branches had weakened so substantially that Reagan actually found himself winning less support on these key override votes than his two Republican predecessors who are so often labelled unfortunate, or victims of the times.

Table 4.3: Major bills vetoed, 1933–86

President	Total	No. involving appropriations	No. involving foreign and foreign economic policy	Major vetoes per year in office	No. over-ridden
Roosevelt	2	0	0	0.16	2
Truman	6	0	0	0.8	5
Eisenhower	2	2	0	0.25	1
Kennedy	0	0	0	0	0
Johnson	0	0	0	0	0
Nixon	13	10^1	1^4	2.4	4
Ford	11	10^2	1	4.4	7
Carter	5	2^3	2	1.3	1
Reagan	10	6	4	1.7	3^5

Notes:
1 Excludes HR 7447 (1973) appropriations bill with a rider prohibiting use of funds for bombing of Cambodia.
2 Excludes S 2662 (1976) involving $3.1 billion for arms sales and military aid. Veto was justified on foreign policy rather than fiscal grounds.
3 Excludes HR 7584 (1980) involving $9 billion appropriations for State, Justice and Commerce. Veto was exercised because of attachment of an anti-busing rider.
4 Excludes 1973 War Powers bill which is coded as of major constitutional import rather than as a challenge to specific aspect of foreign policy.
5 Excludes S 1128 (1986 Clean Water bill) which as HR1 was easily over-ridden in February 1987 by the new Democratically controlled Congress 401-26 and 86-14.
Source: David McKay, 'Presidential strategy and the veto power: a reappraisal', *Political Science Quarterly*, forthcoming, 1989. Table 5. For a definition of major bills, see original.

CONCLUSIONS: THE PRESIDENCY AND THE AMERICAN STATE

None of the above discussion should be taken to indicate that the President's job is getting any easier. Clearly it is not. The point is, rather, that the decline of party and the rise of an individualised politics has, in some contexts, led to increased rather than decreased executive autonomy. In particular, in the absence of alternative sources of policy initiative, the President's agenda-setting power has been enhanced. Presidents are also more prone to use their command resources, if not always to good effect. Unlike the 1930s and earlier, these powers can be exercised independently of any significant social movement for change. So at a time when Congress and state and local governments are becoming more infused with societal influence, the Presidency is becoming more isolated from societal pressures. This is in no way incompatible with the emergence of the plebiscitary Presidency. By definition, a plebiscite is a periodic appeal for approval from the mass of the population. It is not the equivalent of a party mandate or of the sort of organic links engendered by a complex network of party contacts. These developments strongly suggest that Presidents are now closer to embodying the American state than before. Their control over the White House, the bureaucracy and the judiciary is greater. They use their command resources more independently, and the agenda-setting constraints imposed by Congress are weaker.

One crucial question remains. Can such a highly personalised form of state autonomy come to represent the national or the public interest? Almost certainly not. For one thing, the Presidential policies of today often violate Brian Barry's requirement that public interest policies should not in some sense penalise one group or class over another.[46] For another, the very nature of the new presidential powers will render many of the resulting policies ephemeral – a further requirement of public interest policies being extended longevity. With a new President, key personnel in the Executive Office of the President could change in composition and ideology overnight; the greater the political penetration of the rest of the executive branch, the greater is the scope for further policy shifts. Even in the courts, a two-term President could achieve major changes. In theory, then, a liberal or leftist President could utilise the relative autonomy of the office to impose a completely different ideology on the federal bureaucracy and judiciary. Related is the fact that the plebiscitary nature of Presidential power is highly amenable to rapid shifts in policy direction. Of course limits exist on the range of options which incumbents can present to the public, but within these limits, Presidents have considerable freedom to pick and choose – and to change their minds.

Recent institutional changes may have enabled Presidents to act more autonomously in some contexts, but they have not helped move the United States towards acquiring a bureaucratic state in the European or Japanese sense which represents a hierarchy of enduring values which are above and beyond society. Instead, regime fragmentation has helped insulate the American Presidency from societal influence in ways which can encourage short term shifts in public policy, produced with little reference to a popular or party mandate.

NOTES

1 See the discussion in Louis W. Koenig, *The Chief Executive*, New York, Harcourt Brace Jovanovitch, 4th edn, 1981, ch. 2, 'Beginnings'.
2 Samuel Kernell, *Going Public: New Strategies of Presidential Leadership*, Washington, D.C., Congressional Quarterly Press, 1986.
3 Theodore Lowi, *The Personal Presidency: Power Invested, Promise Unfulfilled*, Ithaca and London, Cornell University Press, 1985; Godfrey Hodgson, *All Things to All Men: The False Promise of the American Presidency*, Harmondsworth, Middx., Penguin, 1984.
4 For a discussion, see Lowi, *The Personal Presidency*, ch. 7, 'Restoring the balance'.
5 Richard Neustadt, *Presidential Power: The Politics of Leadership from FDR to Carter*, New York, Wiley, 1980.
6 Neustadt, *Presidential Power*, p. 170.
7 Morris P. Fiorina, 'The Presidency and Congress: an electoral connection?' in Michael Nelson (ed.), *The Presidency and the Political System*, Washington, D.C., Congressional Quarterly Press, 2nd edn, 1988, p. 424.
8 See Fiorina, 'The Presidency and Congress' and sources cited, also, James P. Pfiffner, *The Strategic Presidency: Hitting the Ground Running*, Chicago, The Dorsey Press, 1988, chs. 7 and 8.
9 Kernell, *Going Public*, chs. 7 and 8.
10 For a view of the presidency in comparative perspective, see Richard Rose, *The Capacity of the President: A Comparative Analysis*, Studies in Public Policy Number 130, University of Strathclyde, 1984.
11 See David McKay, *Domestic Policy and Ideology: Presidents and the American State*, Cambridge, Cambridge University Press, 1989, ch. 3, 'Lyndon Johnson and the Great Society: Executive Led Ideology'.
12 See Tom Joe and Cheryl Rogers, *By the Few For the Few: The Reagan Welfare Legacy*, Lexington, Mass., D.C. Heath, 1985, chs. 1 and 2.
13 R. Kent Weaver, 'Social Policy in the Reagan Era' in B. B. Kymlicka and Jean V. Matthews, *The Reagan Revolution?*, Chicago, The Dorsey Press, 1988, Table 2, p. 150.
14 See McKay, *Domestic Policy and Ideology*, ch. 6.
15 James Buchanan and Richard Wagner, *Democracy in Deficit*, New York, Academic Press,

1977; Morris P. Fiorina, *Congress: Keystone of the Washington Establishment*, New Haven, Conn., Yale University Press, 1977.

16 For a discussion see Patrick Dunleavy, 'Bureaucrats, budgets and the growth of the state: reconstructing an instrumental model', *British Journal of Political Science*, vol. 15, 1986, pp. 299–328.

17 For a general discussion of this point see the collection of essays edited by Matthew D. McCubbins and Terry Sullivan (eds), *Congress: Structure and Policy*, New York and Cambridge, Cambridge University Press, 1987.

18 See George E. Peterson and Carol W. Lewis, *Reagan and the Cities*, Washington, D.C., Urban Institute Press, 1986, ch. 2.

19 Samuel H. Beer, 'Federalism, nationalism and democracy in America', *American Political Science Review*, vol. 72, 1978.

20 The two most influential pieces on these themes are David Mayhew, *Congress: The Electoral Connection*, New Haven, Yale University Press, 1974, and Hugh Heclo, 'Issue networks and the executive establishment', in Anthony King (ed.), *The New American Political System*, Washington, D.C., American Enterprise Institute, 1978.

21 See McKay, *Domestic Policy and Ideology*, ch. 2.

22 For a general discussion, see Eric Nordlinger, *On the Autonomy of the Democratic State*, Cambridge, Mass., Harvard University Press, 1981. Also Peter Evans, Dietrich Ruschemeyer and Theda Skocpol (eds), *Bringing the State Back In*, Cambridge and New York, Cambridge University Press, 1985.

23 Stephen Krasner, *Defending the National Interest: Raw Materials, Investments and U.S. Foreign Policy*, Princeton, NJ, Princeton University Press, 1978, p. 62.

24 Krasner, *Defending the National Interest*, part 3.

25 Theda Skocpol and Kenneth Finegold, 'State capacity and economic intervention in the early New Deal', *Political Science Quarterly*, vol. 97, 1982, pp. 255–78.

26 Stephen Skowronek, 'Notes on the Presidency in the political order' in Karen Orren and Stephen Skowronek (eds), *Studies in American Political Development*, vol. 1, New Haven and London, Yale University Press, 1986.

27 Skowronek, 'Notes on the Presidency in the political order', pp. 296–7.

28 Henry J. Aaron points out that a bibliography on the subject in 1963 would run to less than two pages, in Aaron, *Politics and the Professors: The Great Society in Perspective*, Washington, D.C., Brookings Institution, 1978, p. 17.

29 For example, both presidents created policy task forces on coming to power, but of Kennedy's seven task forces only one concerned domestic policy. Of Johnson's fifteen, all but one was devoted to domestic policy.

30 Robert Y. Shapiro *et al.*, 'The Polls: Public Assistance', *Public Opinion Quarterly*, vol. 51, 1987, p. 121.

31 George Bush may also qualify for inclusion, but by 1988, although he was promising to continue the Reagan revolution, he was never as ideologically committed to a New Right agenda as the President. Most commentators have categorised him as a Republican moderate.

32 See Fiorina, 'The Presidency and Congress', Tables 18.1–3.

33 Lowi, *The Personal Presidency*, ch. 5.

34 Nordlinger, *On the Autonomy of the Democratic State*.

35 Pfiffner, *The Strategic Presidency*, chs. 2 and 3.

36 Elizabeth Sanders, 'The Presidency and the bureaucratic state', in Nelson (ed.), *The Presidency and the Political System*; McKay, *Domestic Policy and Ideology*, ch. 7.

37 McKay, *Domestic Policy and Ideology*, Table 6.2.

38 Hearings Before the Sub-Committee on the Civil Service, Post Office and Civil Service Committee, US House of Representatives, *The Senior Executive Service*, Washington D.C., US Government Printing Office, 1984.

39 So much so that OMB was obliged to accept new public disclosure rules in 1986.

A public interest group, OMB Watch, was also established to monitor OMB performance.

40 See, for example, Sanders, 'The Presidency and the bureaucratic state', p. 403.

41 George C. Edwards, *Presidential Influence in Congress*, San Francisco, Freeman, 1980.

42 E. E. Schattsneider, *The Semi Sovereign People*, quoted by Jack Walker, 'Setting the agenda in the U.S. Senate: a theory of problem selection', *British Journal of Political Science*, vol. 7, part 4, p. 423.

43 By 1988 a number of biographies had appeared claiming this. Some of the authors had axes to grind, but this could not be said of the volumes produced by Michael Deaver and David Stockman.

44 Kernell, *Going Public*, ch. 4 and sources cited.

45 David McKay, 'Presidential strategy and the veto power', *Political Science Quarterly*, forthcoming, 1989, Table 4.

46 Brian Barry, 'The use and abuse of the public interest', in Carl J. Friedrich (ed.), *Nomos V: The Public Interest*, New York, Atherton, 1972.

The Least Dangerous Branch no longer: A Reflection on the United States Supreme Court

ABSTRACT

This essay considers the impact of the federal courts, and the United States Supreme Court in particular, on the making of public policy. The starting point of this essay is Alexander Hamilton's remark that the judicial branch of government is the 'least dangerous' branch. However it is argued here that the experience of the last two hundred years suggests that Hamilton's prediction has not come to pass. It has not been fulfilled because the location of the federal courts at a critical juncture of the American constitutional and political process makes federal judges, and above all the justices of the Supreme Court, very important players in the policy making process.

Some two hundred years ago, Alexander Hamilton offered his fellow Americans both an analysis of the power of courts and judges and a prediction of how they would behave within the proposed American constitutional system. He wrote in *Federalist* no. 78:

> The judiciary, from the nature of its functions, will always be the least dangerous to the political rights of the Constitution, because it will be least in a capacity to annoy or injure them ... The judiciary ... has no influence over either the sword or the purse; no direction either of the strength or the wealth of the society ... It may truly be said to have neither FORCE nor WILL, but merely judgement ...[1]

The degree to which Hamilton's contemporaries shared his view is not easy to establish though he was an acute, if occasionally eccentric, critic of American political and social life. However what is readily evident is that such a view would command little support currently. After two centuries, the courts, and in particular the United States Supreme Court, have not conformed to the portrait of a rather powerless and docile branch of government as drawn by

Hamilton. The judiciary has left an indelible imprint on the development of the American polity to the extent that a formidable body of observers today see them through very different eyes. The courts are rarely perceived as less than equal to the legislative and executive branches, by a wide spectrum of opinion, and indeed, the United States Supreme Court, to some of its more trenchant critics, has developed the characteristics of power and arrogance frequently associated with both the Congress and the Presidency.[2] So what has accounted for the transformation of this least dangerous branch of the American constitutional system into an institution of very considerable power and influence?

The transformation, of course, started virtually from the creation of the Republic. The influence and authority of the federal judiciary over most of the last two hundred years has derived from its power of judicial review, or its ability to review the activities of the other branches of government, both federal and state. As a consequence, the United States Supreme Court has been, for most of its existence, the final arbiter of the American Constitution. However, this position of being the constitutional arbiter of last resort was not explicitly allocated to the Supreme Court by the Founding Fathers in 1787, and indeed the historical and scholarly debate still continues over their intentions towards judicial review without any sign of it being definitively resolved.[3] However, in 1803, the Supreme Court in the case of *Marbury v. Madison* claimed the power of judicial review; a claim that was contested but which opponents of the doctrine found difficult to translate into effective political action because they were disarmed by the consummate political skill of Chief Justice John Marshall's majority opinion.[4] The story of *Marbury v. Madison*, however, has been told frequently and consequently need not detain us here other than to note that Hamilton's prognosis on the behaviour of the American judiciary was by 1803 already in some jeopardy.

Marbury v. Madison did not resolve definitively the question of the constitutional incorporation of judicial review. It was a politically contentious doctrine in those decades after the ratification of the Constitution and there were powerful voices in the nation that did not endorse such a development. Consequently the Supreme Court was to return to the issue on subsequent occasions but only to reaffirm *Marbury* and finally to obtain the acquiescence, albeit grudging and reluctant, of those who opposed judicial review.[5]

Certainly by the middle of the nineteenth century the authority of the courts to evaluate the constitutionality of both federal and state legislation was no longer an item on the political agenda. Judicial review had become an accepted part of the political and constitutional landscape, an acceptance that would lead inevitably to the judiciary playing a prominent and significant role in the nation's affairs.

The inclusion of judicial review in the arsenal of the federal courts required politicians, both state and national, to accept the primacy of judges over constitutional interpretation, a fact which American politicians have never found entirely congenial. Presidents and governors, senators and state legislators, have also been aware for most of the past two centuries that judicial review has placed them in a position somewhat different to politicians in most other political systems. They do not retain the final and ultimate authority over the making of public policy. Political solutions that emerge through the very considerable complexities of the American political process can be overturned by the courts. Compromises that are painstakingly and arduously obtained by politicians between the bewilderingly vast array of interests that participate in the political arena can be held unconstitutional. Those who fail to achieve their objectives in the legislature, or are defeated in the electoral process, can turn to the judiciary. In other words, there is a judicial avenue available in the United States; that avenue holds the possibility of altering that which the political institutions have decided. However, if American politicians have found, from time to time, that this state of affairs was not entirely to their liking, so too, on occasion, have judges.

Judicial review has placed American judges at a critical location in the political and constitutional structure, leaving them perhaps more politically exposed and vulnerable than their colleagues in other common law legal systems. Their decisions have immediate political ramifications. They decide the fate of congressional acts, the validity of Presidential actions, and the constitutionality of state laws; when they announce their judgements, the federal judiciary, and in particular the justices of the Supreme Court, are enveloped in political controversy. The controversy is unavoidable, regardless of the specific decision on the issues under consideration, as a significant percentage of the cases are of considerable societal importance, and consequently the political stakes are high. Moreover, because the possibility of overturning a judgement of the Supreme Court is remote and relies primarily on the Court reversing itself, an even greater note is taken and an increased emphasis is placed on the judicial process. So the judiciary, for the past two centuries, have not been able to ignore or underestimate the political ramifications of their activities. Judges in the United States inhabit an intensely political environment and they have not always found it easy to accommodate themselves to this difficult and awkward fact of life. However, while they have had to accept the centrality of the legal process to the political system, the judiciary, nevertheless, have had to maintain the vital distinction and boundaries between the two processes. This task has not been without its problems over the last two hundred years.

One of the central strategies that the federal courts, and especially the Supreme Court, have adopted to maintain this distinction between the legal and political process, has been to seek to convince the body politic that the political impact of a decision has not tainted the process by which the Court has arrived at the decision. In other words the judiciary have sought to disengage the consequences of a judgement from the decision-making process. The Supreme Court may declare an act of Congress unconstitutional, which will antagonise those who supported the act and please its opponents, but the reasons for the Court's decision are not derived from any arguments over the merits or disadvantages of the legislation. The justices' duty and obligation is only to consider whether the act is constitutional. If it is, then the Court will uphold it, regardless of any private view that individual justices might hold on the wisdom of the legislation. And how does a Supreme Court justice arrive at a conclusion on the question of constitutionality? In 1938, Mr. Justice Roberts offered the following description: 'When an act of Congress is appropriately challenged in the courts as not conforming to the constitutional mandate the judicial branch has only one duty – to lay the article of the Constitution which is invoked beside the statute which is challenged and to decide whether the latter squares with the former.'[6] This process of constitutional adjudication, outlined by Justice Roberts, was very straightforward, dispassionate and perhaps somewhat mechanical, but it did distance the Court even further from the everyday activity of politics. If this indeed was the position – that the Supreme Court was interested only in questions of constitutionality and the process of divining constitutionality was both neutral and unproblematic – then the judiciary had a defence against the inevitable claims that politics was intruding into the legal process. However, the history of two centuries of constitutional adjudication suggests that the reality has been somewhat more complex and confused.

The source of the complexity has been the near impossibility of containing the legal and constitutional process within quite such a discrete channel as suggested above. Politics have not been banished from the Court to the extent that some commentators would have us believe. The two propositions – that the Supreme Court was only concerned with questions of constitutionality and that such questions could be readily resolved by the judiciary – have been and continue to be contentious. Indeed there is a substantial and established literature on both of these propositions that raise serious and substantial doubts over them. To take the first notion, have all the justices who sat on the Court over the course of the past two hundred years always been able to distinguish between their constitutional duties and their political preferences? Certainly there is a wide body of scholarly opinion that would dispute the assertion that this dividing line has never been crossed. Indeed, the claim is made that this line has not merely been crossed infrequently by that relatively small group of justices who were either unaware of their actions or derelict in their duty, but that this perimeter has been consistently breached by a large number of justices on numerous occasions. The process of constitutional adjudication, it is argued, on issues of considerable societal importance – slavery, race relations, governmental regulation of the economy and civil liberties, to name but a few – have all been infected to a lesser or greater degree by the politics of the judiciary. If this view is broadly correct, the Supreme Court and all lesser federal courts are both exposed and vulnerable to the charges that the courts are in effect legislatures, and that judges are merely politicians in another guise, who do not have to submit themselves to the inconveniences of the electoral process. The validity of these accusations, of course, depends on whether the justices of the Supreme Court have indeed transgressed and muddied the boundary between the political and judicial process. The answer to this question, however, is not as easy as some would suggest.

The central and constant task that has faced the Court over the past two centuries has been both to interpret the Constitution, and to adapt it to a society whose principal characteristics, perhaps have been its receptivity to innovation and its capacity for change. Neither the interpretation of the Constitution, nor the task of adapting it to contemporary society, have proven to be unproblematic and both of these activities have highlighted the delicate divide between the political and judicial process. The process of constitutional interpretation, for instance, has been consistently fraught with difficulties for the judiciary. Take what appears to be a relatively simple matter, how do judges divine the meaning of the Constitution? Do they rely solely on the document itself, or do they expand their horizons and include a variety of other sources which may cast a light on it? Can they be confident in uncovering the intent of the Founding Fathers, given that it can be far from easy to reconstruct and appreciate fully, as the twentieth century draws to a close, the beliefs and values of an eighteenth-century sensibility? Moreover, even if the justices of the Supreme Court are confident of their interpretation of the meaning and intention of a particular section and clause of the Constitution, are they not obliged to adapt and apply it to the conditions and circumstances that prevail at the moment of adjudication? This activity of adaptation, of course, is fraught with a variety of problems, intellectual, political, legal and constitutional, as the Supreme Court has discovered over the past two hundred years. Perhaps the difficulties inherent in the process of constitutional adjudication will become more evident from a brief examination of a few specific instances of constitutional interpretation.

A particularly good illustration of the complexity of the processes of constitutional interpretation is offered by the Commerce Clause. The words of Article I, Section 8 of the Constitution are fairly clear. 'The Congress shall have power ... To regulate Commerce with foreign Nations, and among the several States, and with the Indian Tribes.' Moreover the intentions of the Founding Fathers, in this instance, are not difficult to divine. The very existence of the Commerce Clause was a reminder that the Articles of Confederation had not been a success; it had not been a success, according to the delegates to the Philadelphia Convention, in large part because of an absence of national power to regulate commerce, and it was this deficiency that the Commerce Clause was designed to rectify. So, in 1787, the framers gave the Congress substantial authority over commerce between the states. However, this authority did not extend to commercial activities within the states, a decision that undoubtedly reflected that other and competing set of beliefs over the concentration of political power and authority that so concerned the Founding Fathers. The constitutional compromise was to place inter-state commerce within the power of congressional regulation, while intra-state commerce came under the jurisdiction of the states. This constitutional arrangement over commerce was accepted in its entirety by courts. The first major Commerce Clause case to come before the Supreme Court was *Gibbons v. Ogden* in 1824.[7] Chief Justice Marshall, speaking for the Court, reaffirmed the division of authority between the states and the federal government over the regulation of commercial activities. However, he also emphasised the very extensive power of the Congress over inter-state commerce, a power that the Chief Justice substantially enhanced by the very broad view of commerce that he adopted. Commerce, according to Marshall was not merely trade but 'the commercial intercourse between nations and parts of nations'.[8] In *Gibbons v. Ogden* Marshall developed the judicial formula for interpreting Commerce Clause cases. Firstly, commerce was more than trade in goods. Secondly, the Congress could regulate the activities of inter-state commerce in a variety of forms, but that thirdly, it could not regulate commerce internal to a state. It was a formula that kept faith both with the intent of the framers and the letter of the Constitution, and in addition, at least on the face of it, appeared to be a formula that the courts could apply, without any great difficulty, to subsequent Commerce Clause litigation. Unfortunately, for the judiciary, Commerce Clause cases post *Gibbons v. Ogden* did not prove to be quite so trouble free.

The principal problem that the courts faced in the years after *Gibbons v. Ogden* concerned the distinction between inter- and intra-state commerce. Neither in 1787 nor in 1824 was this a significant difficulty. The Founding Fathers found it easy to distinguish between these two categories. If production and trade crossed state boundaries, then it ceased to be intra-state commerce and was subject to Congressional control. This categorisation of economic activity was a relatively easy matter in an agrarian economy. However, when industrialisation began to alter the character of the American economy, it also transformed this simple dichotomy. Certainly by the second half of the nineteenth century the economy was increasingly sophisticated, interdependent and national in outlook. Large, complex organisations had emerged that owned manufacturing plants and administrative offices in numerous states, while the financial control of these institutions was increasingly located in those cities of the east and mid-west that had developed sophisticated capital markets. The line between inter- and intra-state commerce was becoming blurred and indistinct. Inter-state commerce had long since passed the stage of goods crossing state boundaries. How did the judiciary respond to these developments in the American economy? They did not, as is sometimes alleged, refuse to recognise these new economic realities. Indeed, in 1905 in *Swift & Co v. United States* the Supreme Court explicitly recognised the changing character of the American economy.[9] The Court spoke of a 'current of commerce' and very deliberately noted that 'commerce was not a technical legal conception but a practical one drawn from the course of business'.[10] Again, seventeen years later, in *Stafford v. Wallace*, the Court reiterated its view that its conception of commerce was derived from experience and that which it could observe, and not from any preconceived or formalistic notions.[11] In *Stafford v. Wallace*, the Supreme Court identified 'streams of commerce' and, using the doctrines of 'streams' and 'currents', the Court was prepared to rule that certain forms of economic activity that took place entirely within one state could, in certain circumstances, be considered inter-state commerce and subject to congressional control.[12] Did this mean that the judiciary, by the early decades of the twentieth century, had abandoned the division between inter- and intra-state commerce? The answer was no, but they did recognise that there was no clear dividing line and consequently they sought to establish further identifying characteristics which would assist them to distinguish between these two increasingly overlapping categories of economic activity. One such characteristic was whether intra-state commercial activities had an indirect or direct effect on inter-state commerce. If it did have a direct effect on inter-state commerce, then it fell within the jurisdiction of the Congress, but if the impact was indirect, then the courts considered such activities to be intra-state and subject to the control of the individual states. Inevitably the direct/indirect rule was contentious and difficult to apply, but it did permit the courts to recognise the economic realities of American industrial life in the twentieth century, while maintaining the constitutionally established limits on congressional power. But did this attempt by the judiciary both to maintain the integrity of the Constitution and take into account the changing economic landscape, remove the courts from political controversy? The answer is a resounding no.

The federal judiciary were unable to insulate themselves from controversy, because the issues raised by Commerce Clause litigation were so politically highly charged. Their collective commitment to propriety and impartiality did not protect them from an all-but-constant litany that the courts, and especially the United States Supreme Court, were partial to the interests of capital and therefore to the limitation of federal intervention in the nation's economic affairs.[13] In the main these claims were without foundation, and they were made, to some extent, by those who were unhappy with the political consequences of particular judicial decisions, when their judgement was perhaps impaired by the disappointment of losing a case. But in addition to the voices of the disappointed, there was a widely expressed view, in the early decades of the twentieth century, that the thrust of Commerce Clause judgements did not take sufficient account of the developments in the US economy. Certainly in the 1930s, these beliefs were expressed with a particular vehemence as several pieces of legislation, including the central provisions of the New Deal, were declared unconstitutional by the Supreme Court because they violated the provisions of the Commerce Clause.[14] The justices of the Supreme Court were accused of underestimating not only the extent of the national and interdependent character of the American economy, but also the unprecedentedly severe economic depression. If there was going to be a recovery from this depression, it required the federal government, according to the Roosevelt administration, to implement a series of measures to restructure and reform the economy. Only the federal government, it was argued, could provide the necessary remedies to the economic malaise confronting the United States, and in those first hundred days of the New Deal it was an argument that was accepted, not only by the Roosevelt administration, but also by the Congress and by a wide spectrum of American opinion. The gravity and severity of the crisis in the 1930s led the Congress to pass several pieces of legislation proposed by President Roosevelt which vastly increased the activities and the role of the federal government in the nation's economy, an increase that was both dramatic and unprecedented.[15] There is little doubt that the Roosevelt administration, at least during the first term, spoke on behalf of a substantial majority of the American electorate, and the popularity of the New Deal was readily and constantly evident. The problem for the Supreme Court was that several of the New Deal programmes paid little heed to the constitutional understandings current at the time. The careful and delicate formula developed over a considerable period of time on the Commerce Clause was ignored as the Roosevelt administration claimed substantial new powers for the federal authorities in managing and regulating the economy. How did the Supreme Court respond to this claim? The answer at one level, of course, is well known. The Court's response created a major political and constitutional crisis which had profound ramifications.[16] But was this conflict avoidable? Could the justices have defused the crisis?

The answer to these questions is that to a considerable extent the Supreme Court found itself, as it has done on numerous other occasions, in a profoundly invidious position. The Court could indeed have prevented the conflict between itself and the Roosevelt administration by giving its constitutional imprimatur to the New Deal. The central difficulty with doing so was that it would have had to set aside the existing judicial interpretations of the Constitution which had evolved over the preceding century. Certainly in the arena of the Commerce Clause, the National Industrial Recovery Act of 1933[17] and the Agricultural Adjustment Act[18] of the same year, two of the central legislative enactments of the first New Deal, or the Bituminous Coal Conservation Act of 1935,[19] could only have been found constitutional if the distinction between inter- and intra-state commerce was abandoned. These Acts gave the federal government authority over activities which hitherto had not been available to federal regulation, and furthermore did not distinguish between the locations of these activities. Now this sharp departure from existing practice was not a problem for politicians in the 1930s, indeed in the context of the depression a break with precedent was welcomed. It was seen as a break with the political failure of the immediate past, as evidence to the electorate of the determination of politicians to solve the problems besetting the nation, and as an indication that the Roosevelt administration and the Congress were prepared to embrace new and even experimental ideas to deal with the depression. The judicial perspective, however, was very different.

The view from the Supreme Court was that the judiciary had in place a formula for dealing with Commerce Clause litigation, a formula that was derived from a reasonable reading of the Constitution and a sympathetic understanding of the intentions of the Founding Fathers. Moreover, the formula was flexible and was able to incorporate the developments and changes that were taking place within the economy. It allowed the judiciary to maintain the integrity of the Constitution in a rapidly changing world. It was, in other words, a successful judicial formula or legal rule which the courts were reluctant to abandon because it had served them very well for a considerable period of time. However, this rule could not incorporate the claim that was being made by the Roosevelt administration that the distinction between inter- and intra-state was no longer germane to the American economy of the 1930s. The interdependence and national outlook of the economy, it was argued, made such a distinction irrelevant, and certainly with the advantage of hindsight, such a claim was far from unreasonable. The line between inter- and intra-state, as the Supreme Court itself had noted, was increasingly difficult to draw, and there were also fewer and fewer industries on the intra-state side of the divide. Consequently, the rule which had served the courts so well for so long was coming to the end of its judicial usefulness and was in need of re-evaluation. So why did not the Supreme Court take the opportunity presented in the cases concerning the New Deal to re-examine the inter/intra-state distinction and the direct/indirect rule? The reason why it did not do so lies in the distinctive character of the judicial process.

If the Supreme Court had accepted the claims of the Roosevelt administration, then it would have meant the immediate overruling of the existing governing rules and the abandonment of the central organising concept of Commerce Clause interpretation, that is, that there was a limitation to the powers of the federal government over commerce and that the role of the judiciary was to establish the precise boundaries of that limitation. It was therefore feasible for the Court to discard the direct/indirect distinction or the inter-state/intra-state divide for a more suitable rule, but it was an entirely another matter for it to say that the Commerce Clause imposed no restrictions on the powers of the federal government. It was certainly unlikely to do so at the first request, for even if the Court should finally adopt the position that the Commerce Clause did limit the authority of the federal government, it was only going to do so after considerable deliberation. The Court would require time and evidence that the existing rules were inadequate and no longer appropriate and that there was no possibility of fashioning other judicial doctrines that were able to cope with the new economic realities. If the Supreme Court had been convinced that this was the position, it could well have been more receptive to the administration, but the judicial process is slow; the courts require time, and though rules do evolve and change, they do so gradually. Politicians both within the Roosevelt administration and outside of it simply expected far too much from the courts. They expected the judiciary to be sympathetic to their belief that the times demanded innovative and drastic remedies. But the nature of the judicial function makes it difficult for the courts to change direction sharply. Politicians can do so, but not judges, and therein lies one of the central problems that has confronted the American courts over the past two centuries.

Judges in the United States have had to accept that the judicial process has been a constant source of frustration to politicians. Judicial mores and behaviour have not endeared judges to their colleagues in the other branches of government. Their emphasis on continuity, certainty and incremental change has frequently clashed with a desire from politicians, and the electorate they represent, to move with far greater rapidity. The last two hundred years of constitutional adjudication is littered with examples of political irritation with the Supreme Court, of which the Commerce Clause cases are but one instance. They are, however, a particularly telling instance because the Court, on the whole, behaved with both propriety and sensitivity, but nevertheless was unable to avoid that friction which appears to have become all but endemic. Indeed, the propriety in a sense was the problem. Let me explain. It has been the reluctance of the Supreme Court to endorse the imperatives of the political process that has been the source of the difficulty. If the Court had accepted the proposition that the economic conditions of the 1930s required the existing constitutional limitations on the federal government's ability to regulate the economy to be swept away, or at least sharply reduced, then the political and constitutional crisis of 1937 would not have arisen. The Roosevelt administration would have welcomed the Court's conversion but, of course, the Court did no such thing. The justices, or at least most of them, retained their distance from the world of the politician; they did not allow those pressures, that Senators and Representatives found irresistible, to influence their opinions. Instead they formed their view after reflecting on those considerations that are at the core of a legal and constitutional decision – the Constitution, its intent and meaning, the cumulative judicial interpretation of the document, and the appropriateness of the extant legal rules to the conditions that prevail at the time. These considerations did not convince the justices on the Court that a hundred years of constitutional adjudication had to be jettisoned forthwith. Did the depression require, as so many politicians believed, unprecedented powers for the federal government? A degree of historical reflection, and history is an important component of the judicial perspective, certainly cast some doubt on such a claim. While the depression of the 1930s was very severe, there had been several other occasions in American history when the economy was far from robust. Indeed, in 1787 the Founding Fathers were aware of the difficult economic conditions that had prevailed during the period of Confederation, but were also deeply unhappy with the measures taken by the legislatures in the individual states to alleviate the subsequent distress, and they sought to ensure, through the Constitution, that these measures would not be repeated.[20] So not only was the claim that the conditions in the 1930s were unique somewhat suspect, but the justices on the Court were also aware that the Constitution was designed to prohibit certain kinds of legislative responses engendered by a difficult economic climate. The Founding Fathers feared that politicians were only too willing to succumb to the immediate and pressing claims of the 'majority faction' and it was this willingness that had led to the abuses during Confederation.[21] Of course this distrust of politics and politicians extended far beyond the period of Confederation. It informed the entire Constitution. It was the reason for the elaborate and complicated structure of government in the United States, the Bill of Rights and, of course, the central role of the courts and the judiciary in the political process. The framers of the Constitution knew and feared the perspective of politicians and they wished to control it. They also knew that it was very different to the judicial perspective, and that sooner or later the differing perspectives would result in conflict between the institutions. Judges would be aloof from those views, beliefs and pressures that politicians, throughout the history of the Republic, have found so persuasive, and the consequence of their adherence to legal and judicial values is that it has led the Surpeme Court to a very different set of conclusions on numerous occasions. Disagreement and tension between the judiciary and the political branches of government, the Congress and the Presidency, was all but inevitable, but in the final analysis the Founding Fathers wanted the political instinct to be subordinate to the judicial instinct.

This brief account of the interpretation of the Commerce Clause illustrates the fact that the Supreme Court has had and continues to have a most profound impact on the American polity. It cannot avoid political controversy because it is the final arbiter of the Constitution. Its central task is that of constitutional interpretation, which means that from time to time it modifies and overrules the considered judgement of the political branches of government and, as been noted above, the judicial perspective does lead the Court in different directions from the Congress and the Presidency. In this respect the interpretation of the Commerce Clause has been no different from that of other sections of the Constitution. The due process clauses of the Fifth and Fourteenth Amendments to the Constitution provide a very similar story. These clauses were understood by the courts to impose limitations on governmental intervention at both federal and state level, in private economic arrangements. However, the courts also had no doubt that government possessed the authority to legislate on behalf of the health, welfare and moral well-being of its citizens, and in order to achieve these objectives, government had the power to modify these private arrangements. For instance, in 1898 the Supreme Court sustained a law passed by the state of Utah limiting the working day of miners to eight hours, because of a danger to their health. In this case the regulation was held to be constitutional because the health considerations overrode the concerns over governmental intervention in the private contractual arrangements between miner and mine owner.[22] In other words, the due process clause protected private property and private economic arrangements, but not absolutely. The judicial task over a period of several decades after the Civil War was to develop a formula, a legal rule, which would create a *modus vivendi* between these two objectives. Understandably, this proved to be a far from easy task. The rapid industrialisation of the American economy brought in its train a variety of social and economic problems. Politicians at both the state and federal level, responding to pressures from their publics, passed legislation to ameliorate the more damaging effects of the new industrial order. For instance, the federal government imposed a tax on incomes over four hundred dollars, and sought to eliminate child labour.[23] The state legislatures passed legislation which regulated the prices that could be charged for a variety of goods and services and which established minimum wage levels.[24] The task of the courts was to decide the fate of this vast outpouring of legislation. Critics of the Supreme Court have accused it, as in the Commerce Clause cases, of being overly sympathetic to the interests of capital, but in reality there is no evidence of systematic partiality by the judiciary.[25] Rather there is, once again, an attempt to grapple with the difficult, if not near-intractable problem, of preserving the constitutional protections of private property and economic arrangements in a polity and society where there is a growing demand for governmental intervention in the economy. Politicians, both state and federal, were not unwilling to respond to these demands, but the task of the Court was different and more complicated. Judges are required to employ criteria other than responsiveness to the electorate, and consequently on several occasions the Supreme Court held statutes, state and federal, to be unconstitutional, although there were far more numerous occasions when it sustained the constitutionality of legislation. Nevertheless, the occasions that lingered in the memory and were the cause of political tension and controversy arose from the Court's rulings against the ability of government to intervene in private economic arrangements. But once again the antagonism and controversy resulted from the Court behaving with judicial propriety, which reinforces the view outlined above about the inherent tension that exists between the political and judicial perspectives. As with the Commerce Clause cases, Due Process litigation also illustrates the centrality of the judicial institutions to the political process and the consequences of that centrality in the making of public policy.

The impact of the Court has not been limited to the arena of economics, but is evident in every area of constitutional adjudication. A similar story is to be found, for instance, with civil liberties and civil rights litigation. Once again federal judges have been critical players in the shaping and formulation of public policy in these areas. Since the 1940s the primacy of economic regulation issues in the docket of the Supreme Court has been supplanted by questions concerning civil rights and civil liberties. As the great and contentious questions over the extent of governmental intervention in the econmy no longer appeared to divide the polity, at least to the same extent, by the 1940s new and equally divisive questions over racial equality and the precise meaning and definition of the Bill of Rights came before the Court. The response of the Court to these questions, especially in the fifties and sixties under the leadership of Chief Justice Earl Warren, was markedly different to that of previous Courts. Whereas the story of Commerce Clause and Due Process adjudication was marked by caution, hesitancy and incrementalism, the attitude of the Warren Court was very different. The Court, or at least the majority on it who controlled the Court, did not appear to endorse those values – stability, continuity and historical analysis – that were critical factors in the judicial decision-making process in the cases concerning the economy. The Warren Court, by contrast, appeared to be more interested in the policy outcomes. Certainly the painstaking and gradualistic attempt to achieve a balance between competing interests and values that characterised the economic regulation cases were replaced by the Warren Court's preference for making dramatic and bold decisions in the arena of civil rights and civil liberties. Perhaps the most dramatic and historic decision concerned the constitutionality of racial segregation.

In 1954, in *Brown v. Board of Education of Topeka*, the Court declared that racial segregation was unconstitutional.[26] It was a momentous and to some extent an unexpected decision which had an extraordinary political impact. It brought severe discomfort to the south and profoundly angered the white population of that region. Conversely, it enormously encouraged blacks throughout the nation and gave welcome inspiration to the civil rights movement. It broke the deadlock in the Congress over the vexed question of segregation and had enduring consequences for the political parties and the political process in general. The Warren Court will not only be remembered for *Brown*, although that by itself is no mean achievement, because it continued to make a series of controversial decisions. If *Brown* withdrew the constitutional authority for legally enforced, or *de jure*, segregation, the position of *de facto* segregation, racial separation that had emerged out of social practice and custom rather than through the force of law, was untouched. However, in *Green v. County Board of New Kent County* the Warren Court sounded the death knell for *de facto* segregation.[27] Away from civil rights, the Warren Court rewrote the relationship between the police and the criminal suspect, substantially limiting the powers of the police and providing the suspect with new rights, particularly during interrogation.[28] These decisions, unsurprisingly, were controversial at a time of growing concern over crime. Indeed, during the 1968 Presidential campaign the Republican candidate for President, Richard Nixon, made the Warren Court and the matter of law and order a principal issue of his campaign. Equally controversially the Court also altered the rules governing the size of legislative constituencies. Until the decisions of the early 1960s, state legislatures could take into account a variety of factors, of which the size of population was usually, but not invariably, the determining one, in constructing constituencies either for the state legislatures or for the House of Representatives. Starting in 1962, the Warren Court began the process of removing all factors other than the size of population to be taken into account.[29] Not only did this infuriate those politicians whose electoral position was now in jeopardy, but it also raised questions about the theory of representation – that population and population only should be represented – that the Warren Court was reading into the Constitution.

This list of controversial and significant decisions made by the Warren Court could be extended without difficulty, but the point is evident; the Warren Court conducted itself in a very different manner to most of its predecessors. Although it is of no particular interest here to evaluate and debate the jurisprudence of the Warren Court, nevertheless and interestingly the same problems came to haunt it. It was at the centre of several political storms, some of which looked as potentially serious as the Court-packing crisis of 1937. There were sustained campaigns to pass constitutional amendments which would have overruled specific decisions, and one such campaign about legislative constituencies came very close to success. Moreover, as was noted above, the Warren Court attracted intense political emotions and became the subject of partisan debate. Of course, the reason for these passions was the fact that the Court was instrumental in resolving contentious issues of public policy. The Court was the critical institution over a range of issues. In that sense, the Warren Court was no different from its predecessors. Like the Courts that struggled with the Commerce Clause or Due Process, it also had a decisive impact on the making of public policy. The location of the United States Supreme Court at a critical juncture in the American political and constitutional process means that, however it conducts itself, it will have a profound effect on public policy. It is not and has not been, for a very considerable time, the institution of Alexander Hamilton's description. It certainly is no longer, if it ever was, the least dangerous branch.

NOTES

1 C. Rossiter (ed.), *The Federalist Papers*, New York, Mentor, 1961, p. 465.
2 See in particular Nathan Glazer, 'Towards an imperial judiciary?', *The Public Interest*, vol. 41, 1975; Raoul Berger, *Government by Judiciary*, Cambridge, Harvard University Press, 1971.
3 For an interesting view on the Founding Fathers and judicial review, see P. Eidelberg, *The Philosophy of the Constitution*, New York, The Free Press, 1968.
4 1 Cranch 137 (1803).
5 See *Fletcher v. Peck*, 6 Cranch 87 (1810); *Cohens v. Virginia*, 6 Wheaton 264 (1821).
6 *United States v. Butler*, 297 US 1,62.
7 *Gibbons v. Ogden*, 9 Wheaton 1 (1824).
8 *Ibid.*, p. 197.
9 *Swift & Co v. United States*, 196 US 375 (1905).
10 *Ibid.*, p. 399.
11 *Stafford v. Wallace*, 258 US 495 (1922).
12 *Houston, E. & W. Texas Railroad v. United States*, 234 US 342 (1914).
13 For an elaboration of this view, see Sidney Fine, *Laisses Faire and the General Welfare State*, Ann Arbor, Mich., University of Michigan Press, 1956; Robert G. McCloskey, *American Conservatism in the Age of Enterprise*, Cambridge, Harvard University Press, 1951; Arthur S. Miller, *The Supreme Court and American Capitalism*, New York, The Free Press, 1968; Arnold M. Paul, *Conservative Crisis and the Rule of Law*, New York, Harper and Row, 1969; Benjamin R. Twiss, *Lawyers and the Constitution*, Princeton, Princeton University Press, 1942.
14 For an example of a contemporaneous and hostile view toward the Supreme Court, see Drew Pearson and Robert S. Allen, *The Nine Old Men*, Garden City, NY, Doubleday, 1937.
15 See, for example, the Agricultural Adjustment Act of 1933; National Industrial Recovery Act of 1933.
16 Of course, the major crisis erupted in 1937, when President Roosevelt unveiled his proposals to reform the federal judiciary; a proposal that is normally referred to as the Court-packing plan. For a lucid and brief account, see William E. Leuchtenberg, 'The origins of Roosevelt's "court-packing plan"', *The Supreme Court Review*, 1966.
17 48 Stat. 195 (1933).
18 48 Stat. 31 (1933).
19 49 Stat. 991 (1935).
20 This is a reference to Article I, Section 10 of the Constitution, otherwise known as the Contract Clause.
21 See *Federalist* no. 10 in Clinton Rossiter (ed.), *The Federalist Papers*, New York, Mentor, 1961.
22 See *Holden v. Hardy*, 169 US 366 (1898).
23 See *Pollock v. Farmers Loan and Trust Co.*, 157 US 429 (1895); *Bailey v. Drexel Furniture Co.*, 259 US 20 (1922).
24 See *Stetler v. O'Hara*, 423 US 649 (1917); *Munn v. Illinois*, 94 US 113 (1877).
25 See Richard Maidment, 'Law and economic policy in the United States: the judicial

response to government regulation of the economy', *The Journal of Legal History*, vol. 7, no. 2, 1986.

26 347 US 483 (1954). For a detailed account of Brown, see Richard Kluger, *Simple Justice*, New York, Alfred A. Knopf, 1976. For a different view see Richard Maidment, 'Changing styles in constitutional adjudication: the United States Supreme Court and racial segregation', *Public Law*, summer 1977.

27 391 US 430 (1968). The final sentence for *de facto* segregation came in *Swann v. Charlotte-Mecklenburg Board of Education*, 402 US 1 (1971), when Chief Justice Warren had retired and was replaced by Chief Justice Warren Burger in 1969.

28 See *Escobedo v. Illinois*, 378 US 478 (1964); *Miranda v. Arizona*, 384 US 436 (1966).

29 See *Baker v. Carr*, 369 US 186 (1962); *Reynolds v. Sims*, 377 US 436 (1966).

Madison v. Madison:
The Party Essays v. The Federalist Papers

ABSTRACT

The most authoritative commentary on the Constitution remains 'The Federalist'. Yet 'The Federalist's' explanation and defence of the Constitution was always somewhat suspect, since, as the authors themselves admitted, 'The Federalist' was a polemic, written to promote the ratification of the Constitution, as well as a work of political philosophy. Moreover, Alexander Hamilton and James Madison, its main authors, soon parted political company, with Madison in the House of Representatives leading a party in opposition to Hamilton's policies as Secretary of the Treasury. Madison, known as the 'Father of the Constitution', was also the father of the party system, grafted onto the Constitution soon after the government went into operation. This chapter displays the departures that Madison's thinking as party leader made from the thinking of Madison the co-author of 'The Federalist', and argues that these departures comprised a very different and in some ways a superior way of conceiving of America's form of government.

While the United States is celebrating the bicentennial of its Constitution, it might be salutary to reflect upon James Madison's second thoughts regarding his original arguments on behalf of that document. Most historians and political scientists and indeed many ordinary Americans identify Madison with the Constitution and especially its defence by 'Publius' – the pseudonym adopted by Madison, Alexander Hamilton and John Jay – in *The Federalist Papers*. Few, however, are aware that in a series of articles published in *The National Gazette* between December 1791 and September 1792 Madison repudiated many of the arguments of *The Federalist Papers*. Marking the beginning of Madison's attempt to organise the republican opposition as a national political party, these essays contained arguments which resembled those of his previous Anti-Federalist opponents.[1]

Norman Jacobson has contrasted the warm fraternal thought of the Articles of Confederation and Thomas Paine's *Common Sense* with the cold, rational, impersonal proceduralism of the Constitution and *The Federalist*. The former abounded with expressions of friendship, affection, American uniqueness and a disdain for mere interest. The latter spoke the harsh language of coercion, interests, threats and calculating rationality.[2] Yet, no sooner had the Constitution been ratified than Madison, one of its principal architects and defenders, in an astonishing act of self-criticism, assailed his previous position as Publius.

Some authors either explicitly[3] or implicitly[4] deny that the thought of Madison as party organiser is significantly different from that of Madison as Publius. Other scholars have asserted that a fundamental antagonism exists; but only John Zvesper has argued the case in any detail, and even he has not delineated the full extent of Madison's transformation in 1791–2 into a trenchant critic of *The Federalist*.[5] This chapter will document the fundamental incompatibility between the thought of the two Madisons. It will also challenge those scholars who concede the contradiction but assume the theoretical superiority of Publius and slight the theoretical worth of Madison's party writings.[6] Madison's essays in *The National Gazette* not only criticised his earlier position as Publius but also adumbrated, if not fully developed, an alternative theory of liberal politics.

Where Publius had sought the greatest possible social heterogeneity as a *sine qua non* of republican government, Madison the party organiser of 1791–2 urged greater homogeneity as essential for preserving a republican regime. Unlike Publius with his expediential defence of equal rights and republican government, Madison as founder of the Republican party sought to touch the soul of Americans by nurturing a principled attachment to republican government and political equality. Furthermore, the extended orbit praised by Publius was now seen as threatening rather than perfecting republican government. What is more, the two Madisons prescribed fundamentally different methods of maintaining the constitutional balance. Finally, Madison's later description of the partisan conflict between republicans and anti-republicans bears no resemblance to the factional politics of *The Federalist*.

HETEROGENEITY VERSUS HOMOGENEITY

For Madison as Publius, the social pluralism generated by a large population inhabiting a large territory provided the principal means of ensuring that a republican government would not become tyrannical. He preferred the greatest possible social heterogeneity in order to fracture public opinion and fragment organised political life, thereby obviating the chief problem of a republic – a majority faction. According to Publius, no faction could be trusted with government power; given the opportunity, it would use government power to advance its own interest at the expense of the national interest or the private interests of others. But removal of the causes of faction would be inexpedient – as it would entail the destruction of liberty, if not impossible – as one could not give citizens 'the same opinions, the same passions, and the same interests'.[7] The answer, then, was to control the effects of faction to ensure that no faction could appropriate government power to benefit itself.

But whereas a minority faction is rendered harmless by 'the republican principle which enables the majority to defeat its [a minority's] sinister views by regular vote', the same principle exacerbates rather than solves the problem of a majority faction. 'When a majority is included in a faction, the form of popular government ... enables it to sacrifice to its ruling passion or interest both the public good and the rights of other citizens.'[8] As events at the state level had demonstrated, even 'auxiliary precautions' such as federalism, separate institutions sharing powers, different terms of office, and different modes of election and selection were unlikely to thwart a majority faction since it would be capable of sweeping aside all such institutional complexity.[9] Furthermore, Madison disparaged any suggestion that virtue could be relied upon to protect Americans from the dangers posed by a majority faction.

> If the impulse and the opportunity be suffered to coincide, we well know that neither moral nor religious motives can be relied on as an adequate control. They are not found to be such on the injustice and violence of individuals, and lose their efficacy in proportion to the number combined together, that is, in proportion as their efficacy becomes needful.[10]

Hence Publius proposed the extensive social pluralism generated by the country's extended orbit as the primary solution to the problem of majority faction. 'Extend the sphere,' Madison wrote, 'and you take in a greater variety of parties and interests; you make it less probable that a majority of the whole will have a common motive to invade the rights of other citizens.'[11] Given sufficient heterogeneity, a governing majority would be a coalition of minorities, each compelled to compromise, if not abandon, its particularistic demands. Thus, 'in the extended republic of the United States, and among the great variety of interests, parties, and sects which it embraces, a coalition of a majority of the whole society could seldom take place on any other principles than those of justice and the general good'.[12]

Shifting his ground in 1791, Madison now argued that political moderation derives from the people's affection for and confidence in one another, not from the exigencies of coalition-building within a pluralist society. 'The greater the mutual confidence and affection of all parts of the Union, the more likely they will be to concur amicably, or to differ in moderation, in the elective designation of the chief magistrate.'[13] If shared republican values do not remove all political differences, at least they minimise them and assure a defeated minority that their rights will be respected. Secure in their knowledge of their fellow citizens' principled commitment to republican liberty, the citizens' mutual concord, sympathy and confidence enable them to trust one another with their interests and rights. Even earlier, Madison had argued that social pluralism and free political institutions were inadequate to preserve republican government if a large number of citizens distrusted the new order. Hence, Madison recommended adoption of a bill of rights to reassure Anti-Federalists that their Federalist opponents were committed to republicanism.[14]

Although *The Federalist* had opposed any possibility of a popular majority acting as a concerted political force, Madison in 1791–2 urged the American people to 'be united' so that they could effectively watch over the national government; greater political and social homogeneity were needed to facilitate common political action in defence of republican government.[15] Adopting the approach of those 'theoretic politicians' disparaged in *Federalist* no. 10, Madison now worked to unify most, if not all, Americans around common interests and opinions; hence the greater substantive homogeneity he now advocated transcended a procedural consensus on the rules of the game. While eschewing any utopian expectation that Americans could share exactly the same interests, he sought to discourage the multiplication of different interests and to reduce differences of interest.

In 1791–2, Madison favoured increased social homogeneity in order to deflect arguments for increased executive discretion. 'In the first place, in proportion as uniformity is found to prevail in the interests and sentiments of the several states, will be the practicability of accommodating legislative regulations to them, and thereby of withholding new and dangerous prerogatives from the executive.'[16] By reducing the difference between the states, Madison hoped to obviate the need for executive discretion in implementing legislation and consequently to confine the executive branch to a narrow sphere of activity.

Ignoring his earlier warnings against a majority faction, Madison now recognised that only a people united by republican sentiment and interest could vouchsafe the efficacy of the fragmented government structure. The American people no longer were to be divided by their different factional interests and the distrust which necessarily accompanied them, but rather were to be united by warm fraternal feelings nurtured by an identity of interests. Madison urged Americans to

> employ their utmost zeal, by eradicating local prejudices and mistaken rivalships to consolidate the affairs of the states into *one harmonious interest*; and let it be the patriotic study of all, to maintain the various authorities established by our complicated system, each in its respective constitutional sphere; and to erect over the whole one paramount Empire of *reason, benevolence, and brotherly affection.*[17]

Madison the party organiser sought to unite the citizenry by inner bonds of fellowship which would supersede the impersonal justice secured by the Constitution's external procedural safeguards.

In pursuit of this republican unity, Madison in 1791–2 began organising the Republican party which he intended to become such a vast majority, that it would not only defeat Hamilton's Federalists electorally, but also obliterate Federalism as a viable political alternative and overwhelm the constitutional structure by securing control of all branches and levels of government. Although describing the division between republicans and anti-republicans as 'natural to most political societies',[18] Madison did not accept the Federalists as a legitimate opposition and consequently did not envisage a party system in which they and Republicans rotated in office, While tolerating Federalism, Madison expected the Republican party to banish its opponents to the political wilderness.[19]

Transcending the heterogeneity produced by the extended sphere, 'the republican party ... will naturally find their [sic] account in burying all antecedent questions, in banishing every other distinction than that between enemies and friends to republican government, in promoting a general harmony among the latter wherever residing, or however employed'. By contrast, the anti-republicans would exploit the nation's heterogeneity in order to disrupt the Republican party and advance their aristocratic purposes. 'It will be equally their [the anti-republicans'] true policy to weaken their opponents by reviving exploded parties, and taking advantage of all prejudices, local, political, and occupational, that may prevent or disturb a general coalition of sentiments.'[20] Far from being a necessary condition for republican government, social heterogeneity was now perceived as a resource available to anti-republicans and hence as a serious danger to a republican regime.

In 1791–2, recognising that the actualisation of republican fraternity required more than exhorting Americans to be friendly towards one another, Madison urged a diminution of social differences in order to encourage fraternal bonds. Unlike Publius who sought political salvation in the multiplication of different interests, Madison now preferred to reduce differences of interest which bred distrust and animosity.

> The less the supposed difference of interests, and the greater the concord and confidence throughout the great body of people, the more readily must they sympathize with each other, the more seasonably can they interpose a common manifestation of their sentiments, the more certainly will they take the alarm at usurpation or oppression, and the more effectively will they *consolidate* their defense of the public liberty.[21]

Now Madison mordantly caricatured his previous advocacy of maximum heterogeneity.

> In all political societies, different interests and parties arise out of the nature of things, and the great art of politicians lies in making them checks and balances to each other. Let us then increase these *natural* distinctions by favoring an inequality of property; and let us add to them artificial distinctions, by establishing *kings* and *nobles* and *plebeians*. We shall then have the more checks to oppose each other; we shall then have the more scales and the more weights to protect and maintain the [constitutional] equilibrium. This is as little the voice of reason, as it is of republicanism.[22]

Although interest groups or factions which are promoted or created by government are qualitatively different from factions which are voluntary creations,[23] Madison as Publius had simply sought the greatest possible social diversity in order to obviate the likelihood of a majority faction. While he had never urged the creation of hereditary classes, Publius had certainly favoured 'the more scales and more weights' in order to forestall the danger of a majority faction.

In contrast to Publius who had insisted that the 'first object of government' is the protection of 'the different and unequal faculties' which produce 'different degrees and kinds of property',[24] Madison as party organiser now urged an approximate substantive equality of condition. To overcome differences of interest so that affection and sympathy might find fertile soil in which to take root, the essay 'Parties' proposed a diminution of economic inequalities although not an absolute equality of condition: '2. By withholding unnecessary opportunities from a few to increase the inequality of property, by an immoderate, and especially unmerited, accumulation of riches. 3. By the silent operation of laws, which, without violating the rights of property, reduce extreme wealth towards a state of mediocrity, and raise extreme indigence towards a state of comfort.'[25] Madison now sought to provide poor citizens with sufficient property in order to secure their political independence and to deprive the rich of excessive wealth in order to prevent them from wielding disproportionate political influence. Although Madison's proposals were marked by moderation and ambiguity, his new determination to reduce economic inequality contradicted Publius' view that inequality was natural. Madison's new concern with attaining a rough substantive equality is apparently traceable to a recognition that large economic inequalities might impede the creation of genuine political community with its inner bonds of affection and trust.[26] It might be easier to subordinate differences of economic interest to common republican values if those differences were negligible.

Unlike Publius, who had simply sought to multiply the number of occupations in order to prevent the existence of a majority faction, and consequently had adopted a stance of moral neutrality towards different occupations, Madison the party organiser favoured greater occupational homogeneity. Abandoning Publius' neutrality, Madison the party organiser now preferred those economic occupations which he considered to be favourable to republican liberty.

The goodness or badness of an occupation now resided in its relation to republican values, not in the individual; 'the best distribution [of citizens into employment] is that which would most favor *health*, *virtue*, *intelligence* and *competency* in the *greater number* of citizens'.[27] According to Madison, husbandry nurtures such characteristics but manufacturing and commerce injure them. While the agricultural work of yeoman farmers fosters 'solid utility', factory work stunts the intellectual and physical development of the operatives; sailors lead morally and physically unhealthy lives; and the fashion industry degrades workers by subjecting them to the whim and caprice of the wealthy followers of fashion. Regarding the fashion industry, Madison asked rhetorically: 'Can any despotism be more cruel than a situation, in which the existence of thousands depends on one will, and that will on the imagination?' Employment in the fashion industry produces a 'servile dependence of one class of citizens on another class' which is inappropriate for republics.[28]

In 1791–2, Madison acknowledged that some occupations benefit a republic by nuturing qualities necessary for active participation in republican politics, while others are harmful since they produce citizens who are less capable, if not incapable, of self-government. Yet Hamilton's financial policies were benefitting and encouraging precisely those occupations which Madison considered injurious to republican citizens. Consequently, Madison now concluded that greater occupational homogeneity rather than increased heterogeneity would be more favourable to republican government. 'The class of citizens who provide at once their own food and their own raiment ... are the best basis of public liberty, and the strongest bulwark of public safety ... The greater the proportion of this class to the whole society, the more free, the more independent, and the more happy must be the society itself.'[29] Although Hamilton's economic policy increased the number of social interests as Madison had recommended in *The Federalist*, Madison now opposed Hamilton's measures because he judged them to be incompatible with the preservation of republican government.

THE EXTENDED ORBIT: A PROBLEM, NOT A SOLUTION

For Madison as Publius, the extended orbit of the United States provided the primary defences against the problem of a majority faction. In addition to increasing social heterogeneity and therefore making it unlikely that a majority would share a common interest, the extended orbit, by posing almost insurmountable problems of communication and co-ordination, would make it less likely that a majority faction could organise around a shared interest if such an interest existed despite the country's heterogeneity.[30]

Representation made an extensive republic possible, and the extended sphere in turn perfected representation. According to Publius, 'the two great points of difference between a democracy and a republic are first, the delegation of the government, in the latter, to a small number of citizens elected by the rest; secondly, the greater number of citizens and greater sphere of country over which the latter may be extended'.[31] Many Anti-Federalists preferred direct democracy and only reluctantly accepted representation as an unavoidable necessity in a large country. In contrast to many Anti-Federalists who favoured a large number of representatives elected for short terms from small districts in order to approximate direct democracy, Madison welcomed the additional safeguards created by the election of relatively few representatives from large electoral districts. Madison rejected direct democracy as inherently flawed since it 'can admit of no cure for the mischiefs of faction'.[32] Because direct democracy could only be practised by a relatively small population concentrated in a compact territory, a pure democracy lacked sufficient heterogeneity to guard against a majority faction. Therefore, even where possible, direct democracy was never desirable; representative government was always preferable since it excluded 'the people in their collective capacity' from government while still permitting free political institutions.[33]

According to The Federalist, representation was a necessary but not sufficient condition to preserve republican government; events in the states had demonstrated that in a small country representation alone could not sufficiently insulate government officials from popular pressure.[34] Additional safeguards were necessary. In order to weaken the immediate pressure of public opinion, to keep popular passions at bay and to favour the election of the better qualified members of the 'conventional' aristocracy who were assumed to be members of a 'natural' aristocracy of talent, representation had to be combined with a large territory, large electoral districts, and a relatively few representatives.[35]

In The Federalist, Madison concluded that large republics 'are most favourable to the election of proper guardians of the public weal'.[36] The larger the electoral district, the greater was the likelihood that well qualified individuals would be elected and appointed to national office. In large districts, the absolute number of talented individuals would be greater,[37] merely local reputations would count for less, and unworthy candidates would be less able 'to practice with success the vicious arts by which elections are too often carried'.[38] As electoral units increase in size and as voters consequently possess less personal knowledge of the candidates, voters increasingly rely upon the education, wealth, status, family connections, and reputations of candidates when deciding between them. Hence regarding both elective and appointive office, the large territory advantages members of the 'conventional' aristocracy at the expense of ordinary citizens because the social position of the former endows them with the extensive reputations necessary for election and selection.[39] In a large country with large constituencies, national legislators, executive officials and judges would be better able than the majority of citizens to identify the national interest, and maximum social pluralism would free them to act according to their conception of the public good. Consequently Madison expected Congress and the entire national government to act as a 'filter' which would improve public opinion.[40]

To help remove government officials from ordinary citizens, Madison as Publius relied upon not only representation and the country's extended orbit but also a wholly formal theory of representation[41] which contrasted with the mirror or reflection theory of representation espoused by many Anti-Federalists. Rejecting Publius' 'filter' theory of representation as 'aristocratic', many Anti-Federalists wanted to make the legislature into a portrait in miniature of society so as to best approximate direct democracy and thereby reduce the distance between officials and citizens. To ensure that representatives would think, act and feel like their constituents, these Anti-Federalists prescribed frequent elections, small districts, and short terms of office.[42] They argued that electoral accountability was insufficient and that a representative would faithfully represent his constituents only if he also resembled them in their occupations, status and opinions. But Publius insisted that the electoral connection was sufficient.

In *Federalist* nos. 35 and 36, Hamilton rejected the Anti-Federalists' 'idea of an actual representation of all classes of the people by persons of each class'[43] and concluded that electoral responsibility, not any resemblance to the voters, ensured the representatives' fealty to their duty. According to Hamilton, there was no need for any organic connection between representatives and represented since the electoral connection sufficed. Echoing Hamilton, Madison as Publius rejected the Anti-Federalists' prescriptions for bringing representatives and represented closer together. Furthermore, when Madison argued in *Federalist* no. 56 that Representatives would have sufficient knowledge of the laws and interests of their states in order to legislate appropriate national taxation, he said nothing to suggest that they should be aware of or pay heed to the opinions of their constituents. Madison assumed that the social pluralism of large electoral districts would free representatives from any need to consult regularly with their constituents.

While emphasising its beneficial effects, Madison did concede that the nation's extended territory might 'expose [Americans] to the inconvenience of remaining for a longer time under the influence of those misrepresentations which the combined industry of interested men may succeed in distributing among them'. To overcome this disadvantage, Madison at this time recommended reliance upon institutional 'auxiliary precautions' to ensure that a single diseased branch would not be fatal to republican liberty. If one branch of the new national government succeeded in manipulating public opinion and hence escaping from popular control, the institutional complexity of the new government would prevent that branch from governing tyrannically.[44]

In contrast to his earlier perception of the nation's large territory as an essential element of republican government, Madison as creator of the Republican party portrayed the nation's extended orbit as a danger. He now argued that the nation's large size endangered republican government by removing government from popular control, by impeding the concerted action of republicans, by thwarting the formation of genuine national public opinion, by encouraging abuses of government power and by vitiating fraternal feelings. Consequently in 1791–2 he sought to diminish the distance between the national government and the governed.

Now as party organiser, Madison perceived a new danger not identified by Publius: 'The more extensive a country, the more insignificant is each individual in his own eyes. This may be unfavorable to liberty.'[45] In a large republic, an individual citizen is likely to conclude that his voice is politically unimportant and hence might become politically apathetic. To encourage political participation by ordinary citizens, Madison's new Republican party mobilised Americans into a common political movement so that a citizen would see himself, not as a weak isolated individual, but rather as an active member of a powerful collectivity.

According to Madison, 'monarchies' suffered from two disadvantages: '1st, That the eyes of a good prince cannot see all that he ought to know – 2nd, That the hands of a bad one will not be tied by the fear of combinations against him.' These disadvantages increased as the size of the country increased.[46] Since Madison alleged that Hamilton's and the Federalists' preference for enhanced executive power betrayed their preference for 'monarchy', Madison was warning that the United States would fall prey to these disadvantages if Hamilton and the Federalists succeeded. Unfortunately, the country's extended orbit favoured Hamilton's designs. In an earlier essay, Madison had argued that an extensive territory contributed to the expansion of executive power by weakening popular control of the legislature which provided the only possible institutional check to executive usurpation.[47] Hence the extended territory jeopardised republican government either because a well-intentioned executive would lack sufficient knowledge of the country or because a tyrannically-inclined executive would exploit the weakness of the legislature.

Although as Publius he had advocated distancing government officials both physically and psychically from the people, Madison the partisan now argued that such removal endangered republican government by providing government with the opportunity to counterfeit public opinion. In a large country where it is more difficult to ascertain genuine public opinion, the government can more easily influence and mould opinion for its own purposes and could even inject its surrogate into the vacuum which results from the people's inability to fashion and discern an independent public opinion. A government's interference in opinion formation, and even outright substitution of its own surrogate for genuine public opinion, threatens republican government since 'public opinion sets bounds to every government and is the real sovereign in every free one'.[48] Laying aside his previous fear that popular passions might overwhelm republican government, Madison acknowledged in a letter to Edmund Pendleton a new fear that the nation's large territory might weaken popular control of government. 'In all

Governments the public censorship is necessary in order to prevent abuses. In such a one as ours, where the members are so removed from the eye of their Constituents, an easy and prompt circulation of public proceedings is peculiarly essential.'[49]

While Publius had praised the obstacles to organisation and communication created by an extensive territory and opted for the institutional 'auxiliary precautions' to safeguard against the problem he associated with it, Madison the party organiser now adopted an anti-institutional solution which proposed to bring the public and government closer together. Although still not adopting the Anti-Federalists' mirror or reflection theory of representation, Madison as party organiser did embrace their anti-institutionalism; he now advocated a regular interchange between representatives and constituents so that the representative's opinions would more closely reflect those of his constituents. To forestall the danger posed by the country's extended orbit, Madison in 1791–2 urged that the government and people be brought into closer proximity. Although the physical territory of the country could not be reduced literally, a figurative shrinkage could be effected.

> Whatever facilitates a general intercourse of sentiments, as good roads, domestic commerce, a free press, and particularly a *circulation of newspapers through the entire body of the people*, and *Representatives going from, and returning among every part of them*, is equivalent to a contraction of territorial limits, and is favorable to liberty, where these may be too extensive.[50]

Repudiating Publius, Madison now hoped to reduce the distance between government and governed in a republic. Far from desiring 'a general intercourse of sentiments', Publius had been hostile to any such intercourse because it could facilitate the formation of a majority faction. However, Madison now played the leading role in organising a national Republican party and establishing a leading republican newspaper in order to facilitate 'a general intercourse of sentiments'.

Unlike Edmund Burke's parliamentary party of family connections, Madison's Republican party reached out into the citizenry in order to mobilise and concentrate a general public opinion, not the fragmented opinions of multifarious factions. Its roots lay in the spontaneous democratic–republican societies which acted out-of-doors to agitate political issues, to arouse public opinion and to pressure elected and appointed officials.[51] While Publius had cautioned against involving the public too strongly in political affairs, Madison's party now sought to unite citizens in all parts of the country in a common endeavour to ensure that genuine public opinion would not only ultimately confine the government, but also govern.

While Publius had favoured an impersonal electoral mechanism to link representatives and represented, Madison now began creating a party in the electorate which rested on face-to-face personal relationships. With its roots in local life, Madison's political party rewarded and favoured exactly those individuals and characteristics scorned by *The Federalist*. Publius had recommended the extended orbit precisely because it would thwart the election and selection of individuals with purely 'local' reputations. Now as party organiser, Madison emphasised inner bonds of affection, sympathy, friendship and trust; however, the nation's large territory prevented the personal knowledge upon which those inner bonds depend for their existence. Requiring proximity among participants, those particularistic qualities can appear only if the participants possess direct personal knowledge of one another. While the Jeffersonian Republican party could not bring all citizens into immediate contact with one another, it could encourage citizens to participate in a common political organisation where they could develop the inner bonds of trust, confidence, and friendship. By providing citizens with the political space where they could develop inner, fraternal bonds, Madison's party helped overcome one deleterious consequence of an extensive territory.[52]

Madison's competing accounts of representation and the extended sphere found in *The Federalist* and his later partisan essays were located at opposite ends of what Samuel P. Hays has termed the 'community–society continuum'.[53] As Publius, Madison had praised the extended territory for removing national politics from the local community and consequently reconstituting the national political arena as one of secondary, impersonal relationships. But Madison's Republican party was rooted in the local life of primary interpersonal relationships. Occupying the 'society' end of the spectrum, Publius spoke the universal language of interest and sought to insulate a wholly popular government from immediate popular control. As a state-builder, the earlier Madison defended the creation of free political institutions which were as separate from and independent of the citizenry as popular government would allow.[54] Yet Madison the party organiser adopted a more anti-institutional approach which blurred the line of demarcation between government and people.

REPUBLICANS FROM EXPEDIENCY OR PRINCIPLE?

In *Federalist* no. 51, Madison explained that self-interested calculation or expediency would induce Americans to endorse the proposed Constitution with its supposedly neutral decision-making process. Since no faction wanted to see any other faction armed with government power, and since each desired protection from the others, all could agree to a government that would ensure minimal justice by punishing crime, enforcing contracts and repelling foreign attacks.

> In a society under the forms of which the stronger faction can readily unite and oppress the weaker, anarchy may as truly be said to reign as in a state of nature, where the weaker individual is not secured against the violence of the stronger; and as, in the latter state, even the stronger individuals are prompted by the uncertainty of their condition, to submit to a government which may protect the weak as well as themselves; so, in the former state will the powerful factions or parties be gradually induced, by a like motive, to wish for a government which will protect all parties, the weaker as well as the more powerful.[55]

Although every faction desires to tyrannise, calculations of self-interest or expediency, especially the impossibility of becoming a tyrant and the fear of being tyrannised over, lead weak and strong alike to edorse an impartial government guaranteeing equal protection of the laws. According to *Federalist* no. 51, Americans, who are divided by their competing factional interests, accept as a second-best compromise a republican government which impartially protects the rights of the weak as well as the strong. Lacking a principled commitment to republican government, Americans still consent to it for expediential reasons.

However, if given an opportunity, an individual who only consented to impartial republican government for expediential reasons would be only too eager to deprive his fellow citizens of their liberty and to govern tyrannically. As Publius, Madison did not attempt to remove such tyrannical desires, but instead relied upon free government and the minority status of all factions to prevent Americans from acting upon those desires. Only if a governing majority was a coalition of minorities would liberty be safe. In a republic, the minority status of all factions would preserve liberty.

> In a free government the security for civil rights must be the same as that for religious rights. It consists in the one case in the multiplicity of interests, and in the other in the multiplicity of sects. The degree of security in both cases will depend on the extent of country and number of people comprehended under the same government.[56]

For Madison, neither the weak parchment barriers of a bill of rights nor, by implication, any principled commitment, but rather a plethora of minority religious sects in the context of free political institutions preserved religious liberty in Virginia and the United States. Madison insisted that if a majority belonged to a single religious sect that majority would inevitably institutionalise its religious practices and beliefs as the state church and state religion since no sect had principled objections to such establishments.

> Is a bill of rights a security for religion? Would the bill of rights in this state [Virginia] exempt the people from paying for the support of one particular sect, if such sect were established by law? If there were a majority of one sect, a bill of rights would be a poor protection for liberty. Happily for the states, they enjoy the utmost freedom of religion. This freedom arises from that multiplicity of sects, which pervades America, and which is *the best and only* security for religious liberty in any society. For where there is such a variety of sects, there cannot be a majority of any one sect to oppress and persecute the rest. Fortunately for this commonwealth [Virginia], a majority of the people are decidedly against any exclusive [religious] establishment – I believe it to be so in the other states ... It is better that this security should be depended upon from the general legislature, than from one particular state. A particular state might concur in one religious project. But the United States abound in such a variety of sects, that it is a strong security against religious persecution, and is sufficient to authorise a conclusion, that no one sect will ever be able to out-number or depress the rest.[57]

According to Madison's analysis, despite every sect desiring to establish itself as the state church, religious freedom survives in Virginia and the United States for two reasons: extensive social pluralism ensures that no religious sect can claim the allegiance of a majority of citizens; and in a republic, a majority will always have the power as well as the motive to prevent any minority from establishing its beliefs and practices as the official religion and church. Since its more extensive territory encompasses a greater variety of religious sects than the individual states and therefore increases the probability that all sects will be minorities, the United States better protects religious liberty than does a single state. Since minority status and republican government prevent each sect from attaining its first preference of establishing itself as the official church, all sects can and do agree on a second-best alternative of religious freedom and equality.

Madison's insistence that republican government could not survive without virtue in the people[58] and his declaration that 'republican government presupposes the existence of these qualities ['which justify a certain portion of esteem and confidence'] in a higher degree than any other form'[59] apparently contradict this view that Madison thought that Americans lacked any principled commitment to republican government. Yet even if officials and citizens in *The Federalist* might be capable of transcending narrow self-interest and acting so as to realise a broader public interest, Americans still are not virtuous in the sense of possessing a principled commitment to free government. At this time, Madison mistakenly equated an expediential American preference for republican government with virtue, although this preference originated in unvirtuous expediency and self-interest and was devoid of any principled commitment. Hence Madison confused an expediential preference with a virtuous motive; but a reluctant, expediential acceptance of republican government is not equivalent to a virtuous, principled commitment to it.

The 'virtue' of the rulers and the more limited 'virtue' of the ruled which Madison invoked to rescue the essentially mechanical system of *The Federalist* are the products of placing officials and ordinary Americans in an institutional context where it is in their interest to act according to a broader public interest.[60] Hence, Publius derives the virtue of officials from their electoral incentive in a heterogeneous society to behave themselves and to act in the public interest since various factional interests cancel one another; but electoral calculation is hardly equivalent to virtue. Similarly, if voters in a sufficiently heterogeneous society must turn to representatives who can discern a broader public interest and eschew electing potential despots because they do not want to become subjects, their expediential decision hardly makes the voters virtuous in the conventional sense; rather these voters are merely prudential. According to Publius' mistaken logic, an individual who is deterred from committing a crime because he fears punishment is just. However while the behaviour may be just, the individual is not.

Madison's ideological rebirth began in late 1788 during the movement for adoption of a national bill of rights. Although he continued to think that parchment barriers were ineffective in resisting a tyrannical majority, he now acknowledged that a bill of rights had an expressive role which might significantly impede the appearance of a majority with despotic intentions; within three short years, he perceived the Jeffersonian Republican party as a united majority whose commitment to republicanism innoculated it against any desire to deprive its Federalist opponents of their rights.[61]

While advocating a national bill of rights a few months after the Virginia ratifying convention, Madison continued to adhere to his previous arguments that social pluralism was the best guarantor of religious liberty and that a bill of rights could not prevent a majority from depriving a minority of its rights. However, he now appreciated that a bill of rights could positively shape public opinion so that a united majority might never desire to violate the rights of a minority.

> What use ... can a bill of rights serve in popular Governments? 1. The political truths declared in that solemn manner acquire by degrees the character of fundamental maxims of free Government, and as they become incorporated with the national sentiment, counteract the impulses of interest and passion. 2. Altho' it be generally true as above stated that the danger of oppression lies in the interested majorities of the people rather than in usurped acts of the Government, yet there may be occasions on which the evil may spring from the latter sources; and on such, a bill of rights will be a good ground for appeal to the sense of the community.[62]

Madison's advocacy of a national bill of rights manifested a new anti-institutional concern for the formation of the citizenry's political beliefs. By symbolising the entire nation's commitment to shared republican values, a bill of rights would encourage a firmer, more general attachment to liberty so that Americans would not desire to deprive their fellow citizens of liberty. Although a bill of rights could be employed as a standard by which to limit executive power or even to check a usurping minority, it primarily functioned in a republic to safeguard minorities against a tyrannical majority, not by legally checking a majority, but by instilling republican beliefs and thereby forestalling the formation of 'interested majorities' which desired to tyrannise. Hence the ultimate value of a bill of rights extended beyond its legal properties to its role in politically educating the citizenry. Despite Publius' conclusion that constitution-makers could only strive to control the effects of faction,[63] Madison now recommended a bill of rights as an antidote to 'the impulses of interest and passion'.

Unwilling to rest republican government upon the insecure foundation of expediential calculation, Madison the party organiser relied upon 'good' citizens[64] who possessed a firmer, more principled commitment to liberty and republican government. 'As the metes and bounds of government, they [charters of government] transcend all other land-marks, because every public usurpation is an encroachment on the private right, not of one, but of all.'[65] Since Publius' expediential calculators are only too eager to encroach upon the rights of others, this assertion that 'every public usurpation is an encroachment on the private right, not of one, but of all' holds only if citizens are committed to liberty and republican government from firm principle. Free of the trammels of prudential calculation, Madison's good citizens oppose all abuses of government power, regardless of whether such abuses rebound to their private advantage.

While Publius' self-interested calculator measured all government action against the standard of his private interest, principled republicans 'are naturally offended at every public measure that does not appeal to the understanding and to the general interest of the community, or that is not strictly conformable to the principles, and conducive to the preservation of republican government'.[66] Although a faction might object for self-interested reasons to partial legislation which benefits another faction, factions are not 'naturally offended' by 'all' partial legislation; rather the factions of The Federalist, and especially a majority faction, are a problem precisely because they seek and welcome partial legislation which will benefit themselves.

While Publius' factions with their hunger for governmental favours are willing to sacrifice impartial republican government to their self-interest, the good citizen of Madison the party organiser does not calculate whether a government policy which encroaches upon the rights of others benefits or injures himself. Possessing a principled commitment to republican government, a good citizen will not sacrifice the liberty of others for his own advantage; he disinterestedly subordinates his private interest to the value of liberty. His firm, strong attachment to liberty becomes part of his second nature so that he 'naturally' opposes all narrowly self-interested legislation even when it would benefit his own private interest.

Good citizens reject selfish advantage as a proper motive or as a legitimate criterion for evaluating governmental activity. They insist that public policies should 'appeal to the understanding and to the general interest of the community'. Hence good citizens or principled republicans repudiate partial legislation even when it appeals to their own selfish interest. Madison complained that by appealing 'less to the reason of the many than to their weakness',[67] anti-republicans lured citizens away from their attachment to liberty by promising private economic benefits. Such anti-republican appeals tempted citizens with only an expediential preference for republicanism to sacrifice the liberty of others to their private advantage.

Having previously co-authored *The Federalist* with Alexander Hamilton, Madison now opposed the new Secretary of the Treasury's economic policies which sought to create a class of citizens who would have a strong economic interest to support the new national government. Worried that such an appeal to naked self-interest reduced the grand republican experiment to nothing more than an economically profitable arrangement, Madison objected that Hamilton's economic policy transplanted the English system of corruption to the United States.[68] Yet Hamilton's proposal to provide economic incentives to entice some individuals to defend the national government simply made Madison's earlier expediential calculus in *Federalist* no. 51 and in the Virginia ratifying convention more concrete.

PUBLIC OPINION AND THE CONSTITUTIONAL BALANCE

As Publius, Madison insisted that the preservation of liberty depended upon the maintenance of the constitutional balance; hence he described as despotic popularly elected state legislatures which overwhelmed the other branches and appropriated all effective government power. He defined tyranny procedurally: 'The accumulation of all powers, legislative, executive, and judiciary, in the same hands, whether of one, a few, or many, and whether hereditary, self-appointed, or elective, may justly be pronounced the very definition of tyranny.'[69] Madison formulated the political equivalent of Adam Smith's 'invisible hand' of the free market which was supposed to produce the public interest from the individual pursuit of self-interest; Publius counted upon the self-interested competition of officials in independently powerful government institutions to preserve the constitutional balance although no political actor actually willed its preservation.

When disputes between the different branches and different layers of government occurred, how would those disputes be resolved without disrupting the constitutional equilibrium? Who or what would adjudicate? To preserve the constitutional balance, Publius could not simply rely upon the Constitution's formal demarcation of the separate government institutions and their respective powers, since events at the state level had demonstrated the inefficacy of mere parchment barriers.[70]

Federalist nos. 49 and 50 also disparaged the suggestion that public opinion could be safely entrusted with the delicate task of preserving the constitutional balance whenever a conflict arose over the power of the different branches or levels of government. *The Federalist* feared that appeals to public opinion would inflame dangerous passions, thereby generating additional turmoil and fanning unrest: 'The danger of disturbing the public tranquility by interesting too strongly the public passions is a still more serious objection against reference of constitutional questions to the decision of the whole society.' Furthermore, Publius heeded the lesson learned at the state level that public opinion usually favoured the legislature whenever it came into conflict with the other branches: 'But the greatest objection of all is that the decisions which would probably result from such appeals would not answer the purpose of maintaining the constitutional equilibrium of the government. We have seen that the tendency of republican governments is to an aggrandizement of the legislative at the expense of the other departments.'[71] Hence Publius concluded that both mere parchment barriers and public opinion were inadequate to protect the constitutional balance between the different levels and branches of government.

Fashioning an institutional solution internal to the Constitution, Publius counted upon social pluralism, the fragmentation of governmental power and the self-interest of officials to maintain the dynamic equilibrium of the constitutional structure. Publis expected self-interest to motivate officials to assert the independent power of their institutions when confronted by challenges from other levels or branches of government. To preserve the Constitution's distribution of power, Madison relied upon a 'policy of supplying by opposite and rival interests, the defect of better motives'.[72] Although officials would not have to be public-spirited, their self-interested defence of the power of their offices would still contribute unintentionally to the maintenance of the constitutional balance.

> But the great security against a gradual concentration of the several powers in the same department consists in giving to those who administer each department, the necessary constitutional means and personal motives to resist encroachments of the others ... Ambition must be made to counteract ambition. The interest of the man must be connected with the constitutional rights of the place.

Therefore, within the constitutional structure, 'the private interest of every individual may be a sentinel over the public rights'.[73] Publius concluded that constitutional liberty could survive and even flourish although no individual consciously upheld it. The private pursuit of interest within the Constitution's elaborate structure was supposed to protect liberty as an unintended consequence, just as the pursuit of self-interest in Adam Smith's free market ostensibly served the public good unintentionally.

Although later worried by the threat of executive, rather than legislative, usurpation, Madison in 1791–2 agreed with Publius about the necessity of maintaining the constitutional balance: 'Power being found by universal experience liable to abuses, a distribution of it into separate departments, has become a first principle of free governments.'[74] Still associating the Constitution's institutional balance with republican government and liberty, Madison now eschewed Publius's reliance upon self-interested officials and his political version of the invisible hand. Instead, he argued that the regime of republican liberty could be maintained only if citizens willed its defence. Hence Madison the party organiser substituted an anti-institutional reliance upon virtuous public opinion for Publius' mechanical solution. 'To secure all the advantages of such a system [that is, a confederated republic], every *good citizen* will be at once a centinel over the rights of the people; over the authorities of the federal government; and over both the rights and the authorities of the intermediate governments.[75] Although Publius had confidently expected the self-interested competition of office-holders in separate institutions with overlapping powers to preserve constitutional liberty, Madison the party organiser declared: 'Let it be the *patriotic* study of all, *to maintain the various authorities* established by our complicated system, each in its respective constitutional sphere.'[76] Abandoning Publius' political version of the invisible hand, Madison now sought citizens who would consciously act to preserve the constitutional balance. In order for a citizen to be a 'centinel over the rights of the people', he now had to be 'good' and 'patriotic'; but Publius had only required them to be self-interested or ambitious. Madison now expected Americans to possess those 'better motives' which Publius had thought superfluous.

Expounding a new anti-institutionalism, Madison in 1791–2 subordinated institutional arrangements to public opinion as the ultimate guarantor of republican government and denigrated the importance of the Constitution's institutional complexity: 'In bestowing the eulogies due to the particular and *internal checks* of power, it ought not the less to be remembered, that they are *neither the sole nor the chief palladium* of constitutional liberty. The people who are authors of this blessing, must also be its guardians.'[77] Madison the party organiser belittled institutional arrangements as sterile and inefficacious unless supported by republican opinion. Madison now contended that public opinion, not the social pluralism and 'internal checks' celebrated by Publius, determined whether governments respected liberty.

According to Madison the party organiser, republican opinion constrains even tyrannical governments; and the best, most elaborately constructed republican government will go awry if republican opinion ceases its active oversight.

> All power has been traced up to opinion. The stability of all governments and security of all rights may be traced to the same source. The most arbitrary government is controlled where the public opinion is fixed ... *The most systematic governments* are turned by the slightest impulse from their regular path, where public opinion no longer holds them in it.[78]

Since the new United States Constitution obviously qualified as one of 'the most systematic governments', Madison now disparaged his earlier overweening concern for mechanical solutions. Not only are institutional arrangements inferior to republican opinion in protecting republican government, but also even the most perfected and developed institutional arrangements alone cannot preserve republican government. Only the citizenry's republican opinion, not the social pluralism and 'auxiliary precautions' of *The Federalist*, determines the republican character of American government.

At this time, Madison offered a new anti-institutional explanation of the preservation of English liberty. Institutionally-inclined thinkers like Publius attributed the existence of liberty in Britain to the equilibrium of the British constitution, with its tripartite division and the association of each branch with a different social order. According to this Whig analysis, the social complexity of three distinct estates conjoined with institutional complexity to generate a dynamic equilibrium protective of liberty. Derisively dismissing this argument which, with the necessary modifications to accommodate the absence of three permanent social orders (or estates), had served as the model for the new United States Constitution, Madison now declared: 'The boasted equilibrium of this [the British] government (so far as it is a reality) is maintained less by the distribution of its power, than by the force of public opinion.'[79] Madison's new position echoed Thomas Paine's heretical *Common Sense*. Repudiating the Whig constitutionalism of the pre-Independence resistance literature,[80] Paine had written: 'It is wholly owing to the constitution of the people, and not to the constitution of the government, that the crown is not as oppressive in England as in Turkey.'[81]

PARTIES BEYOND FACTION

Publius had accepted an interest-based factional politics as natural in a free society: 'The latent causes of faction are thus sown in the nature of man.' Furthermore, while acknowledging the multitude of differences which generated political divisions, Publius had concluded: 'the most common and durable source of factions has been the various and unequal distribution of property.'[82] Earlier Madison had avowed an even more extreme position by distinguishing 'natural' divisions based on economic interest from 'artificial' cleavages arising from political or religious opinions.[83]

In contrast, Madison the party organiser distinguished partisan conflict from the factional competition of *The Federalist*; by linking parties to ideological disagreements which transcended economic differences, Madison defined political parties as qualitatively different from factions. The two concluding essays in his series postulated the ideological antagonism between republicans and anti-republicans as the essential core of American political conflict.

As party organiser, Madison sought to make political parties respectable by divorcing them from mere factional squabbles. Madison periodised American history into four periods of partisan conflict, but 'general' or national parties existed in only three of these periods. The conflict between the supporters and opponents of independence defined the first period; but Madison implied that the latter might not qualify as a proper political party since there were so few members of that 'disaffected class'. The peace treaty with Britain ushered in the second period from 1783–7 which lacked 'general' parties although there were 'local' 'parties in abundance'.[84] The third period witnessed the reappearance of 'general' parties which were divided by their support for and opposition to the new Constitution. The struggle for ratification, however, did not mark a resumption of fundamental political conflict since most of the members of both these national parties were good republicans, although both also contained some opponents of republican government. While 'the great body [of Federalist supporters of the Constitution] were unquestionably friends to republican liberty', they also contained 'some who were openly or secretly attached to monarchy and aristocracy; and hoped to make the constitution a cradle for these hereditary establishments'. Similarly, the 'great body' of the Anti-Federalist opponents of the Constitution 'were certainly well affected to the union and to good government, tho' there might be a few who had a leaning unfavourable to both'.[85]

Resembling the first party period, the fourth period renewed the original conflict between republicans and anti-republicans. This current conflict was far different from the local divisions of the second party period and from the less fundamental differences of the third. In both the first and fourth periods, the friends and enemies of free republican government were segregated into competing, even if unequal, national parties.

Contradicting his earlier teaching about the naturalness of factional politics, Madison described the conflict between republicans and anti-republicans as 'natural to most political societies';[86]

this partisan division was at heart an ideological disagreement. Abandoning Publius' earlier emphasis upon (economic) self-interest as the mainspring of political conflict, Madison defined the anti-republican party ideologically as that party which

> consists of those, who from particular interest, from natural temper, or from the habits of life, are more partial to the opulent than to the other classes of society; and having debauched themselves into a persuasion that mankind are incapable of governing themselves, it follows ... that government can be carried only by the pageantry of rank, the influence of money and emoluments, and the terror of military force. Men of those sentiments must naturally wish to point the measures of government less to the interest of the many than of the few, and less to the reason of the many than to their weaknesses.[87]

Although some anti-republicans were self-interested and some anti-republican ideas benefitted a few wealthy individuals, anti-republicans could not be accurately described in terms of factional interest.

According to Madison, the anti-republicans sought to rule by imitating the British use of 'place' and force. Fearful that 'the people are ever ready to fly off from the government', the anti-republicans recommended that the national government be supplied with additional military capacity for compelling obedience and increased financial resources to bribe some citizens to be loyal.[88]

Distrusting the people's capacity for self-government, the anti-republicans urged that the protection of the people's liberty be entrusted to 'their wise rulers'.[89] As Publius, Madison had argued that the election and selection of relatively few national officials from an extensive territory and population would transform the national government into a 'filter' by ensuring the elevation of the virtuous and wise to government posts. But as party organiser, Madison now identified as anti-republican the teaching that the people should trust 'their wise rulers' to protect their liberty.

Acknowledging that the people had often erred in self-government, Madison the party leader refused to accept such error as sufficient reason for proscribing self-government.

> Too true it is, that slavery has been the general lot of the human race. Ignorant – they have been cheated; asleep – they have been surprised; divided – the yoke has been forced upon them. But what is the lesson? That because the people *may* betray themselves, they ought to give

themselves up, blindfold, to those who have an interest in betraying them? Rather conclude that the people ought to be enlightened, to be awakened, to be united, that after establishing a government they should watch over it, as well as obey it.[90]

Madison now identified the latter as the republican course, but it hardly resembles the path taken by Publius four years earlier. Publius had never proposed to enlighten the people, had feared a united citizenry, and had argued that the citizenry could not be relied upon to preserve the constitutional order. Although in less extreme form, Madison as Publius had opted for the former 'anti-republican' solution.

Just as Madison described the anti-republican party in terms of its political ideas so he also defined republicans, not in terms of their interests, but rather by their commitment to free government. Republicans have faith in the people's capacity to govern themselves and to preserve their liberty. The republican party

> consists of those who believing in the doctrine that mankind are capable of govering themselves, and hating hereditary power as an insult to the reason and an outrage to the rights of man, are naturally offended at every public measure that does not appeal to the understanding and to the general interest of the community, or that is not strictly conformable to the principles, and conducive to the preservation of republican government.[91]

Not just their preference for republican government but also their principled commitment to it distinguishes republicans from their anti-republican opponents.

CONCLUSION

Madison as Publius endorsed maximum heterogeneity, but as party organiser he favoured greater homogeneity. While Publius praised the beneficial consequences of the extended sphere, Madison in 1791–2 emphasised its deleterious effects. The later Madison's call for a principled devotion to republican liberty rejected Publius' expediential logic. Publius thought that the constitutional balance could be preserved as the unintended by-product of political competition mediated by a complex institutional structure; but Madison the party organiser recognised that Americans would have to will its preservation. Madison's later description of the partisan conflict between republicans and anti-republicans hardly accords with the factional politics of *Federalist* no.10.

In part, these differences are attributable to the two Madisons responding to different political problems. Confidently assuming that majority rule automatically prevents minority factions from gaining and abusing government power, Madison as Publius had emphasised that in a republic a majority faction posed the real danger to liberty. Contradicting this assumption, Madison the party organiser stressed that a minority had usurped government power. Similarly, Publius had sought to prevent the legislature from unilaterally exercising legislative, executive and judicial powers; but in 1791–2, unchecked, expanding executive power worried Madison.

Another, more important reason for the differences between Madison as Publius and as party organiser was their competing conceptions of a liberal politics. John Zvesper has suggested that Madison's commitment to liberalism provides the continuity in his thought. As Publius and as party organiser, Madison offered different defences of a liberal political order, but at all times he 'was more consistently attached to the principles of liberalism and prudence than to the devices of pluralism and party government'.[92] However, Zvesper's cogent conclusion should not obscure the fact that Madison's twin devices defended two fundamentally different liberal regimes.

As Publius, Madison had accepted economic inequality as the inevitable outcome of the individual pursuit of interest; but Madison the party organiser sought greater equality of condition. While Publius simply sought the greatest possible number of social interests, Madison in 1791–2 evaluated different occupations according to their compatibility with republican politics. Transcending the usual point that individuals who desire to pursue their self-interest must be willing to respect the right of others to do the same, Madison the party organiser now deemed some occupations to be harmful and others beneficial, not because the former (criminally) violated, and the latter respected, the rights of others, but because some occupations stunt and others nurture the capacities needed by self-governing republican citizens. The earlier, institutionally-inclined Madison had placed his primary faith in the extended republic, the 'auxiliary precautions', and expediential calculation; but emphasising that only a principled commitment to republican government ensured its survival, the later Madison concerned himself with the moral health of Americans.

Revealing that a liberal consensus does not necessarily preclude fundamental political conflict, the later argument between Stephen Douglas and Abraham Lincoln about how best to deal with the slavery extension issue recapitulated this earlier intra-liberal antagonism between Madison as Publius and as party organiser. On behalf of a procedural politics divorced from questions of ultimate value, Stephen Douglas refused to judge slavery as immoral and condemned Lincoln's willingness to interject moral considerations into politics. Douglas insisted that private opinions about the morality and immorality of slavery should not intrude into politics. In contrast, Lincoln called upon Americans to give political force to the moral judgement that slavery was sinful. While Douglas proclaimed that he was indifferent to whether the people of a territory decided to permit or prohibit slavery, Lincoln argued that a liberal republic could survive only if its members publicly judged slavery to be immoral and incompatible with free government. Like the two Madisons, Douglas and Lincoln not only disagreed about how to preserve a liberal political order but also offered competing liberal visions.[93]

Despite the disagreement between the two Madisons, Madison in 1791–2 never directly criticised the Constitution; however, his criticism of Publius' defence of it implied a criticism of the document itself. In 1791–2, Madison expected his national Republican party to embody the virtue needed to ensure the proper functioning of the Constitution. If, according to Madison the party organiser and even according to some of Publius' comments, virtue in the people and statesmanship in the leaders are necessary to preserve republican government, then Madison's loyalty to the Constitution seems misplaced, since that document does not attempt to ensure the availability of the required virtue and statesmanship. If, as Madison the party organiser thought, the moral health of the citizenry is more important than institutional arrangements, can one praise a Constitution which eschews responsibility for nurturing inner virtue?

NOTES

The author thanks Paul Cammack and John Stachniewski for their assistance.

1 Marvin Meyers (ed.), *The Mind of the Founder: Sources of the Political Thought of James Madison*, Indianapolis, Bobbs-Merrill, 1973, p. xliv.

2 Norman Jacobson, 'Political science and political education', *American Political Science Review*, 57, 1963, pp. 561–9.

3 Neal Riemer, *James Madison*, New York, Washington Square Press, 1968; and 'James Madison's theory of the self-destructive features of republican government', *Ethics*, 65, 1954, pp. 34–43.

4 Robert J. Morgan, 'Madison's analysis of the sources of political authority', *American Political Science Review*, 75, 1982, pp. 613–25.

5 Meyers, *Mind of the Founder*, pp. xliii–xlvi; Edward J. Erler, 'The problem of the public good in *The Federalist*', *Polity*, 13, 1980–81, pp. 649–67; Harry V. Jaffa, 'A phoenix from the ashes', a paper delivered at the annual meeting of the American Political Science Association, Washington, D.C., 1977; John Zvesper, *Political Philosophy and Rhetoric: A Study of the Origins of American Party Politics*, Cambridge, Cambridge University Press, 1977, pp. 110–19.

6 Meyers, *Mind of the Founder*, pp. xliii–xlvi; Adrienne Koch, *Madison's 'Advice to My Country'*, Princeton, Princeton University Press, 1966.

7 Alexander Hamilton, John Jay and James Madison, *The Federalist Papers*, ed. Clinton Rossiter, New York, New American Library, 1961, no. 10, p. 78. Henceforth, all citations from *The Federalist* refer to this – the Rossiter – edition.

8 *The Federalist*, no. 10, p. 80. See letter to Jefferson, 17 October 1788, *The Papers of James Madison*, eds. William T. Hutchinson, William M. E. Rachal, Robert A. Rutland, *et al.*, Chicago, University of Chicago Press and Charlottesville, University Press of Virginia, 1962 to date, 11, p. 298. Henceforth this source is cited as *Papers*.

9 The defenders of the new Constitution interpreted stay laws and paper money as unjust infringements of property rights perpetrated by majority factions; state constitutions with the greatest institutional complexity had proved inadequate to check these tyrannical actions by unified majorities. Even the institutionally complex constitution of Massachusetts which served as a model for the new federal constitution had failed to protect property rights. When poor farmers led by the Revolutionary War captain Daniel Shays had resorted to illegal direct action to close the state courts in western Massachusetts with the aim of preventing mortgage foreclosures, the state government had used the militia to quell the rebellion; but then the Shaysites discovered that they could achieve their factional objective legally. Defeated militarily, the Shaysites triumphed electorally, and their duly elected representatives then enacted stay laws prohibiting mortgage foreclosures. Gordon Wood, *The Creation of the American Republic, 1776–1787*, New York, W. W. Norton, 1969, pp. 463–7; Isaac Kramnick, 'Editor's introduction', in Alexander Hamilton, John Jay and James Madison, *The Federalist Paper*, New York, Penguin Books, 1987, pp. 55–6.

10 *The Federalist*, no. 10, p. 81.

11 *The Federalist*, no. 10, p. 83.

12 *The Federalist*, no. 51, p. 325.

13 James Madison, *The Writings of James Madison*, ed. Gaillard Hunt, New York, Putnam, 1900–10, VI, p. 68. Henceforth this source is cited as *Writings*.

14 Meyers, *Mind of the Founder*, p. 213. Also see *Papers*, 11, pp. 404, 415.

15 *Writings*, VI, p. 120.

16 *Writings*, VI, p. 68.

17 *Writings*, VI, pp. 68–9, emphasis added.

18 *Writings*, VI, p. 114.

19 The later Jacksonian Democrats developed the idea of a party system. Richard Hofstadter, *The Idea of a Party System: The Rise of a Legitimate Opposition in the United States, 1780–1840*, Berkeley, University of California Press, 1970, esp. pp. 84–6; Michael L. Wallace, 'Changing concepts of party in the United States: New York, 1815–1828', *American Historical Review*, 74, 1968, pp. 453–91.
20 *Writings*, VI, p. 119.
21 *Writings*, VI, p. 68, original emphasis.
22 *Writings*, VI, p. 86, original emphasis.
23 See Theodore J. Lowi, *The End of Liberalism: The Second Republic of the United States*, New York, W. W. Norton, 2nd edn, 1979; and Grant McConnell, *Private Power and American Democracy*, New York, Vintage, 1966.
24 *The Federalist*, no. 10, p. 78.
25 *Writings*, VI, p. 86.
26 Jean Jacques Rousseau, *The Social Contract and Discourses*, tran. G. D. H. Cole, New York, E. P. Dutton, 1950, p. 50.
27 *Writings*, VI, p. 96, original emphasis.
28 *Writings*, VI, p. 100.
29 *Writings*, VI, pp. 98–9.
30 *The Federalist*, nos. 10 and 63.
31 *The Federalist*, no. 10, p. 82.
32 *The Federalist*, no. 10, p. 81.
33 *The Federalist*, no. 63, p. 387, original emphasis.
34 *The Federalist*, no. 10, pp. 82–3; Wood, *Creation of the American Republic*, ch. 10.
35 *The Federalist*, nos. 10 and 63.
36 *The Federalist*, no. 10, p. 82. See no. 10, pp. 82–3; no. 3, p. 43.
37 *The Federalist*, no. 10, p. 82.
38 *The Federalist*, no. 10, pp. 82–3.
39 Jean Yarbrough, 'Thoughts on *The Federalist's* view of representation', *Polity*, 12, 1979, pp. 65–82; Wood, *Creation of the American Republic*, pp. 475–83, 495–9.
40 *The Federalist*, no. 10, p. 82. See Yarbrough, 'Thoughts', pp. 68–73; Kramnick, 'Editor's introduction', pp. 41–3; Wood, *Creation of the American Republic*, pp. 506–18.
41 *The Federalist*, nos. 35, 36, 56, 57; Yarbrough, 'Thoughts'.
42 Kramnick, 'Editor's introduction', pp. 43–6.
43 *The Federalist*, no. 35, p. 214.
44 *The Federalist*, no. 63, p. 385.
45 *Writings*, VI, p. 70.
46 *Writings*, VI, p. 80.
47 *Writings*, VI, p. 67.
48 *Writings*, VI, p. 70.
49 Letter to Edmund Pendleton, 6 December 1792, *Writings*, VI, p. 121.
50 *Writings*, VI, p. 70, original emphasis.
51 Eugene Perry Link, *The Democratic-Republican Societies, 1790–1800*, New York, Columbia University Press, 1942; Richard Buel, Jr., *Securing the Revolution: Ideology in American Politics, 1789–1815*, Ithaca, N.Y., Cornell University Press, 1972, pp. 97–105, 129–34.
52 According to Eldon Eisenach, except for its possession of government coercion, Jefferson's proposed 'ward system' of government resembled Madison's Republican party. 'The American Revolution made and remembered', *American Studies*, 20, 1979, p. 89.
53 Samuel P. Hays, 'Political parties and the community–society continuum', ch. 6 in William Nisbet Chambers and Walter Dean Burnham (eds.), *The American Party Systems*, New York, Oxford University Press, 1967.
54 Kramnick, 'Editor's introduction', pp. 67–75.
55 *The Federalist*, no. 51, p. 325.

56 *The Federalist*, no. 51, p. 324.

57 Speech, 12 June 1788, *Papers*, 11, pp. 130–31, emphasis added. Madison repeated this argument in a letter to Jefferson dated 17 October 1788. *Papers*, 11, p. 298.

58 *Papers*, 11, p. 163.

59 *The Federalist*, no. 55, p. 346. Also see nos. 10, 51, 57. Some scholars see no difficulty in reconciling Madison's description of self-interested factional politics and his assumption of virtue in the rulers and ruled. However, other, more sceptical scholars doubt that *The Federalist*'s sudden shifts from self-interested factional politics to disinterested republican virtue are compatible. Erler, 'Problem of the public good'; Jaffa, 'A phoenix from the ashes'; Zvesper, 'The Madisonian systems', *Western Political Quarterly*, 37, 1984, pp. 236–56.

60 *The Federalist*, nos. 51, 55, 57.

61 *Writings*, VI, p. 123.

62 Letter to Jefferson, 17 October 1788, *Papers*, 11, pp. 297–9.

63 *The Federalist*, no. 10, p. 80.

64 *Writings*, VI, p. 82.

65 *Writings*, VI, p. 84.

66 *Writings*, VI, p. 118.

67 *Writings*, VI, p. 117.

68 *Writings*, VI, pp. 94, 120–23.

69 *The Federalist*, no. 47, p. 301.

70 *The Federalist*, no. 48.

71 *The Federalist*, no. 49, pp. 315–16.

72 *The Federalist*, no. 51, p. 322.

73 *The Federalist*, no. 51, pp. 321–2.

74 *Papers*, 14, p. 217; *Writings*, VI, p. 91.

75 *Writings*, VI, p. 82, emphasis added.

76 *Writings*, VI, p. 68, emphasis added.

77 *Writings*, VI, p. 93, emphasis added.

78 *Writings*, VI, p. 85, emphasis added.

79 *Writings*, VI, p. 87.

80 Thomas Paine, *Common Sense and Other Writings*, Indianapolis, Bobbs-Merrill, 1953, p. 9.

81 Stephen Newman has demonstrated how Paine's *Common Sense* broke radically with the Whig constitutional theory of the resistance literature. 'A note on *Common Sense*', *Political Theory*, 6, 1978, pp. 101–8.

82 *The Federalist*, no. 10, p. 79.

83 *Writings*, V, p. 29.

84 *Writings*, VI, pp. 109–10.

85 *Writings*, VI, pp. 112–13.

86 *Writings*, VI, p. 114.

87 *Writings*, VI, pp. 114–17.

88 *Writings*, VI, pp. 94, 120–23.

89 *Writings*, VI, p. 120.

90 *Writings*, VI, p. 120, original emphasis.

91 *Writings*, VI, p. 118.

92 Zvesper, 'The Madisonian Systems', p. 254.

93 See J. David Greenstone, 'Political culture and American political development: liberty, union and the liberal bipolarity', in Karen Orren and Stephen Skowronek (eds), *Studies in American Political Development: An Annual*, New Haven, Yale University Press, 1986, I, pp. 1–49; Harry V. Jaffa, *The Crisis of the House Divided: An Interpretation of the Lincoln–Douglas Debates*, Seattle, University of Washington Press, 1959; and Major L. Wilson, *Space, Time and Freedom: The Quest for Nationality and the Irrepressible Conflict, 1815–1861*, Westport, Conn., Greenwood Press, 1974.

American Political Parties
and Constitutional Government

ABSTRACT

Many of the problems of the American political system in the late twentieth century can be traced to the decline of the party system. This chapter presents a portrait of the development of the party system and examines the shifting relationship between the party system and the Constitution. It argues that much of the dysfunctioning of the party system, and therefore of the political system as a whole, can be traced to an unproductive tension between the party system and the Constitution. It is natural for there to be some tension between the party system and the Constitution, but an unhelpful level and kind of tension has emerged with the development of the reformed party system of the twentieth century.

A formal constitution is the way that politics is seen to work in a country. Underneath or alongside this constitution are always less formal and less publicly respectable political devices: the 'invisible government' of the country. Perhaps the most prominent of these somewhat murky devices in the modern world is the political party. This device has become so prominent that it has become in many places almost as visible and respectable as the more formal constitution itself. Yet even in countries, and in those individual American states, where the constitution accommodates political parties more readily than does the Constitution of 1787, party government is not identical to constitutional government. Even in one-party regimes, the party is distinct from the government. Parties and partisanship, as the words themselves indicate, are and are seen to be partial, neither comprehensively representative nor directly tending towards the public good, however indirectly they may represent and advance the good of all the citizens. Party government was first advocated as a healthy system by that arch realist, Niccolo Machiavelli, and in spite of the more idealistic versions of party that have emerged during the last two centuries, the original Machiavellian air of conspiracy against the public still clings to the theory and practice of party politics. The tension between constitutionalism and party politics is one of the animating tensions of all modern political systems. This tension is clearly illustrated in the American political system, where it has been visible from the very beginning. Exploring the American example should illuminate this more general modern political phenomenon, even while revealing any uniqueness of the American version of this phenomenon. In addition, seeing how parties and the Constitution have more or less successfully meshed in the past can highlight some of the dysfunctioning of the American political system in more recent decades.

THE FIRST PARTIES

The party politics that was to become a well established feature of the American political system by the middle of the nineteenth century was invented only after the Constitution of 1787 had become the framework of American government. As Douglas Jaenicke's exposition of James Madison's thought makes clear, the 'Father of the Constitution' himself had some second thoughts about the way that he described and defended the Constitution after he had begun to invent modern party politics in the 1790s. Yet even supposing that a national party politics had been anticipated by the framers of the Constitution, it is difficult to imagine how they would have changed the Constitution in order to accommodate political parties, apart from such minor adjustments as the one that was actually made shortly after these parties appeared on the scene, by the Twelfth Amendment (which separated Presidential from Vice Presidential voting in the Electoral College, so Electors' partisan fidelity does not repeat the result of 1800, when a tie in their voting threw the election into the House of Representatives). It is a mistake to assume that the framers' dim views of parties would have made them all recoil in horror from the presence of a national party or parties, and try to counter party with constitutional devices. Their condemnations of parties were condemnations not of political parties as they later developed (with the help of many of the framers themselves), but of 'factions', that is, entirely non-public-spirited interests and cliques. The prior existence of national political parties might actually have reassured the framers on some points; for example, many feared that the Electoral College – at least after the departure of George Washington, the obvious first candidate for the Presidency – would regularly fail to produce a majority for any candidate, thus breaking down the separation of powers by making Presidents owe their election to the House of Representatives.[1] But the prior existence of such parties would probably not have altered very much the considerations that went into the deliberations that produced the institutional arrangements set up by the Constitution. So the mere fact that the Constitution was framed before political parties were developed does not explain the tension between constitutional government and party politics in America; if parties had already been developed, the Constitution would still have worked to some extent against the grain of party politics. Constitutional government, with its attempt to treat all citizens evenhandedly, is necessarily somewhat at odds with party government, with its bias against some citizens in favour of others, the party faithful.

It may sound a bit naive to talk about a situation in which national parties did not exist. The framers of the Constitution were quite familiar with a kind of partisanship at the national level. The contest between patriots and loyalists in the struggle for independence from Britain was a national party contest. So was the contest between the framers themselves – the Federalists, as they somewhat misleadingly called themselves – and their Antifederalist opponents in the ratification battles of 1787 and 1788. The framers of the Constitution had experienced national party conflict, as well as numerous factional conflicts at the state and local level. When Madison explained and defended the incipient Republican party opposition to Alexander Hamilton's policies in 1792, he cited the nation's previous experience of 'general' party conflicts – patriots *versus* loyalists, and Federalists *versus* Antifederalists – as precedents.[2] He and other framers had failed to foresee that the need to appeal to these precedents would arise so soon after the Constitution was adopted. But the precedents were at hand, and were more or less recognised as such in Madison's and even Hamilton's reflections in *The Federalist*.[3] It was not necessary for Madison and other Federalists to abandon their support for the Constitution in order to lend their support to a general political party.

However, the tension between Constitution and party remained.

It was necessary for Madison and others who moved from support of the Constitution to party action against Hamiltonianism to stop emphasising the need to strengthen the central government and to start emphasising the need to strengthen the influence of public opinion outside the government, public opinion marshalled by the Republican party. Of course, the Constitution provided many limitations on central government, but it was the product and the vehicle of a movement designed to increase the 'energy' of the central government, a movement which could be seen to culminate logically in Hamilton's economic programme. Opposition to that programme was based not only on hard economic interests but also on Madison and other Republicans' judgement that partisanship was needed to erect public opinion as a supervisor over 'the various authorities established by [the] constitutional system'.[4]

The first modern partisans were not quick to reach for the weapon of mass partisanship. At first they hoped that Congressional re-apportionment following the census of 1790 would produce a Congressional majority against Hamilton's policies. When this technical tactic failed, they tried to challenge the constitutionality of those policies in the courts, and privately to persuade President Washington to abandon Hamilton. None of these tactics worked, and in the end the leaders of the Republican party had to inspire a popular electoral revolution – the 'revolution of 1800' – by which the Republicans captured control of the Presidency as well as Congress. This strategy of focusing popular attention on the Presidential election has been repeated by successful American parties ever since, and has thereby altered the balance between the legislative and executive branches, which the framers of the Constitution had expected to tilt clearly in the direction of Congress.

However, the Republican leaders themselves did not seek to set a precedent that would be repeated regularly or routinely. Having beaten the unrepublican party (except in the judiciary, where Federalists clung on), there seemed to them to be no reason to maintain a permanent party system in the republic. Party politics was, they thought, an emergency device, to be used only when there was a real danger of successful unrepublican policies and policy-makers. Although Madison and Thomas Jefferson came to speak of the naturalness of an opposition between republicans (optimists, who love popular government) and antirepublicans (pessimists, who fear it), they did not think it was necessary for this natural antagonism to be institutionalised in republican government. While defeated Federalists might share the hopeful prediction of John Adams – the defeated incumbent in the Presidential election of 1800 – that American government was becoming 'not a national but a party government',[5] with regular transfers of power from one party to the other, Republican leaders had other ideas, and over the years they and events did largely succeed in reducing national party competition by eliminating the Federalist party from that competition. The tension between this 'first party system' and the Constitution was in this way perhaps somewhat reduced: a party system that was expected to wither away – and during the Presidency of James Monroe, the third Republican President, did in fact do so to an extent that now seems incomprehensible – was an unlikely permanent rival to the Constitutional ways of policymaking.

A second reason that this tension was less than it might have been was that the Republican policies were in a sense quite negative. The Republicans were trying not so much to get the central government to act in certain ways as to get it to stop acting in certain ways. Hamilton's programme was the one that required central government action; the Republicans required less energetic central government. (Patronage rewards for their party workers were therefore thinner on the ground than they would have liked.) Perhaps it would be more accurate to say that Hamiltonianism required – and Republicans attacked – central *administrative* action. Hamilton was less a politician than an administrator. Federalists had a large administrative agenda but (even with George Washington on their side) insufficient political support; Republicans had political support but much less on their administrative agenda. At some later times in American political history, and at almost all times in American political science, the expectation has been the other way around: that parties would be the source of active and ambitious policy, and that governmental inertia, based on the constitutional separation of powers, federalism, and socio-economic pluralism, would be the resisting object of partisan attentions. But American parties 'were first organised at a time when popular rule meant the limitation of government power'.[6] The Jeffersonian Republicans saw themselves as the true conservators of the Constitution, which was (they said) being distorted into a nationally consolidated (rather than federal) and monarchical (rather than republican) system by Hamilton's policies. As explained by a Republican campaign pamphlet in 1800,

Hamilton's 'funding system begets and perpetualizes debt; debt begets intrigue, offices, and corruption; those beget taxation ... a standing army ... monarchy, and ... an enslaved and impoverished people.'[7] The decentralising and limiting purposes of America's first real party – the Jeffersonian Republicans – have never entirely disappeared from major American parties, and this feature has made them appear very unpartylike to many foreign observers as well as to many Americans dissatisfied with their peculiarly unambitious parties.

However, there remain two important ways in which even the first American party – the Jeffersonian Republicans – did establish a tension between party and Constitution. The first way has already been noted: the role of extra-governmental public opinion as a power in the land. The first partisans, very like later (and current) ones, enhanced this role by their partisan use of the media and ideological political action committees (the Democratic-Republican Societies of the 1790s, which were modelled on the committees of correspondence of the Revolution). In earlier thinking about this role, such as in *The Federalist*, popular protests against governments had been conceived as occasional, *ad hoc* movements, appealing to natural right and working through informal, extra-constitutional channels – a democratic response inspired by tyrannical government or by imprudent use of executive prerogative, a response and an inspiration fully provided for in Lockean political philosophy. The institution of party politics reduced the occasional quality (at least in appearance) and made the channels more formal, but maintained the anti- or extra-constitutional bearing of this role. Party statesmen who can lead and direct the force of partisan public opinion can thereby overcome some of the limitations on statesmanship imposed by the necessity of acting in a party. Party can thus serve as an instrument of popular or statesmanlike discretion, *versus* rigid constitutionalism. The philosophic appeal to natural standards, *versus* adherence to established constitutional procedures, can thus play a part in American politics, and appeal not only to the Revolutionary precedent of 1776 but also to the Jeffersonian partisan precedent. The defects of the rule of law and constitutionalism – their overgenerality and relative insensitivity to different and changing circumstances – can be addressed and to some extent corrected by partisan politics. Reinterpretation and amendments of important provisions of the Constitution have resulted from the pressures of party action, especially after those watershed realigning elections of the 1790s, 1850s and 1930s.

This brings us to the second way in which the Jeffersonian Republicans established a durable tension between party and Constitution. A qualification must be added to our observation of the relatively unambitious policy agenda of the Republicans. That agenda was not blank, and even if it had been, various decisions – perhaps the most important was the purchase of Louisiana – thrust themselves upon it. Relative to Hamiltonian Federalism, the Republicans may have had a negative approach to central government, but they had policies, some of them quite positive, and they did not hesitate to use the machinery of their party to gain support for these policies in Congress and in the country. The development of party politics by the Republicans facilitated popular majority mandates, bursting through the constitutional restraints of separated powers and federalism. This potential for majoritarian party government was more fully developed by Jacksonian, Progressive and New Deal Presidents, but they owed something to the Jeffersonian precedent. One of the reasons for the insistence upon strict construction of the Constitution's grants of power to the central government by Madison and other thoughtful Republicans after the emergence of parties was precisely their recognition of the danger that Republican partisanship could lead too easily to the assumption that the majority party was always right – that *vox populi vox dei*. Popular partisanship can address the defects of constitutionalism, but popularised constitutionalism can also address the defects of popular partisanship.

Given these tensions between the Constitution and party government, one important question to address to the subsequent history of American politics is, has this tension been healthy or destructive? The answer explored in the rest of this essay is that it was in some important ways healthier in the nineteenth century, especially in the mature party system built after the first parties died down, than in the twentieth century, which has seen a series of attempts to reform the party system to make it more progressive and less partisan.

THE MATURE PARTY SYSTEM

The second set of major parties in American national politics were the Jacksonian Democrats and the Whigs, whose conflicts lasted from the 1830s to the 1850s. This period of American party history is generally and not altogether inaccurately characterised as the period during which the party system reached 'maturity'. In part this maturity consisted in structural democratisation and organisational perfection: the replacement of state legislatures by popular elections in the choice of Presidential Electors, the expansion of the electorate, the expansion of the number of elective offices, the election of Congressmen by districts (rather than at large, as had been the case in some states), the introduction of the Presidential and lower-level nominating conventions (replacing caucuses), and the proliferation and perfection of local party organisations. It is a little misleading and rather patronising to look back from the vantage point of this mature 'second party system', with its close resemblances to the current party system, and see the 'first party system' as a case of immaturity and 'arrested development'.[8] The first partisans developed such organisation as they thought they needed (it was actually quite extensive and sophisticated);[9] they did not intend for that organisation to endure, so they should not be chastised too much for setting up a system that 'failed to survive'.[10] Nevertheless, the 'second party system' did exhibit much more of that characteristically American exuberant if rather chaotic participation and organisation seemingly for the sake of participation and organisation rather than for the sake of some programmatic set of policies.

However, one must beware of letting the party organisational and structural innovation in this period lead one to conclude that here we truly have the first real American party system, with patronage and party loyalty proving themselves to be sufficient forces to hold the system together and to keep it functioning with only a marginal, insincere and halfhearted recourse to the kind of programmatic or ideological appeals that had been so rife in the first party system. It is true that the kind of party being developed in this period was based in part on the Albany Regency model, the New York type of party that stressed orgaisational solidarity above policy and ideology, and that often involved 'that lack of consistency and clarity on ideas and issues that is so often the despair of critics of the American party system'[11] (and the point admired by some of its conservative defenders). But organisational virtuosity was not enough.

In the first place, it was not enough to make it durable. If one is considering systems that 'failed to survive', one must consider the fate of this second party system. For it, too, 'failed to survive'.

In the 1850s and 1860s it was replaced by the third American party system. If it was organisationally so 'mature', and it even lacked the handicap of 'immature' attitudes towards the necessity of party politics, why did it so soon collapse?

But in the second place, organisational virtuosity was not as a matter of fact enough to define and to energise the second party system. It also had a strong ideological element. The Jacksonian Democrats could not have endured as long as they did, nor have become the nationally dominant party in this period, if they had been characterised solely by politicians like Martin Van Buren, the 'Sly Fox' and 'Magician' of the Albany Regency, unaccompanied by politicians like 'Old Hero', Andrew Jackson. While there was significant organisational and structural innovation in the second party system, there was also some significant continuity between these parties and the first parties in terms of issues and ideologies. The Jacksonian crusade against the Bank of the United States and the federal patronage of business enterprise and internal improvements was an updated and westernised version of the Jeffersonian crusade against Hamiltonianism;[12] and as the Jacksonians revived Jeffersonianism, so the Whigs inherited Federalist policies. The Whigs were more successful electorally than the Federalists had been, partly because they were better at mimicking the Jacksonians than the Federalists had been at imitating the Jeffersonians. As their name indicates, the Whigs presented themselves as opponents or at least sceptics of executive power, especially of Jackson's populistic executive aggrandisement; in other words, they engaged more fully in the popular rhetoric of American party politics than had their Federalist precursors. They also prudently chose military heroes as Presidential candidates, rather than party regulars who might emphasise too much the Whig party platform and policies, which were politically less marketable. In short, the Whigs learned better than the Federalists the role of the lesser of the two major parties in each successive American 'party system': the role of moon to sun (as Samuel Lubell put it).[13] Each historical 'party system' – with the possible exception of the current one – has had a dominant party, a natural party of government, whose glory must be reflected 'me too' fashion by the subordinate party if it is to survive and to prosper at all. In the first system the dominant party was clearly the Jeffersonians, and in the second it was clearly the Jacksonians. It is not at all clear that the Jacksonians would have been able to become the dominant party – or even that party politics at the national level would have been revivable in this period – if 'the Jacksonian persuasion' had not revived ideological issues. 'Party is organised opinion.' Benjamin Disraeli's compact definition of political parties points to their two-sided nature: they need and are organisation, but they also need and are opinion. Major American parties have conformed to this nature. Successful parties of interest and patronage have also been parties of principle and issue, most clearly in their origins and establishment into hegemony, but also in their sub-sequent lives. American political parties have not been uniquely unideological parties, although their critics and their defenders have often criticised and defended them for being so.

If this dual nature of American political parties had not been passed on from the first parties to the second ones, it would have been not easier but more difficult for this generation of politicians to develop a justification for partisanship, as they did, that accepted and encouraged the permanent place of parties alongside the Constitution. In politicians' and citizens' changed opinions about the desirability of a permanent party system, and about the way in which such a system can be compatible with the Constitution, there is real novelty in the second party system, and some reason to rename it the *first* party *system* – the first coincidence of the practice of party with its systematic justification.

Martin Van Buren left us the best statement of that justification, and of the more (not to say perfectly) complete integration of parties with the Constitution and with democratic constitutionalism that was possible in the generation that succeeded the framers. Van Buren is the true founder of the American party system. The subtlety and depth of his views on that system deserve the close attention of students of American politics.[14]

When Van Buren was elected to the Senate in 1821, he left for Washington, D.C., consciously intending to repeat at the national level what he had done in New York: to revive the party conflict, to end the blurring of party lines, and to overcome 'the Utopian notion of … the amalgamation of all parties'.[15] This was not an easy or straightforward project. He backed the wrong horse in 1824, when he hoped to revive the old alliance between New York and Virginia by supporting William Crawford for the Presidency. He soon became willing to see the Democratic Party basing itself farther west, and resting on – or rather, supplying the basis of – the candidacy of

Andrew Jackson. Jackson won the Presidency in 1828, after the election of 1824 had been 'stolen' from him by the 'corrupt bargain' between John Quincy Adams and Henry Clay. (Clay, having been eliminated from the race,[16] threw his weight to Adams, and become Adams' Secretary of State.) The alliance between Jackson and New York was crucial to Jackson's victories in 1828 and again in 1832. From the beginning, Van Buren insisted that Jackson's candidacy should depend on and perpetuate not his personal appeal as a candidate, but 'old party feelings.' Jackson's 'personal popularity' was an asset, but also a danger; it would be a grave error to let Jackson get himself elected because of 'his military services without reference to party'. For the sake of the future of the country as well as of the Party (including, of course, Van Buren's own future, as Jackson's successor in 1836), Jackson's election must be, and be perceived to be, 'the result of a combined and concerted effort of a political party, holding in the main to certain tenets and opposed to certain prevailing principles'.[17]

Why was Van Buren so confident that a system of political parties, openly avowed, would be a valuable addition to the American political system? Forty years before, when the Constitution was composed, and even thirty-five years before, when the first parties under the Constitution were forming, political parties (as distinguished from 'factions', which meant interest groups or personal followings) had been treated as secret weapons, to be deployed only in emergencies, not in everyday politics. How had circumstances changed to make public principled parties more desirable? Following Edmund Burke's reasoning that political parties need to be made more respectable when great statesmanship becomes rare or extinct,[18] one could argue that the departure of the great statesmen of the Revolutionary and Constitutional eras did make a system of parties more desirable in America.

> The visit of Lafayette and the laying of the cornerstc ne of the Bunker Hill monument in 1825 reminded Americans that half a century had passed since the Revolution. The passing of the founding fathers caught the attention of the nation. The remarkable coincidence of the deaths of Jefferson and Adams on the Fourth of July 1826, brought home the fact that most of the old heroes were gone.[19]

Party principles and regularity can provide a democratic substitute for the discretion and discrimination of heroic statesmanship.

Moreover, 'years of work in party-building and ... the exacting discipline of party loyalty'[20] can be the democratic politician's answer to the rather oligarchic assumption of some of the older-style anti-party politicians that they were born to rule, as well as to the demagogic danger of an ambitious and popular leader like Jackson, unconstrained by party ties. Richard Hofstadter describes the Albany Regency politicians in these terms: 'They were ... modern political professionals who loved the bonhomie of political gatherings, a coterie of more-or-less equals who relied for success not on the authority of a brilliant charismatic leader but on their solidarity, patience, and discipline.'[21]

In addition to the need to compensate for the limits and dangers of democratic politics – limits and dangers not always modestly acknowledged by democratic politicians, citizens and intellectuals, but confronted by Van Buren – it is reasonable to speculate that the passage of time itself made party politics more tolerable under the less-than-brand-new Constitution: 'Only after our institutions of government were well-established could politicians look to differences of opinion as something that might be organized to serve as a positive political force in American politics.'[22]

But perhaps the crucial difference between Van Buren and the anti-partisan generation of American politicians that preceded him was not a difference in circumstances, but Van Buren's disagreement with their judgement that American citizens could all be expected to be of one party, the republican party. Van Buren thought it was too optimistic to expect all Americans to become and to remain loyal to truly republican ways of thinking; there would always be un-republican partisans, who (because of their wealth and connections) could organise covertly more easily than republicans, so it was best to have them openly identifiable, by open party organisation. Van Buren argued that the 'Utopian' expectations of anti-partisanship led to a corruption of the good, republican party, as well as to an unsafe obscuring, rather than an obliteration (which was impossible), of the bad, anti-republican party. The experience of the country under Monroe and John Quincy Adams supported Van Buren's less utopian view: Federalist policies and partisans had not disappeared from the political arena, they had simply infiltrated the ranks of the Republicans themselves. John Quincy Adams – the son of the last Federalist President – presented himself as a Republican, but proposed (quite unsuccessfully) transparently Federalist policies.

Van Buren thought the American people would support the right policies if only the choice were made clear to them, rather than obscured by this blurring of party lines.

In fact, Van Buren argued – again, with a fair degree of support from American experience – that trying (with President Monroe) to amalgamate the old parties and to suppress principled partisanship merely made partisanship break out in forms that were not only messier, less manageable and less comprehensible (a disadvantage particularly important in democratic politics), but also – and more seriously – lower, meaner, and pettier. Van Buren had experienced this problem in New York politics; in 1824, it manifested itself in the Presidential election. Personal rivalries produced unedifying campaigns that began years before the election itself. Van Buren began his *Inquiry into the origin and course of political parties in the United States* (written largely during his retirement in the 1850s, and published posthumously in 1867) by contrasting the successful administrations of Jefferson and Madison – who had, 'throughout, recognized and adhered to the political party that elected them' – with the political atmosphere presided over by the party amalgamator, Monroe, which became 'inflamed to an unprecedented extent' by a regression to unprincipled rivalries:

> In the place of the two great parties arrayed against each other in a fair and open contest for the establishment of principles in the administration of Government which they respectively believed most conducive to the public interest, the country was overrun with personal factions. These having few higher motives for the selection of their candidates or stronger incentives to action than individual preferences or antipathies, moved the bitter waters of political agitation to their lowest depths.[23]

It is important to appreciate the extent to which Van Buren regarded his novel and detailed defence of a party system as a defence also of political moderation and constitutionalism. He made his defence of political partisanship with the understanding that 'the inviolate sanctity of a written Constitution [is] the life of a republican government'.[24] As already noted, systematic partisanship depersonalises politics to some extent. This moderates personal political ambitions, and makes the necessary concessions to the compromises and coalitions of a moderate politics less personally painful. Van Buren's solution to the problem of strong personal ambitions in the pursuit of the Presidency – ambitions tempted (as in 1824) to resort to extreme and inflammatory appeals – was his system of parties, which 'would restrain presidential aspirants, inducing them to take moderate positions'.[25] Van Burenite partisanship is not partisanship that is constantly challenging the moderating influences of the Constitution.

However, it is also important to appreciate the occasionally less moderate, more decisive, more fully partisan function of the party system founded by Van Buren. This function is implicit in Van Buren's descriptions of the seriousness of the points at issue between the major parties, even if he does not explicitly draw attention to this function, and even though he does concentrate on the parties' differences on 'specific programs and policies instead of general theories'[26] (the former being closer to party interests and farther from convulsive regime politics). This function is also apparent, if only as an 'amendment to his earlier views',[27] in Van Buren's becoming the Presidential nominee of a third party in 1848 – the highly principled Free Soil Party (with Charles Francis Adams, the grandson of the last Federalist President, as his running mate!) – which challenged the stable, moderating competition between Democrats and Whigs.

James Ceaser offers a reasonable synthesis of these two views of the functions of partisanship, both contained within Van Buren's system – the moderating, 'inside', 'institutional' view, and the 'insurgency', 'outsider', more highly partisan view:

> Normally, the electoral system should work to prevent major pressure for change from translating itself too quickly into party policy. This bias is built into the system in the belief that an open system removes restraints on presidential aspirants and encourages them to appeal to dangerous and immoderate currents of opinion. Yet the moderation of the existing parties itself needs a check; occasional demands for change and renewal must be accommodated. These objectives can be accomplished by permitting a new party to be created or an old one to be reconstituted. Under this method, change takes place when a party sets forth a new program in response to some particular substantive problem and then attempts to win the political power to enact it.[28]

In this synthesis, most of the time American parties are rather *status quo*-oriented, and quite compatible with and protective of Constitutional government; but occasionally they respond to a powerful issue outside of the current party mainstream, and pursue policies that require radical changes, extending possibly to the Constitutional

fabric itself. The tension between American constitutional government and American political partisanship remains within the
mature party system founded by Van Buren. Perhaps that tension
is reduced by this system's institutional bias against radical change.
Those proposing such change have to persevere against this bias, and
can only hope to thrive from time to time, not in every election.
Nevertheless, the openness of the system to such proposals –
whether from 'third parties' (which are thus 'integral elements of
the so-called two-party system')[29] or from major party insurgents –
constitutes an advantage of the mature party system, although or
rather because it reintroduces, at least potentially, the tension
between the party system and the calmer politics anticipated by the
Constitution.

The answer to the question posed above – if the second party
system was so perfect and mature, why did it 'fail to survive'? – is
thus that this 'failure' was actually a success: the decision to stop
compromising on the issue of freedom and slavery was a just
decision, made through the party system itself, by the replacement
of one of the major parties – the Whigs – with a 'third party' –
the Republicans – and by the realignment of the electorate to
support the dominance of the Republicans. Of course, Van Buren
himself did not see it that way when these events occurred, towards
the end of his life (he died in 1862). In spite of his previous support
for the Free Soil cause, he supported Stephen Douglas in 1860. He
had always been deeply concerned with sectional rivalries; these
were one of the kinds of conflict that his party system had been
intended to suppress. Nevertheless, it was clearly Van Buren's party
system that made and reinforced the realigning decision of 1860, and
it is not against the spirit of Van Buren's work to contend that the
second party system was mature because it gave way to the third.
True, Van Buren had consciously chosen not to call up a new party
alignment so much as to recall and to reinstate the old one, and he
did this with one eye on the necessity of having such issues as were
embodied in this alignment as sustainers of party morale. And true,
there had always been something suspiciously artificial about the
issues of the second party system; the 'Jacksonian persuasion' (like
the Jeffersonian persuasion to which it was the heir) was a nostalgic
protest against an inevitable socio-economic reality – call it the
dynamics of capitalism – as much as it was an affirmation of 'substantial goods'.[30] Nevertheless, the invocation of such a moralising

persuasion as an essential element in the mature second party system made more possible the more genuinely moral decision of 1860.

THE REFORMED PARTY SYSTEM

Van Buren succeeded, perhaps better than he knew, in establishing not only a relatively open party system (open to challengers such as the Free Soil and Republican Parties, as well as to darker ones such as the Know Nothings), but also relatively closed parties (biased in favour of party discipline and regularity, and against incorporation of new issues). Following the Civil War and Reconstruction, the party system brought forth a line of Presidents whose lack of charisma and indebtedness to party were all that Van Buren could have asked for and more. The closed parties, especially the dominant Republican party, helped keep Presidents relatively weak, and Congress relatively strong. The strong moderating effects of party were complemented and boosted by social and economic developments. Industrialisation ensured that parties were by no means at odds with strong economic interests; in fact, the party system and the economy ran rather more in tandem than Van Buren, with his suspicion of the money power, would have liked. After all, the Republican party was the heir of the Whigs' pro-business policies. Abraham Lincoln's fear that after the Civil War the businessmen would enjoy too much political power proved to be well founded. The celebration of the robber baron businessman in turn made corrupt party machines seem acceptably American. Urbanisation and immigration ensured that there was a large market in which the party machines could trade their favours – to the poor as well as to the rich – for votes and organisational help; the party drilling became even less likely to turn into a radical force than it was in Van Buren's day. In short, the moderate or Constitutionalist tendency of the party system became extremely narrow and absolute.

Not surprisingly, the reaction against that tendency, when it came, was a rather extreme reaction, offering to reform the party system in the opposite direction, and even attacking the Constitution in order to make that reformation seem desirable and possible. The all-too-realistic profile assumed by parties during the last thirty years of the nineteenth century inspired a particularly strong anti-party ethos in America, in contrast to other liberal democracies.

'Nowhere else in the western democratic world did parties look so evil, at least to middle-class citizens, as they did in the United States.'[31] This was partly because the ideal of participation – difficult even for a party organisation of the European mass membership kind to live up to – was higher in America than elsewhere, but it was also partly because the realities of party organisation were often actually considerably lower than elsewhere. In twentieth-century America, the understanding of the party system, and the practical changes proposed for and made in that system, have alternated between two extreme viewpoints: a hardheaded 'conservative' one (accepted, sometimes reluctantly, by many liberals with a realistic political education), defending an exclusively Constitutionalist, consensus, patronage, professional, Congressional, status-quo orientation;[32] and a high-minded 'liberal' one, proposing an exclusively anti-Constitutionalist, alternatives, issue, amateur, Presidential, change orientation. Rarely has there appeared, much less dominated, in either theory or practice, a balance between these two sets of tendencies comparable to that achieved by the mature party system founded by Van Buren.

The party reforming reaction, most effective in the Progressive period and in the post-1968 and post-Watergate reforms of the 1970s, has produced a host of legal and institutional changes affecting the practice of party both at the state and local levels and at the national level: 'professionalisation' of the civil service (including city managers), non-partisan municipal elections, referenda, initiatives, recall devices, voter registration, government-printed ballots, heavy regulation of internal party activities (forbidding such terrible conspiracies as communication between county committees and the state committees: an extreme example, but a real one), widespread use of the direct primary election (with primaries coming to dominate nominations at the Presidential level as well since 1972) and (the most recent large innovation) public financing of some campaigns in seventeen of the fifty states and in Presidential primary and general elections. The experience in various places and in various elections differs, but the general tendency of these reforms clearly has been to promote voters' independence from partisanship, and to discourage existing party organisations, thus encouraging candidates' own organisations and campaign efforts, rather than dependence on parties. Furthermore, insofar as party organisations have also been helped by these reforms, it has been the duopoly of

Democrats and Republicans that has been propped up, thus closing the party system even while opening up the major parties. Primaries and other party-opening reforms allow new groups to compete within the existing major parties, thus disinclining them to work through new or existing third parties; legal regulations burden minor parties more than major ones; and public financing helps major parties far more than minor ones. The party reform movements have promoted candidate-centred politics, as a replacement for a party system that they have made in some ways even more stale and *status-quo*-directed than it was before they started complaining about this failing.

The subordination of party to candidate was one of the effects most clearly intended by the reforms, and one which most clearly sets the reformed party system apart from the mature party system. The founding father of the reformed party system, the moving spirit to set against Van Buren, was Woodrow Wilson.[33] Wilson, a Progressive intellectual and politician, outlined at the beginning of the party reform era the essential purposes and shape of this reformation. Most prominent in Wilson's view of the party system − and in the characteristic liberal view ever since − is the necessity of using this system to add to the constitutional system as a whole a constantly active 'leadership' with energy and 'vision'. In this view, the need for such leadership is (at least in the contemporary world, as distinct from the sleepier world of eighteenth- and early nineteenth-century America) not occasional, as the mature party system assumes, but continuous. Party power, especially at the state and local levels, must be made to yield to candidate and leader power.

At first Wilson had proposed the abolition of the separation of powers, to produce a more parliamentary system of government in America, to achieve the levels of governmental unity, leadership, activity, and change that he thought were necessary. But he later accepted the difficulty of such a proposal, and urged instead the transformation of the Presidency into a constant source of such leadership. The stasis of '*Congressional government*' (the title of Wilson's famous critique of American government, published in 1885) − which he recognised was caused by the fragmentation of Congress into 'committee government' − could be overcome by Presidential government, with a more national party, designed not to limit him but to 'be an instrument at the leader's command helping to further the principles and programs for which he had won approval in his direct appeal to the people'.[34] Not the 'worn-out' traditional principles and programmes of his party, but newer, more up-to-date principles and programmes, were to comprise the popular leader's mandate. Party leaders need to be in direct contact with a public opinion from which all traces of Constitutionalism have been removed, because they must owe their power not to the Constitution but to the people. For their proper function is not Constitutionally definable. It is moral leadership which requires them to interpret the sometimes vague longings of the public into a coherent public policy. It is to have a 'vision' that is a privileged glimpse at the next stage of the historical process, and to be able to move the public in that direction, by building on the public's progressive opinion and helping it to suppress its non-progressive opinion. This process needs to be repeated again and again, in fairly rapid succession; therefore it was insufficient for Wilson simply to replace the worn-out principles of the existing parties with new ones, in the relatively difficult and rare manner allowed by the mature party system. It was necessary rather to change the party system itself, to make it much more productive of continual change, to keep the country in step with historical progress.

One of the major problems with reforming the party system in this way is that it makes the whole notion of party loyalty and discipline more than a little suspect. The supremacy of political leadership and political leaders over party entails a denigration of the respectability and usefulness of party. Parties are required to be sources of constant change, and with no particular end in view, for historical progress is seen to be endless. The strong party government intention of the American party system in its reformed condition is thus distinct from other western party governments, which have generally taken as their model party a socialist movement, with a well-defined end justifying party activity. Lacking that final justification, progressive American parties have lacked a firm justification for their existence. Every party is 'worn-out' as soon as it makes its particular contribution to political progress. The usefulness of political parties can be no more durable than that of individual political leaders – perhaps less so, since parties are if anything more constrained by their own histories. In this perspective, can any party system, formed however differently from the mature party system, produce parties that are anything but instantly obsolete? Must a party system always be by nature not mature but senile?

Thus, there is a distinctly non-partisan or anti-partisan cast to Wilson's and the general reform view of parties. (There are other reasons for the decline of party in recent decades, but a hundred years of reform and of reform-minded political education is prominent among them.)[35] In this view, elected offices, especially the Presidency, as the representative of the whole nation, but other elected offices as well, are seen as above partisanship. Voters themselves are expected to avoid or to be easily weaned away from 'irrational', habitual partisan attachments, which may be essential to parties but are clearly obstacles to the rapid change demanded by progressive politics. This position recalls the originally anti-party attitudes of the framers of the Constitution, but it incorporates a much more sanguine, plebiscitary view of elections and of elective offices. The party reformers' emphasis on the need for government leadership and activity is comparable to the framers' emphasis on the need for energetic government, but they do not supplement this emphasis with a comparable insistence on maintaining some distance between elected officials and the electorate, and on maintaining the separation of powers as a means of controlling as well as of enabling officeholders. Thus, the system proposed by the party reform view is much more hostile to the Constituion than is the mature party system. Since Wilson, it has been more common among political scientists and practising politicians to condemn the Constitution as a worn-out 'Newtonian' political system, which needs to be replaced, in effect if not in fact, by a more progressive, more easily evolving, 'living', 'Darwinian' political system.[36] The greater hostility to party in the reformed party system makes it more, not less hostile to Constitutional government.

For the past century, then, a 'conservative' version of the mature view of the party system, emphasising the parties' production of consensus and playing down their production of alternatives, has coexisted uneasily with the 'liberal', reform view, emphasising alternatives and relegating consensus-building to the darker and unacceptable side of party politics. The first view has been quite compatible with the Constitution – although inclined to overlook those elements of the Constitution itself that anticipate the need for periodic renewal, such as the provision for amendments and the stipulation that Presidents undertake to 'preserve, protect and defend the Constitution' (not merely, as other officials, 'to support this Constitution'). The second view has been compelled to go on living with the Constitution, but has been bent on altering it to make the political process less fragmented, by altering the party system.

The reform view has succeeded in moving the party system and the larger political system in the desired direction to some extent, although the anti-party thrust of party reform has tended to undermine its unifying leadership thrust. Plebiscitary leadership has been encouraged, but, as might have been expected, the unifying and enduring qualities of this leadership have not been so apparent. It is now commonly expected of both conservative and liberal politicians, especially executives, that they will lead in a Wilsonian manner, relying less on Constitutional powers or party ties than on popular leadership, based on their whole constituency and on public (not party) opinion. The 'modern Presidency' and the modern administrative state are Wilsonian in spirit, although they have not succeeded in reducing the 'extraordinary isolation' of the Presidency noticed by Wilson. Furthermore, it is now widely accepted that the best voters are independents, not party regulars. Not even potential party regulars: the dealigning American electorate are more decidedly dealigned than other dealigning electorates; their attitudes to their major parties are less hostile than they are neutral, viewing them as irrelevancies in the political system.[37]

Even the New Deal in the 1930s, which is often seen as an episode that revived American partisan politics for a time, can be seen more penetratingly as an attempt by Franklin Roosevelt's leadership to replace partisan politics with Presidential administration, pursuing not Jefferson's or Van Buren's lead, but Hamilton's. The New Deal, like its successor the Great Society in the 1960s, and not unlike the Reagan assault on the Great Society in the 1980s, was less a partisan programme than an exercise in extending 'non-partisan administration'; it was intended to be 'a party to end all parties'.[38] Roosevelt tried – inconsistently and unsuccessfully – to reinforce partisanship by making the Democratic party a more purely liberal party. But apart from the fact that ideological purity and partisan loyalty are two different things (so success with this project might not have revived so much as stultified partisanship), Roosevelt easily consoled himself when this project failed, because he saw (as he said in 1940 – in his Jackson Day Speech!) that

> the future lies with those wise political leaders who realize the great
> public is interested more in government than in politics, that the

independent vote in this country has been steadily on the increase, at least for the past generation, that vast numbers of people consider themselves normally adherents of one party and still feel perfectly free to vote for one or more candidates of another party, come election day, and on the other hand, sometimes uphold party principles even when precinct captains decide 'to take a walk'.[39]

The overt and covert hostility of the reform view to partisanship itself, and therefore to any party sytem, however formed or reformed, has helped to create the current situation, in which weak partisanship both in the electorate and in elected officials makes durable partisan and governing coalitions difficult if not impossible for politicians to construct, and therefore makes political leadership itself more difficult. Political leadership is (as expected by the reformers) in greater demand but (contrary to their expectations) shorter supply. Partisan majorities, when they appear, are extremely short-lived. Policy sucesses, when they appear, are equally ephemeral. This situation can be attributed in significant part to the failure of twentieth-century political science and politicians to achieve a healthy level and kind of tension between the party system and Constitutional government.

NOTES

1 Some, on the other hand, foresaw a degree of communication and co-operation among the Electors of the various states that would be sufficient to produce a decision by the Electoral College. See Madison's speeches of 4 September and 5 September 1787, *The Records of the Federal Convention of 1787*, ed. Max Farrand (4 vols.), New Haven, Yale University Press, 1966, II, pp. 500, 513.
2 'A candid state of parties', *The Writings of James Madison*, ed. Gaillard Hunt (9 vols.), New York, Putnam, 1900–10, VI, pp. 106–19.
3 See in particular nos. 40 and 43 (Madison), and 26 and 28 (Hamilton).
4 'Consolidation' and 'Public opinion', *Writings*, VI, pp. 67–70.
5 Letter of 27 September 1808, *Correspondence Between the Hon. John Adams and the Late William Cunningham, Esq.*, ed. E. M. Cunningham, Boston, E. M. Cunningham, 1823.
6 James Piereson, 'Party government', *The Political Science Reviewer*, XII, 1982, p. 48.
7 'Marcus Brutus', *Serious Facts ...*, n.p., 1800, p. 4.
8 Paul Goodman, 'The first American party system', in William Nisbet Chambers and Walter Dean Burnham (eds), *The American Party Systems: Stages of Political Development*, New York, Oxford University Press, 1967, p. 85.
9 Noble E. Cunningham, Jr., *The Jeffersonian Republicans: The Formation of Party Organization 1789–1801*, Chapel Hill, The University of North Carolina Press, 1957.
10 Goodman, *loc. cit.*; Richard P. McCormick, 'Political development and the American party system', in Chambers and Burnham, *American Party Systems*, p. 95.
11 Richard Hofstadter, *The Idea of a Party System*, Berkeley, University of California Press, 1970, p. 246.

12 See Marvin Meyers, *The Jacksonian Persuasion*, Stanford, Stanford University Press, 1957.

13 *The Future of American Politics*, New York, Harper and Row, 1951.

14 For fuller statements of these views than that which follows, see James W. Ceaser, *Presidential Selection*, Princeton, Princeton Univeristy Press, 1979, ch. 3; and Donald V. Weatherman, 'From factions to parties: America's partisan education', in Thomas B. Silver and Peter W. Schramm (eds), *Natural Right and Political Right*, Durham, Carolina Academic Press, 1984, pp. 401–13, and his 'America's rise to a mature party system', paper presented to the American Political Science Association Annual Meeting, 1982.

15 *Albany Argus*, 29 January 1822, quoted by Donald B. Cole, *Martin Van Buren and the American Party System*, Princeton, Princeton University Press, 1984, p. 104.

16 By coming fourth: the House has to choose from the top three when there is no one with an Electoral College majority.

17 Letter to Thomas Ritchie, 13 January 1827, quoted by Ceaser, *Presidential Selection*, pp. 160–61.

18 Harvey C. Mansfield, Jr., *Statesmanship and Party Government*, Chicago, University of Chicago Press, 1965.

19 Cole, *Martin Van Buren*, p. 102.

20 Hofstadter, *Idea*, p. 241.

21 Hofstadter, *Idea*, p. 242.

22 Weatherman, 'America's rise', p. 9.

23 *Inquiry*, New York, Hurd and Houghton, 1867 (reprinted New York, Augustus M. Kelley, 1967), pp. 3–4.

24 *Inquiry*, p. 213.

25 James W. Ceaser, 'Political change and party reform' in Robert A. Goldwin (ed.), *Political Parties in the Eighties*, Washington, D.C., American Enterprise Institute, 1980, p. 102.

26 Weatherman, 'America's rise', p. 13.

27 Ceaser, 'Political change', p. 103; see also Ceaser, *Presidential Selection*, pp. 142–3.

28 Ceasar, 'Political change', p. 103.

29 V. O. Key, *Politics, Parties and Pressure Groups*, quoted by Ceaser, *Presidential Selection*, p. 326.

30 Meyers, *Jacksonian Persuasion*, p. 274.

31 Leon D. Epstein, *Political Parties in the American Mold*, Madison, University of Wisconsin Press, 1986, p. 159.

32 An excellent example of this type of apology for the low-minded party system is Edward C. Banfield, 'In defense of the American party system', in Robert A. Goldwin, (ed.), *Political Parties, USA*, Chicago, Rand McNally, 1961, reprinted in Goldwin (ed.), *Political Parties in the Eighties*, pp. 133–49; the classic of this type is probably Pendleton Herring, *The Politics of Democracy*, New York, W. W. Norton, 1940.

33 On Wilson, see Paul Eidelberg, *A Discourse on Statesmanship*, Urbana, University of Illinois Press, 1974; Harry M. Clor, 'Woodrow Wilson', in Morton J. Frisch and Richard G. Stevens (eds), *American Political Thought*, New York, Charles Scribner's Sons, 1976, pp. 192–218; Ceaser, *Presidential Selection*, ch. 4; and Charles R. Kesler, 'Woodrow Wilson and the statesmanship of progress', in Silver and Schramm (eds), *Natural Right*, pp. 103–27.

34 Ceaser, *Presidential Selection*, p. 174.

35 It is worth noting that the rise of the use of the non-partisan media as part of the new candidate-centred campaign techniques, one of the most often-noticed of the other causes of party decline, was itself prompted by the Progressive antiparty legislation of the early twentieth century.

36 Progressive evolutionism denies the fixed natural right purpose of the Constitution. The best gloss on Wilson's call for a more 'Darwinian' constitution is Charles Edward

Merriam, *A History of American Political Theories*, New York and London, Johnson Reprint Corporation, 1968 (first published 1903), pp. 305–27.

37 Martin P. Wattenberg, 'Party identification and party images', *Comparative Politics*, XV, 1982, pp. 23–40.

38 Sidney M. Milkis, 'Franklin D. Roosevelt and the transcendence of partisan politics', *Political Science Quarterly*, C, 1985, pp. 479–504; see also Milkis, 'The Presidency, democratic reform, and constitutional change', PS, XX, Summer 1987, pp. 628–36.

39 Milkis, 'Roosevelt', p. 498.

Foreign Policy and the Constitution: 'Invitation to a Perpetual Institutional Struggle'?

ABSTRACT

This essay explores one of the more fundamental contemporary criticisms of the constitutional arrangements for the formulation and implementation of foreign policy, namely that the separation of powers inhibits the wise conduct of the nation's foreign affairs. It describes the rather ambiguous nature of the constitutional arrangements for the control of foreign policy as well as interpretations of what the intentions of the Founding Father's might have been in this regard; but the central thrust of the argument in this paper is that the underlying problems of foreign policy have little to do with the Constitution, but rather are intimately connected to the process of hegemonic decline.

INTRODUCTION

In all liberal–democratic states the formulation, as well as the conduct, of foreign policy pose a unique challenge to the fabric of democratic government. Put most crudely, the problem is that, in an uncertain and dangerous world, the pursuit of national security may, at times, lead to a neglect of established democratic processes. As the Irangate affair has demonstrated, together with the many similar abuses of the Nixon Presidency, those most committed to the defence of democracy may in their fervour unintentionally undermine it. Writing almost two hundred years ago in support of the newly drafted Constitution, Alexander Hamilton warned his fellow citizens of such dangers: 'Safety from external danger is the most powerful director of national conduct. Even the ardent lover of liberty will, after a time, give way to its dictates ... To be more safe ... [nations] at length become more willing to run the risk of being less free.'[1]

In the year in which Americans celebrate the bicentennial of the Constitution, Hamilton's perceptive warning has much greater resonance than even he may have expected, and certainly desired. For in the aftermath of Irangate, the constitutional arrangements for the conduct of foreign policy have come under intense public scrutiny and criticism. Deep concern has been expressed about the efficacy of these arrangements and whether, given they were designed for an eighteenth-century agricultural state, they still remain appropriate for a hegemonic world power in the nuclear age. Two hundred years on from the efforts of the Founding Fathers, the principles of liberal democracy and the requirements of national security have still to be finally reconciled.

Commenting upon the constitutional design of American government with regard to foreign policy, the distinguished historian Louis Halle remarked that 'American government is about as badly designed for the conduct of foreign affairs as it could be'.[2] Such a view has a distinctly respectable heritage, commencing with De Tocqueville's observation that democracies lack all the requisites which the conduct of an effective foreign policy demands. Underlying these widely accepted 'truths' is the conviction that the pursuit of national security in the nuclear age, together with the requirements of America's hegemonic world role, demand an unfettered executive which can act decisively to articulate and to protect the national interest. However, the problem is that the Founding Fathers, in their desire to avoid executive tyranny, made foreign affairs subject to the same separation of powers which applied with respect to all aspects of domestic government. In the context of an eighteenth-century Eurocentric international system, such a peculiar constitutional arrangement for the conduct of the nation's foreign policy mattered very little, except perhaps to constitutional lawyers. But the emergence of the United States as a global superpower has transformed this situation. Whether the Constitution actually hinders, or assists, the prosecution of a rational and effective foreign policy now matters crucially, not just to 270 million Americans, but equally to the whole western world whose security and survival are ultimately tied to that of the United States.

In recent years there has been strongly voiced opinion that the separation of powers in respect of foreign policy is now a major inhibition to the effective pursuit of the national interest and America's global responsibilities. Many examples abound of major

Presidential foreign policy initiatives, like the SALT II treaty or aid to the Contra rebels in Nicaragua, being thwarted by what some would regard as Congressional interference. This concern with the inability of even the most popular Presidents to pursue strategic foreign policy objectives is not confined to any particular section of political opinion, liberal or conservative. Rather, there appears to be a unanimity of views amongst many professionals and politicians that the existing system fails the nation in this most critical of areas, the defence and the security of the Republic.

In this essay I want to explore critically this contemporary surge of dissatisfaction with the Constitution, commenting particularly upon the validity of the arguments and evidence which sustain it. More specifically, the essay will suggest that the critics of the existing foreign policy process exaggerate its defects, ignore its strengths, and overlook some of the more striking continuities in the conduct of foreign affairs. Moreover, contrary to much popular opinion, it will be argued that the problems of the foreign policy process are not so much institutional as political and therefore are not amenable to constitutional reform. Associated with this is also the view that the perpetual institutional struggle for mastery of the nation's foreign affairs, witnessed almost every day in contemporary media reports, reflects more accurately the Founding Fathers' intentions than the era of the 'Imperial Presidency' in which the rationality of international power politics took precedence over the democratic process. Accordingly, the essay commences with a brief exploration of how the Constitution shapes the contours of the foreign policy process.

THE CONSTITUTION AND FOREIGN AFFAIRS

There is little doubt amongst students of the Constitution that, at least in respect of responsibility for foreign affairs, the Founding Fathers' prescriptions are extremely ambiguous. Indeed on the matter of foreign affairs, the Constitution has been described as essentially 'an invitation to struggle'.[3] One of the reasons for this ambiguity over who should make foreign policy stemmed from the great uncertainty which the Founding Fathers themselves had as to how to answer this question. Although they believed that a strong national government was essential in dealing with foreign powers they were equally concerned to ensure that the most vital decisions about war and peace could not be left to the executive. The experience of European states had convinced them that the executive had to be constrained in the foreign policy arena since foreign entanglements, as George Washington noted, could so easily undermine the fragile domestic polity.[4] According to Thompson the Founding Fathers were therefore somewhat 'ambivalent and uncertain about who should make foreign policy and their uncertainy is reflected in the Constitution'.[5]

This ambiguity arises partly because the Constitution says very little about the respective powers and responsibilities of the three branches of government in respect of foreign affairs. There is, for instance, no reference in the Constitution itself to the terms foreign affairs or national security. Indeed Henkin remarks that 'the constitutional blueprint for the governance of our Foreign Affairs has proved to be starkly incomplete'.[6] But even where the actual Constitution is explicit, such as for example over the legislature's right to declare war, this suggests nothing about either the power to terminate war or the power to engage American military forces in hostilities not involving a declaration of war. Although the (in)famous War Powers Resolution of 1973 attempted to define the respective responsibilities of the executive and legislature with respect to the use of American armed forces abroad it has not removed the original ambiguities present in the Constitution. In this respect at least the Constitution is without doubt a clear invitation to perpetual struggle.

At best the Constitution established little more than the broad framework within which the nation's foreign affairs were to be managed. Whilst the President was granted the authority to negotiate treaties, make Ambassadorial appointments and act as Commander-in-Chief of the armed forces, such powers were made subject to Congressional review. International treaties and ambassadorial appointments had to be approved by the Senate, whilst only Congress was awarded the right to declare war, raise and finance the armed forces, and regulate foreign commerce. Other than these specific powers the respective roles of the executive and legislative branches in the management of foreign affairs were assumed to flow from the broader constitutional division of authority between both institutions.

One of the consequences of this constitutional ambiguity is that much effort has been devoted to divining precisely what the

Founding Fathers intended with respect to foreign affairs. Since, as noted above, they too were largely ambivalent and divided on this matter the exercise has not proved decisive. However, there does appear to be agreement amongst most constitutional experts on three points. Firstly, the actual day-to-day conduct of foreign policy was regarded by the framers as the province of the executive – 'executive altogether'.[7] Secondly 'except for repelling sudden attacks on the US, the founders of our country intended decisions to initiate either general or limited hostilities against foreign countries to be made by Congress, not by the Executive.'[8] Thirdly, the general legislative and financial powers of Congress clearly invite its (active or passive) involvement in those areas of foreign policy which require legislative action or the expenditure of public money.[9] However, even though there may be a general consensus on these three particular points there still remains considerable uncertainty as to how the framers expected the separation of powers, with respect to foreign affairs, to operate in practice.

Since the days of the framing of the Constitution, three competing schools of thought have been engaged in a rather intense conversation, with important practical consequences, concerning the question of who should make foreign policy. One school, perhaps best expounded by Hamilton in *The Federalist*, is that foreign and national security policy is the province of the executive since only the President can effectively articulate a coherent national interest and pursue it consistently. In this view, the executive is supreme both with respect to the formulation and the conduct of foreign affairs. A second school considers that the powers granted to Congress by the Constitution clearly signal the framers' intention that the legislature should exercise control over the direction of foreign affairs. Meanwhile a third school argues that foreign policy is an arena of shared powers and responsibilities in which Congress was to have ultimate authority but a vigorous and independent executive was essential for a balanced and effective foreign policy.[10] At various times in American history each of these views has informed the living Constitution, the actual practice of government. Thus Washington, Jefferson, Madison and Lincoln, as with many post-war Presidents, operated largely on the principle of executive dominance of foreign policy. Yet throughout much of the nineteenth century Congress appeared to be the dominant institution. In comparison, the period from the early 1970s into the late 1980s might be best described as an era of permanent conflict, in which these two powerful institutions, Congress and the Executive, are locked into a struggle to establish control over the direction of foreign policy. Indeed it is this struggle between the executive and Congress which has fuelled much of the current dissatisfaction with the existing constitutional arrangements for the conduct of the nation's foreign policy.

Over the years since 1787, whilst these three distinct prescriptions for the management of external affairs have clashed and collided, with one then another coming to dominate the 'living Constitution', the Supreme Court has remained curiously absent from the public debate. Apart from the Chadha judgement in 1983 and the Pentagon papers judgement in 1971, the Supreme Court has tended to avoid, whether consciously or not, those issues connected with the proper constitutional conduct of foreign affairs.[11] The matter of who should make foreign policy has thus always been a political, as opposed to a legal, question to be 'settled' between the executive and legislative branches. Consequently, the institutional politics of executive–legislative relations have always been an important factor in shaping foreign and national security policy even during the period of the 'Imperial Presidency'.

THE IMPERIAL PRESIDENCY: A CONSTITUTIONAL ABERRATION?

Underlying many of the criticisms of the contemporary foreign policy process is a certain misplaced 'nostalgia' for the 'golden age' of executive primacy which lasted for the first two decades of the post-war era. During this period Presidents were able to act decisively, as in the case of Truman's commitment of troops to Korea in 1950 or Eisenhower's dispatch of forces to the Lebanon in 1958, without fear of Congressional interference or retribution. Given a societal political consensus upon the strategic objectives underlying the conduct of foreign policy there was a genuine reluctance to challenge executive actions in the international arena, or to withhold Congressional authority for the effective implementation of the President's foreign policy initiatives, since this could so easily be presented, in the face of a global communist threat, as unpatriotic behaviour. By comparison the foreign policy process of the late 1970s and 1980s appears to verge on the anarchical, to be unpredictable, and to lack coherence. This, some have argued, is a product of excessive Congressional interference.[12]

Writing in 1981 Senator John Tower argued, somewhat surprisingly for a Senator, that 'the balance between Congress and the President has swung dangerously to the legislative side with unfavorable consequences for American foreign policy'.[13] His comments reflected concern, not just in conservative but also in liberal political circles, with the apparent 'damage' which a decade of Congressional activism had done to the fabric of national security. Whilst many Republicans pointed to the relative decline of American military power as one consequence of a 'parochial' Congressional activism, Democrats too were equally unhappy with the Senate's 'sabotage', through its failure to ratify SALT II in 1979, of the central plank of Carter's policy of detente with the Soviets; an action which had even more profound consequences for the whole tenor of east–west relations since it contributed directly to the emergence of what Halliday refers to as the 'second cold war'.[14]

As Bailey has noted, the 1980s witnessed a growing belief in some very powerful circles that foreign policy was being undermined by excessive Congressional interference.[15] In this context a return to executive primacy had great appeal to the critics of Congress, including President Reagan who, exasperated with yet a further defeat for his policy on arming the Contra forces in Nicaragua, commented in 1985: 'We have got to get to where we can run a foreign policy without a committee of 535 [the combined membership of the House and Senate] telling us what we can do.'[16] Reform of the foreign policy system was aired.[17] Some even suggested that the situation was so serious that the Constitution itself had to be altered to enable the executive to pursue a rational and coherent foreign policy.[18] But critics and reformers overlooked the fact that the 'golden age' of executive primacy in foreign policy, which many regarded as the 'norm', could not be reinvented through tinkering with the Constitution. For the period of the 'Imperial Presidency', even if it was desirable, was underwritten by a constellation of historical and political factors which made it more of an aberration than the norm. It might assist the argument here to enquire briefly as to what these factors were.

From the late 1940s through until the late 1960s successive Presidents dominated the conduct of foreign policy. Only rarely did Congress challenge the President's authority to lock the nation into foreign policy commitments or to prosecute policies which were considered 'unwise'. Moreover, even when Congress threatened to or actually voiced dissent, as it did over the formation of NATO in 1948 and the Korean War in the early 1950s, this did not dislodge Presidents from pursuing their intended course of action. For two decades Presidents set the agenda and controlled the implementation of American foreign policy. The 'Imperial Presidency' emerged despite what the framers of the Constitution intended since it was nurtured by a unique combination of domestic and international political conditions.

In the aftermath of the Second World War it was evident to victors and vanquished alike that world politics had been dramatically transformed. With the major European powers either devastated by or recuperating from war the United States was thrust into the role of a hegemonic power for which it was not fully prepared. Although, early in the war, Roosevelt had initiated planning for the post-war world order, this was predicated upon a peace settlement and international co-operation amongst the allies, including the Soviet Union. But the failure to conclude a European peace treaty, combined with the rapidly developing Cold War rivalry, imposed global responsibilities upon the United States. As the western world's dominant economic and military power, the United States had to provide the leadership which was vital to the continued existence of liberal democracy and western capitalism. Imperial responsibilities, however, required an imperial style of government. 'Pax Americana' therefore contributed enormously to the extension of presidential power over foreign policy.

Although George Washington had warned the American people of the domestic political dangers which flowed from foreign entanglements, this had little impact on successive Presidents who sought to construct and police a new 'liberal' world order. By the early 1950s the United States had anchored into place the United Nations, together with its functional agencies, and a new world economic order 'governed' by a series of multilateral organisations, such as the International Monetary Fund. In the process Congress willingly devolved extensive powers to the President, since to exercise the leadership responsibilities of a hegemonic power the executive had to be unfettered by domestic constraints. Presidents could no longer simply pursue the parochial national interest, but rather had to be concerned with ensuring stability and order in the international system. Where international necessities clashed with the isolationist tendencies in American domestic politics, as evidenced in the Congressional debates on the formation of NATO and the Marshall Plan in the late 1940s, Presidents almost always gave priority to global commitments. For instance, legislation to implement Eisenhower's 'Atoms for Peace' proposal in 1953 passed Congress despite Senator Bricker's protestations that it undermined the constitutional powers of the Senate.[19] At issue was the fact that the administration devised a legal mechanism which allowed the executive branch to enter into international agreements for cooperation in nuclear matters without the Senate's approval, so bypassing the latter's power with respect to the ratification of international treaties. This is just one instance of how the requirements of America's hegemonic role contributed to the gradual expansion of Presidential power. But there were many more.

Executive dominance of the foreign policy process rarely proved to be a source of great controversy since Congress recognised that domestic economic prosperity and security was underwritten by 'Pax Americana'. Throughout the post-war period Congress acquiesced in the executive's accretion of power because this came to be accepted as both a natural consequence of the nation's hegemonic role in the world and a requirement for continued prosperity.

Of course Cold War rivalry too contributed enormously to the diminution of Congressional authority over foreign affairs. One of its consequences was to create, under the control of the President, a huge, permanent national security apparatus. By its very nature this apparatus operated under a greater shroud of secrecy than any other sector of government, making it especially difficult for Congress to exercise its oversight function. Moreover, the dynamics of military competition with the Soviet Union created a strong interlocking set of mutual interests between Congressional politicians, the military and defence contractors. Although its significance is often exaggerated, this 'iron triangle' nonetheless facilitated executive dominance over the defence policy process, for the Pentagon retained considerable control over the allocation of defence contracts. With increasing shares of the defence budget going to weapons and equipment procurement, Presidents had vital levers with which to generate Congressional support for their national security policies. But it was the very nature of the Cold War itself which legitimised executive primacy over defence and foreign affairs.

In commenting upon the origins of the 'Imperial Presidency' Mandelbaum stresses the critical influence of Cold War rivalry: 'There was no retiring from the Cold War, no respite from it, and virtually no conflict anywere – on the Korean peninsula, in Indochina, or in the former Belgian Congo – that did not get caught up in it. The power of the American Presidency has always swelled in time of emergency, and the Cold War made emergency a permanent condition.'[20] In 'fighting' the Cold War, Presidents had to be able to react quickly and in a determined fashion, with military force if necessary, to contain the expansion of Soviet power anywhere on the globe. In the face of the Soviet threat and the dangers it posed to American global interests Congress had little political scope to challenge the growing authority of Presidents over foreign policy without appearing to be unpatriotic or, even worse, 'soft' on communism. With a fervently anti-communist public mood, combined in the early Cold War years with the McCarthy witchhunts, either path would have been political suicide for most Congressional politicians.

But it was in respect of the deployment and use of military forces abroad that Presidents, relying upon their Constitutional authority as Commander-in-Chief, usurped Congressional power. Since the Cold War, by definition, involved an absence of any formal declaration of war Congress, as the Korean and Vietnam conflicts demonstrated, had negligible influence over decisions to use force abroad. As one Congressional report complained: 'Almost every post-war President has made decisions to use US Armed Forces without consulting Congress in advance, but instead, informing them after the decision.'[21] On each occasion Presidents justified their actions in terms of the exigency of the situation and the necessities of maintaining a global balance of power. But the cumulative consequences of such actions was to erode the constitutional and political power of Congress to participate in the most fundamental decisions about war and peace. This too was compounded enormously by the advent of nuclear weapons. Growing reliance upon nuclear weapons and the advent of sophisticated delivery systems awarded unprecedented power to the Presidency. Faced with negligible time within which to make decisions about war, perhaps no more than an order of minutes, Presidents sat atop an elaborate military structure of nuclear command and control with the ultimate power of decision over the fate of the whole nation.

Congress, except perhaps for the Speaker and Congressional leadership, was (and remains) excluded from this most critical aspect of national decision making. The advent of nuclear weapons reinforced the erosion of Congressional power since it effectively involved delegating to the President the constitutional right of Congress to declare war. As the 1962 Cuban missile crisis demonstrated, in times of national emergency it was the President, not Congress, who had control of the nation's destiny.

What legitimised this tremendous expansion of Presidential power over foreign affairs was the underlying domestic political consensus about America's global role and responsibilities. Despite different interpretations of means, there was a genuine convergence of partisan views on the goals and objectives of American foreign policy. As Holsti's examination of American public opinion demonstrates, from the late 1940s through until the mid-1960s there was a consistently high level of support, both amongst elites and the general public, for an internationalist foreign policy.[22] Containing the Soviet Union and 'managing' the Western world, including protecting specifically Western, as opposed to purely American, interests in the developing world – the new arena of Cold War rivalry – were accepted by both Democrats and Republicans alike as the central objectives of foreign policy. For two decades these objectives were largely unquestioned by Congress. In turn this enabled Presidents to dominate the foreign policy process since there were no politically viable alternatives on offer from which the American public could choose. Even those politicians critical of the growth of the 'Imperial Presidency' recognised that the Soviet threat and the dynamics of Cold War rivalry made any challenges to Presidential primacy in foreign policy largely counterproductive. As Senator Javits remarked only recently: 'The reluctance to challenge the President is founded in an awareness that he holds, in large degree, the fate of the nation in his hands. We all wish to assist and sustain the Presidency.'[23] The existence of a powerful societal consensus upon foreign policy acted to strengthen Conressional loyalty to the President even when, as in the case of the Vietnam war, there was considerable concern over the direction which policy took. But Congressional loyalty to the President also flowed from the workings of the seniority system on Capitol Hill.

One of the consequences of the seniority system for the making of foreign policy was that it strengthened the President's power.

If the President could enlist the support of the Congressional 'establishment' (those favoured by the seniority rule) he could largely ensure Congressional acquiescence to his policy initiatives. Lyndon Johnson, for example, was extremely effective in extracting Congressional support for the war in Vietnam by manipulating the system. Even when Congress was dominated by a different party from that of the President, as in the case of much of Eisenhower's period in office, the combination of a bipartisan consensus and the seniority system effectively marginalised Congressional opposition to any major Presidential foreign policy initiatives.

Although the era of the 'Imperial Presidency' led to a considerable diminution of Congressional power over foreign affairs this should not be exaggerated. For it is evident from the recent histories of post-war foreign policy that Presidents were always acutely aware of the limits to their relative autonomy from domestic political con-straints. Allison's account of the deliberations in EXCOM (President Kennedy's crisis management team) during the Cuban missile crisis illustrates this vividly.[24] Moreover, it is now also clear that, for much of the post-war period, even on those occasions when force or covert intervention was used abroad, Presidents consulted or informed the Congressional leadership of their intentions.[25] What all this implies is that Presidents did not aggressively usurp the powers of Congress, but rather that the latter consciously acquiesced in adopting a minimalist role in the formulation of foreign policy.

The 'Imperial Presidency', as the discussion has shown, resulted from a particular constellation of domestic and international conditions. Once those conditions began to dissipate, as they did by the 1970s, the 'Imperial Presidency' too was undermined. Contrary to much popular wisdom, the era of Presidential dominance of foreign affairs was therefore more of an aberration than the norm. Underwritten by a domestic political consensus, as well as intense ideological and military rivalry with the Soviet Union, it represented no more than an imperfect and temporary solution to the conflicting demands of America's hegemonic role in the global system and the domestic requirements of constitutional democracy. Indeed the combination of detente, the Vietnam war and the excesses of the Nixon administration conspired together to dismantle the awesome edifice of the 'Imperial Presidency'.

THE POLITICISATION OF FOREIGN POLICY

In 1979 Franck and Weisband entitled a brief article on United States foreign policy 'Congress as a world power'.[26] This symbolised what they viewed as a 'revolution that will not be unmade', a radical restructuring of executive–legislative relations with respect to the making of foreign policy.[27] Since the late 1960s foreign policy has become increasingly politicised with the consequence that Presidential primacy was directly challenged by a reformed Congress no longer willing to accept a secondary role in determining the fate of the nation. By the 1980s Congress had reasserted its constitutional authority over the conduct of foreign affairs and this, as noted earlier, prompted calls from many quarters for a return to the halcyon days of executive primacy. But, as Franck and Weisband have argued, this is unlikely to transpire given the radical transformation in executive–legislative relations that took place during the 1970s.

The Vietnam war proved to be one of the most traumatic catalysts for change. It contributed directly to demolishing the bipartisan consensus on foreign policy; it also encouraged Congress to recover its constitutional powers with respect to the use of armed force abroad. The revelations of the Pentagon papers, the secret bombing of Cambodia in 1970, growing internal repression of antiwar dissenters, combined with the apparent failure of a military solution to the Vietnam problem, undermined totally public and Congressional confidence in the 'Imperial Presidency'. A more 'youthful' and aggressive Congress, which had thrown off the shackles of the seniority system and party discipline, asserted its constitutional rights over foreign affairs. Commencing with the War Powers Resolution in 1973, Congress voted to impose considerable constraints upon executive action in foreign affairs and to ensure that the whole national security apparatus, including intelligence agencies, became more directly accountable to the legislature. Moreover, Congressional vetos were incorporated into almost every significant piece of foreign policy legislation thereby imposing sometimes severe limits upon Presidential autonomy. Congress, for instance, linked the sale of arms abroad to questions of human rights and nuclear proliferation.

But it was not simply the breakdown of the national consensus upon foreign policy, and the political backlash resulting from the Vietnam war, which contributed to greater Congressional intervention in foreign affairs. For the 1970s, the era of the oil crisis and the devaluation of the dollar, brought home to Americans the consequences of a more interdependent world. From the gas pump to the factory floor, to the local church and community, many Americans became increasingly aware of how international forces impinged directly upon their daily lives. A whole range of 'intermestic issues', in which it was impossible to disentangle foreign and domestic policy interests, became apparent. Growing Japanese imports, the sale of wheat to the Soviet Union, environmental issues, relations with South Africa, US corporate investments abroad, human rights, and many other issues sensitised different segments of American society to the fact that foreign affairs could no longer be separated from domestic politics.

Congress became the focal point of a plethora of organised interests trying to shape US policy with respect to everything from foreign trade, international economic managment, human rights, and relations with South Africa, to detente with the Soviet Union, strategic arms control, and even the exploitation of nuclear power abroad. Kissinger's detente strategy, for instance, was 'sabotaged' by a combination of conservatives, human rights activists, and the Jewish lobby. These together forced the passage of the Jackson-Vanik resolution in 1974 denying the Sovet Union most favoured nation treatment and trade loans until they amended their policy with respect to Jewish emigration. Across a whole range of intermestic issues, this politicisation of foreign affairs contributed directly to the 'opening up' of the foreign policy process. One of the consequences of growing recognition of international interdependence was therefore to 'democratise' the foreign policy process 'to a degree hitherto unseen.'[28]

Facilitating this 'democratisation' of the foreign policy process was a series of very significant changes in the pattern of American domestic politics. The secular decline of party loyalty and identification, alongside the rising importance of political action committees and single issue groups, fed on and contributed to a more assertive Congressional role in foreign affairs. Reforms too, in the internal organisation of Congress, together with its sophisticated and well staffed committee machinery, made it difficult for the executive to escape extensive Congressional scrutiny and oversight without resorting to improper behaviour. Taken together with the lack of any clear political consensus on the appropriate global role for the United

States in the post-Vietnam era, these changes contributed to a remarkable fragmentation and decentralisation of the foreign policy process. As a result the foreign policy initiatives of the executive can now be readily blocked, as President Reagan found in his many attempts during both periods of office to direct aid to the Contra forces in Nicaragua, by a determined minority of Congressional politicians and organised interests. And it is this fact which has provoked concern about 'excessive' Congressional intervention in the management of the nation's foreign affairs.

What has further compounded this increasing politicisation of foreign policy is the process of hegemonic decline. Although still the dominant economic and military power in the world, since the 1960s the United States has witnessed a significant erosion of its relative power. Strategic parity with the Soviet Union, their increasing ability to project military power globally, combined with the emergence of Japan and West Germany as major economic powers has led to the loss of United States dominance in world politics. The global system is now much more pluralistic and polyarchic and much less susceptible to United States control than at any time in the post-war period. Moreover, as the largest 'debtor' nation the United States has become increasingly sensitive to developments in the global financial and trading communities. As Gilpin has observed, 'the fundamental task of the United States in the realm of foreign affairs has become one of responding to its changed position in the world as new powers arise on the world scene.'[29]

The domestic political consequences of hegemonic decline have been (and continue to be) dramatic. Relative decline has strengthened the ideological fragmentation and polarisation amongst foreign policy elites, and among the public, which fed off the breakdown of the post-war foreign policy consensus. In a recent study of the foreign policy beliefs of policy-making elites Holsti and Rosenau point to the entrenched fragmentation of opinion which gives little hope for the evolution of any new consensus.[30] Quite simply, the question of how to manage hegemonic decline has provoked a deeply rooted intellectual and ideological crisis within the domestic polity.

Equally, relative decline has brought home to the American public, more so than perhaps at any time in the past, the domestic political and economic costs of 'Pax Americana'. The growing forces of protectionism and the voicing of significant neo-isolationist tendencies have been reflected in greater Congressional activism in the foreign policy arena. Combined with the other factors mentioned above, the lack of enthusiasm amongst the American public for bearing the costs of hegemony, whether it be in terms of unqualified opposition to interventionism in the Third World or support for a liberal world economic order, has fuelled the irreversible re-assertion of Congressional power over foreign affairs.

Hegemonic decline means that increasingly the choices facing American politicians and the public will be between sustaining its international commitments and investing in domestic programmes. Hunt has stated the dilemma simply:

> ... by attempting to honor the claims the world ostensibly makes on us, an activist foreign policy dims our capacity for domestic renewal. Such a foreign policy diverts us from the public issues raised by rapid technological, economic, and social change. It also devours the funds essential to improving the quality of our lives, whether measured in terms of health, education, environment, or the arts. Currently more than half of the federal budget is committed to international programs and military operations past, present and future.[31]

Given (as the British experience demonstrates) the secular nature of hegemonic decline, the struggle between Congress and the executive for the control over foreign policy is therefore likely to remain a permanent feature of American government.

THE CONTEMPORARY INSTITUTIONAL STRUGGLE

One of the consequences of renewed Congressional intervention in the management of foreign affairs has been, as mentioned earlier, a very powerful counter-reaction. Critics of Congress, amongst whom are numbered leading Congressional politicians, argue that the balance of power between the executive and legislature has swung too much in favour of the latter. This, it is suggested, has made it virtually impossible for recent Presidents to pursue rational and consistent policies in the international arena. As the Reagan administration's proposed sale of AWACs to Saudi Arabia in 1981 demonstrated, even a very popular, newly elected President was forced to mobilise all his political resources simply to defeat his Congressional opponents.[32] But the ramifications of renewed Congressional activism go much deeper.

According to a number of critics the contemporary institutional struggle between Congress and the executive presents a profound challenge to the wise and effective conduct of American foreign policy. Four specific criticisms are reflected in many of the commentaries upon contemporary foreign policy. Firstly, there is the view that the openness of the policy process makes effective diplomacy and the pursuit of strategic objectives almost impossible. In the case of the AWACs sale, the administration's whole Middle East strategy was virtually held 'ransom' to the demands of a powerful ethnic lobby represented by the American Israeli Public Action Committee and other Jewish organisations. Secondly, the fragmentation of power in the foreign policy arena allows minorities and sectional interests working through Congress to block Presidential foreign policy initiatives. This makes it virtually impossible for the executive to articulate and promote a coherent national interest. It also makes it exceedingly difficult to construct and pursue a consistent policy on any issue. The failure of Congress to ratify the SALT II treaty is but one vivid illustration of how even United States relations with the Soviet Union are often more dependent upon the President's handling of Congress than his relationship with the General Secretary of the CPSU. As one critic has noted, the fragmented nature of the policy process means that: 'Rather than optimally serving our national interests, [foreign policy] decisions are 'contaminated' by parochial political forces acting to serve disparate institutional, organisational, commercial, local, or personal interests.'[33] Thirdly, because of these factors, some have argued that Presidents are forced to adopt a less publicly visible and more covert style of foreign policy. The recent revelations of the Iran–Contra scandal seem to suggest that the President's advisors were 'driven' to a covert foreign policy because they knew only too well that such a policy would be unacceptable to Congress. Thus some critics seem to place the responsibility for scandals like Contragate on the excessive constraints imposed upon Presidential action in the foreign policy arena by Congress. Fourthly, and finally, concern is expressed that the politicisation of the foreign policy process has made policy outcomes much less 'rational'. This, it is argued, is a very unwelcome and dangerous development; in the nuclear age, with both superpowers permanently poised for conflict, it merely invites catastrophe.

Taken together, all these arguments present a strong case that, as far as foreign affairs is concerned, the separation or sharing of powers is somewhat incompatible with the United States role as a global superpower. However, the critics of Congressional activism in foreign affairs greatly exaggerate the deficiencies of the contemporary foreign policy process and misinterpret the underlying causes of the current 'crisis'. Indeed, there are several good reasons for believing that the 'crisis' (if there is one) does not derive so much from the nature of the Constitution as from the traumas of hegemonic decline.

Although recent Presidents and Secretaries of State castigate Congress for undermining vital foreign policy initiatives, significantly, all are equally critical of the bureaucracy. Even if Congress adopted a largely passive role in the foreign policy process it is hard to believe, given the constant bureaucratic struggles within the executive branch, that policy would be either more coherent or more rational. For instance, although the Carter administration bemoaned Congress's failure to ratify the SALT II treaty, it is also clear that segments of the bureaucracy and military were not fully united on this matter. Disagreements within the bureaucracy over verification issues and other aspects of the agreement spilled out into the Congressional arena where they were utilised by the administration's opponents. More recently the Reagan administration has bitterly condemned Congress for thwarting its whole Central American policy by refusing to grant military aid to the Contra forces fighting the Nicaraguan regime. Yet, as Rubin and others have observed, within the executive branch there is no coherent policy towards Central America.[34] On the contrary the CIA, the Department of Defense and the State Department are locked in fairly fundamental disagreements about how to deal with the Central American crisis. As a consequence messy compromises are often reached which merely compound the lack of coherent policy and virtually condone each agency's pursuit of its own mini 'foreign policy'. The problems of foreign policy fomulation are thus by no means simply a product of Congressional activism.

Studies of the existing foreign policy process confirm that on most issues decision making within the executive branch is dominated by inter-agency strife and bureaucratic politics. Talbott's investigation of the first Reagan administration's strategic arms control policy described the process of policy formulation as 'untrammelled bureaucratic warfare.'[35] Even Kissinger, who deliberately by-passed the bureaucracy on most major policy issues, refers in his memoirs to the enormous bureaucratic obstacles which face any President or Secretary of State attempting to develop and pursue a coherent and consistent foreign policy.[36] Entrenched bureaucratic interests and conflicting visions of the national interest make it almost impossible for the executive branch to establish a rational implementation of policy. The whole Irangate debacle illustrates an extreme, but not necessarily atypical, example of different segments of the executive branch pursuing quite contradictory policies toward the same country, Iran. Yet here is a case in which Congress had no role whatsoever since, along with other important bureaucratic actors in the foreign policy process, it was totally excluded from any policy deliberations.

Accompanying this bureaucratic strife, foreign policy is also subject to a more permanent institutional struggle between the President's national security advisors and the State Department. As one recent study commented: 'White House mistrust of State and its search for alternatives have been familiar features of the Washington scene for so long as to seem the norm rather than some heretical deviation.'[37]

Throughout both the Carter and Reagan Presidencies the conflict between the State Department and the White House national security staff contributed enormously to the inconsistency and incoherence of many policy initiatives. At various times, the outcome of this institutional struggle has led to the resignations of Secretaries of State, or the President's National Security Advisors, the most recent casualties being General Haig and Robert McFarlane.

The politics of foreign policy formulation within the executive branch suggests that curtailing Congressional intervention in foreign affairs, even if it was possible, would by itself do little to improve the actual quality or coherence of the nation's foreign policy. This merely tends to confirm the view that the reassertion of Congressional authority over foreign affairs is not by itself the primary cause of (what some have labelled) the current crisis in foreign policy. This conclusion is further confirmed by a recognition of the fact that Congressional influence over the substance and conduct of foreign affairs varies enormously between different types of policy decisions.

As mentioned earlier, critics of Congressional activism in foreign affairs argue that one of its consequences is to severely constrain or fetter the executive's autonomy. Thus, so the argument goes, Presidents are often unable to pursue policies which may be strategically necessary, or vital to the national interest, because they are likely to be blocked or undermined by Congress. Yet on major foreign policy questions it is hard to find many examples of Presidents being totally defeated by Congressional opposition. The Senate has refused only five treaties this century, the most important ones being the Versailles Treaty and SALT II. Yet in the latter case the executive continued to operate as if the treaty was in place. On foreign policy matters Presidents have considerable scope for pursuing their objectives even though Congress may be opposed, and particularly if doing so does not require the expenditure of public monies. Moreover, on many of the most vital questions of national security Congress has a negligible influence on policy formulation.

Whilst Congressional politicians play a significant role in shaping policy outcomes across the whole range of intermestic issues (foreign policy problems like trade, energy, etc. which have domestic impact, or vice versa) their influence over other equally vital matters on the foreign policy agenda is less marked. Congressional power and activism appear to be most visible on those 'distributional' issues, such as defence procurement decisions, which can have a significant impact upon the well-being of politicians' constituents, or with respect to those issues which directly challenge the values and interests of vocal and well-organised lobbies, such as ethnic or corporate groups. But in the critical areas of defence strategy, the use of force and crisis decision making, Congress has dwindling influence. Equally, it is largely impotent in shaping the executive's strategic objectives and priorities which every post-war President on coming to office has articulated in the form of a foreign policy 'doctrine' such as the 'Reagan doctrine' or the 'Truman doctrine'. Such 'doctrines' are important since they amount to a declaration of the principles and objectives which guide the administration's approach to foreign affairs whilst also providing a 'vision' of the proper nature and purposes of America's role in ensuring world order.

When it comes to the use of force abroad Presidents, even in the post-Vietnam era, can still act quite autonomously. Despite the existence of the War Powers Act, Presidential discretion with respect to the use or threat to use force abroad has been only marginally constrained. As President Carter's hostage rescue mission in 1979 demonstrated, like President Reagan's military intervention in

Grenada 1983 and the bombing of Libya in 1986, Congress tends to be informed after the event, not consulted beforehand. Moreover, the imprecise wording of the War Powers Act offers such fertile ground for conflicting legal interpretations that Presidents may readily by-pass its requirements. Thus President Reagan despatched American marines to the Lebanon in 1982 and subsequently opposed Congressional attempts to invoke the act. A compromise was eventually reached with the result that the marines were allowed to stay for up to eighteen months.[38] Only the horrific bombing of the marines' quarters, in which many men died, led to the withdrawal of US forces. Passage of the War Powers Act then has not in practice given Congress the degree of control over the exercise of US military force abroad that its proponents in the 1970s argued it would. As Senator Javits has remarked: 'The pressure of the threat of armed conflict is such that even I found myself willing to compromise, to lean in the direction of the presidency, by giving either more time or a wider latitude of discretion to presidential actions than warranted by the specific provisions of the War Powers Resolution.'[39]

But it is not just with respect to the use of force abroad that Presidents still retain a substantial degree of autonomy. For when it comes to managing crises, which in the nuclear age may involve decisions about national survival, Presidents and their advisors in the White House Situation Room have no time to consult the Congress. Since the stakes are also so high and since centralised control over both decision making and implementation is so crucial to successful crisis management, Congress has always accepted Presidential primacy in this domain. When the nation's vital interests are threatened, Congress always rallies to support the President. As Walter Lippman commented, in crises Americans prefer the President to take the decisions because they believe that 'the flexibility of one mind [is] superior to the inertia of many.'[40]

If Congressional activism has not, as indicated above, 'infected' some of these more vital areas of foreign policy decision making, there is also reason to suspect that it may not, as critics suggest, have undermined the continuity and consistency of the nation's foreign policy. Whilst there may be no domestic political consensus on the direction which foreign policy should take, there still remains much common ground on its essential features. Containing Soviet power, maintaining a stable world order, and fulfilling alliance commitments are all central objectives upon which Congress and a President of any political persuasion would agree. Over the years Congressional activism has not led to the undermining of American commitments to Western Europe, or to the abandonment of the policy of containing Soviet power and influence in the world. Indeed, Congress may have been more consistent in its approach and commitment to these objectives than many recent Presidents. As noted above each President's desire to establish an identifiable foreign policy 'doctrine' has undoubtedly contributed to some of the more dramatic shifts in policy over the last two decades, particularly towards the Soviet Union. Contrast, for example, President Carter's handling of relations with the Soviet Union with that of President Reagan. Congress cannot be charged as the sole culprit responsible for the lack of continuity in foreign affairs.

Finally, there seems little evidence to suggest that the more visible role of Congress in foreign affairs has forced Presidents to rely more upon secret diplomacy and covert activities. Whilst some critics have voiced concern that Irangate would probably never have occurred if foreign policy was less open to Congressional inter-ference, this seems a rather perverse logic. Any study of United States foreign policy in the 1950s and 1960s, the halcyon years of Presidential primacy, would reveal that even with a 'passive' Con-gress the executive abused its power and engaged in a vast range of 'covert' activities as well as secret diplomacy. Indeed, the abuse of executive power in the foreign policy arena, as the history of the 'Imperial Presidency' illustrates, is largely a consequence of weak Congressional oversight.

Where, then, does this discussion leave the arguments of the many contemporary critics of Congressional activism in foreign affairs? What is suggested is that they may have wrongly diagnosed the underlying causes of the current problems which afflict both the process and the conduct of American foreign policy. In crude terms not only do they exaggerate the damage which the reassertion of Congressional power has had on foreign affairs but they even exaggerate just how far its influence penetrates the processes of policy formulation within the executive. Moreover, there is a strong tendency for critics to ignore the real problems which afflict the conduct of foreign affairs.

Adapting to the position of a declining hegemony, with no domestic political consensus on how interests and commitments should be reshaped to fit this new situation, is without doubt the fundamental problem confronting the American foreign policy establishment. The argument that the current 'crisis' in United States foreign policy stems from the constitutional separation of powers, which encourages a perpetual struggle between Congress and the executive for control over foreign affairs, therefore appears a somewhat crude and inaccurate over-simplification.

FOREIGN POLICY AND THE LIVING CONSTITUTION

In reviewing the contemporary arrangements for the management of foreign policy Henkin comments: 'If we have not verged on a constitutional crisis, few have been moved to declare that the constitutional arrangements for conducting the foreign affairs of the United States are worthy of celebration.'[41]

But are things really that bad? Probably not, for the reassertion of Congressional authority in the foreign policy arena is a sign of the vitality and strength of the Constitution and not, as some would argue, a sign of its antiquity or its irreconcilability with America's role as a global power. Indeed, as this essay has suggested, the real problems of United States foreign policy are not constitutional ones but rather those connected with the domestic politics of hegemonic decline.

As Americans come to celebrate the bicentennial of the Constitution, many appear to be, for quite varied reasons, distinctly unhappy with the arrangements for the conduct of foreign affairs established by the Founding Fathers. On the one hand, some politicians, influential commentators and political analysts regard the separation of powers as being a major barrier to the formulation and implementation of an effective and coherent foreign policy. On the other hand, many ordinary Americans are dismayed by recent events, such as Irangate, which tend to inflame deeply held suspicions and distrust of executive dominance of foreign affairs. As a consequence, in the bicentennial year few Americans may actually wish to celebrate the constitutional arrangements for the conduct of the nation's foreign affairs. Yet, as this essay has argued, it is not the separation of powers which is primarily responsible for this 'crisis of confidence' afflicting foreign policy. Rather, it is the lack of any domestic political consensus upon America's global role and how that should be managed, given the problems of a declining hegemony, which underlies the present 'crisis'.

Undoubtedly, the struggle between Congress and the Presidency for control over foreign policy has contributed to the current malaise. But, as has been suggested, it is simply not the case that constitutional reform, or a return to the ways of the 'Imperial Presidency' (even if this were possible) would actually guarantee a more coherent, consistent and rational foreign policy. Indeed, even in those aspects of foreign affairs which still remain virtually 'executive altogether', there is little comforting evidence that policy is in some sense arrived at, or implemented, by an inherently more rational or superior process to that embodied in the Constitution.

If the Founding Fathers could comment upon how foreign policy is made today in the United States they would probably conclude that it reflects their own constitutional vision much more than did the era of the 'Imperial Presidency'. Ornstein wisely observes in his analysis of the Constitution and the contemporary foreign policy process: 'As the constitutional debates make clear, the Founding Fathers perceived the institutional struggle to take place between two strong and self-confident institutions. In the post-reform, post-Vietnam, and post-Watergate era, we have come closer to this image than in decades.'[42]

NOTES

1 Alexander Hamilton, *The Federalist*, no. 8 in *The Federalist Papers*, London, Penguin, 1987.

2 L. J. Halle, 'Foreign policy and the democratic experience' in L. J. Halle and K. W. Thompson (eds), *Foreign Policy and the Democratic Process*, Washington, D.C., University Press of America, 1978.

3 The phrase comes from Cecil V. Crabb and Pat M. Holt, *Invitation to Struggle: Congress, the President and Foreign Policy*, Washington, D.C., Congressional Quarterly Press, 1984.

4 On this point consult R. H. Ullman, 'Washington, Wilson and the Democrats' dilemma', *Foreign Policy*, 21, 1975–6, pp. 99–127.

5 K. W. Thompson, 'The President, the Congress and foreign policy' in Edmund S. Muskie *et al.* (eds), *The President, the Congress and Foreign Policy*, New York, University Press of America, 1986, pp. 8–9.

6 L. Henkin, 'Foreign affairs and the Constitution', *Foreign Affairs*, v. 66 no. 2, 1987, pp. 284–310.

7 See *ibid*.

8 This is quoted from *Background Information on the Use of US Armed Forces in Foreign Countries*, prepared by the Foreign Affairs Division of the Congressional Research Service for the Committee on International Relations, Washington, D.C., USGPO, 1975, p. 15.

9 See the discussion in Henkin, 'Foreign affairs'.

10 Thompson, 'The President', p. 11.
11 On the role of the Supreme Court in foreign affairs consult Henkin, 'Foreign affairs'.
12 See John G. Tower, 'Congress versus the President: the formulation and implementation of American foreign policy', *Foreign Affairs*, v. 60 no. 2, 1981, pp. 229–46.
13 Quoted in C. J. Bailey, 'President Reagan, the US Senate, and American foreign policy 1981–86', *Journal of American Studies*, v. 21 no. 2, August 1987, pp. 167–81.
14 On the links between these events, see F. Halliday, *The Making of the Second Cold War*, London, Verso Press, 1987.
15 See Bailey, 'President Reagan'.
16 Quoted in R. Maidment and Anthony McGrew, *The American Political Process*, London, Sage, 1986, p. 173.
17 On the question of reform consult I. M. Destler *et al.*, *Our Own Worst Enemy – the Unmaking of American Foreign Policy*, New York, Simon and Schuster, 1984.
18 This is discussed in J. Q. Wilson, 'Does the separation of powers still work?', *The Public Interest*, 86, Winter 1987, pp. 36–52.
19 On this particular issue consult ch. 2 of A. G. McGrew, 'Competing perspectives on the United States domestic nuclear power policies and nuclear technology relationships with Japan, 1954–1974', unpublished Ph.D. thesis, University of Southampton, 1988.
20 M. Mandelbaum, *The Nuclear Revolution*, Cambridge, Cambridge University Press, 1981, p. 186.
21 Quoted in *Background Information on the Use of US Armed Forces*, p. 2.
22 See O. R. Holsti, 'Public opinion and containment' in T. L. Deibel and J. L. Gladdis (eds), *Containing the Soviet Union*, London, Pergamon-Brassey, 1986.
23 Senator Jacob J. Javits, 'War Powers reconsidered', *Foreign Affairs*, v. 64 no. 1, Fall 1985, pp. 130–41.
24 See G. Allison, *Essence of Decision*, Boston, Little Brown, 1971.
25 Hastedt notes that from 1949 onwards Congressional committees were informed about CIA covert operations. See G. P. Hastedt, 'The constitutional control of Intelligence', *Intelligence and National Security*, v. 1 no. 2, May 1986, pp. 255–71.
26 See T. Franck and E. Weisband, 'Congress as a world power', *Worldview*, October 1979, pp. 4–7.
27 *ibid.*
28 Quoted from S. S. Rosenfeld, 'Pluralism and policy', *Foreign Affairs*, v. 52 no. 2, January 1974, pp. 263–72.
29 R. Gilpin, *War and Change in World Politics*, Cambridge, Cambridge University Press, 1981, p. 241.
30 Consult ch. 1 and concluding chapter of O. R. Holsti and J. N. Rosenau, *American Leadership in World Affairs – Vietnam and the Breakdown of Consensus*, London, Allen and Unwin, 1984.
31 M. H. Hunt, *Ideology and US Foreign Policy*, New Haven, Yale University Press, 1987, pp. 177–8.
32 On the details of the AWACs case consult Bailey, 'President Reagan'.
33 See A. Clark and R. M. Pious, 'Waging war: structural versus political efficacy', *Armed Forces and Society*, v. 14 no. 1, 1987, pp. 129–47.
34 Consult B. Rubin, *Secrets of State – the State Department and the Struggle over US Policy*, Oxford, Oxford University Press, 1985.
35 S. Talbott, *Deadly Gambits*, London, Picador, 1985.
36 Consult H. Kissinger, *Years of Upheaval*, London, Weidenfeld and Nicolson, 1982, chs. 10 and 22 specifically.
37 Rubin, *Secrets of State*, p. 140.
38 On the details consult Javits, 'War Powers reconsidered'.
39 *ibid.*

40 Quoted in Maidment and McGrew, *The American Political Process*, p. 160.
41 Henkin, 'Foreign affairs'.
42 This is the firm opinion of Ornstein. Consult N. J. Ornstein, 'The Constitution and the sharing of foreign policy responsibility' in Muskie *et al.*, *President, Congress and Foreign Policy*.

Obituary for the 'Living' Constitution? Policy Making and the Constitutional Framework Two Hundred Years On

ABSTRACT

In this essay, the author evaluates the performance of the policy-making process established by the Constitution of 1787. In particular, consideration is given to whether the original values and capacities of the system are appropriate to an age in which government has accepted a host of positive responsibilities toward society. Through an examination of governmental policy making on the issue of equal rights for women, the author argues that policy-making structures and processes in the United States offer both advantages and disadvantages to those seeking fundamental reforms; and that American feminists have secured gains from the American political system that easily stand comparison with those obtained in similar societies with less fragmented policy-making systems. Thus, while progress on equality for women still leaves much to be desired in the United States, the problem lies less with the policy-making process than it does with the ideologies of democratic capitalism and patriarchy. Consequently, there seems little reason to expect that simply amending the policy-making process will produce better public policies.

Since the mid-1960s, Americans have had good reason to be dissatisfied with government policy. There has been confusion and disaster in foreign policy, as Irangate and the Vietnam War bear witness; there has been failure to produce coherent and effective policies on basic domestic issues, such as the energy crisis and the budget deficit; and social policies of the most well-intentioned kind have created turmoil, as with busing and abortion, or have been derided as 'throwing dollars at problems', as was the case with President Johnson's War On Poverty. These policy failures have, reasonably enough, raised the question of whether the roots of the problem do not lie wholly or partly in the processes by which policy is made in the United States. Above all, the question has been squarely put whether the system of government established by the Constitution of 1787 is any longer capable of dealing with the major problems of the nation, as it nears the twenty-first century. Just recently, for example, the Committee on the Constitutional System, composed of respected academics and former policy makers, has been discussing possible constitutional amendments aimed particularly at improving co-operation and agreement on policy between Congress and the Presidency.[1] The implicit theme of all such discussions is that the fragmentation of governmental power designed by the Founding Fathers as a defence against tyranny, has now become an almost insurmountable hurdle in the path of effective policy making. In this chapter, we shall take up this theme and examine it critically: for although it seems 'obvious' that a governmental system established to fill the policy needs of an eighteenth-century agrarian society can scarcely be expected to cope with the demands of a highly complex post-industrial nation, further reflection may suggest that the case against the Constitution of 1787 has been overstated and, in some respects, misconceived.

However, before embarking upon an analysis of the relationship between the constitutional framework and the policy-making process in the United States, we need to remind ourselves of two fundamental truths about the production and evaluation of public policy. The first is that many factors other than the structure of the policy-making process determine a nation's policies. Indeed, factors such as the practices and ideologies of democratic capitalism are much more important in influencing policy outcomes than, say, the separation of powers. This is not to belittle the impact of particular policy-making structures, but simply to suggest that they are not determining forces in the same fundamental sense as shared societal values and economic systems. For example, the failure of the United States government to enact a comprehensive national health insurance plan is certainly due in part to the opportunities afforded by a fragmented system to powerful groups who wish to prevent policy initiatives, in this case, the American Medical Association: but much more important here are the strong American belief in individual self-sufficiency and the great American fear of socialism. Similarly, the separation of powers undoubtedly helped southern politicians to thwart Presidential initiatives on civil rights; but more important in explaining the failure to make progress on these issues until 1964, was a legacy of racism throughout the country which made many Americans either hostile or indifferent to civil rights legislation. The examples are endless, but that should not distract us from this crucial point: that no particular arrangement of policy-making structures in a liberal democracy will produce policies that consistently transcend its ideological and economic lifeblood. Thus, as Charles Lindblom put it, 'the policy-making process can explain partially how governments pursue their various policy targets, but not why the targets are chosen'.[2]

The second point to emphasise at this stage is that good public policy consists of much more than merely a smooth policy system. For if efficiency of policy delivery were the sole aim, then central-isation and even authoritarianism might well be best suited to achieving it: the fewer institutions and individuals playing a role in the making of public policy, the greater is the chance for agreement and efficient policy making. However, this ignores the vital fact that most Americans want not only efficient policy making, but also democratic, or at least open, policy making. And open policy making is not simply a good thing in itself, it is also a precondition of effective policy making. Thus, democracy and effectiveness suggest that the policy-making process should be open to numerous participants, since this would help ensure that policy is neither 'dictated' nor made in ignorance of a wide range of policy alternatives. The rub, of course, is that structures which support more open policy making may run counter to the demands of an efficient policy-making process: the more interests and viewpoints represented, the more likely it is that decisive policies will be watered down to effect compromise and thus will lose their original logic and force. In this sense, open policy making may also have a detrimental effect upon the effectiveness of policy. Those who would defend the fragmented policy-making process in the United States concede this point, but do not see it as fatal to the system:

> In the age of omnipresent government, everyone ought to have a chance to slow government down before it acts in order to search for alternatives, including no government action at all. This may cause some inefficien-cies, but it maintains democratic values through a more representative politics and policy making. The compromises inherent to an open politics with dispersed power may alter a policy's objectives and reduce its

effectiveness, but they seem to be the essence of representative policy making in a large heterogeneous society.[3]

Seen in the light of this conflict between openness and efficiency, the best policy-making process is not that which sacrifices the one for the other, but rather that which balances the two in the manner most appropriate to serving the particular values and policy needs of any given society. And since these values and needs change and develop over long periods of time, a further condition of a constitutionally-determined policy-making system is that it is sufficiently flexible to recognise and incorporate such developments. These qualities of openness and efficiency, effectiveness and adaptability, provide the major criteria by which we may evaluate the contemporary operation of the policy-making structures of the Constitution of 1787. And that evaluation must, of course, begin with an examination of the intentions and aspirations of those who designed it in Philadelphia, some two hundred years ago.

As has often been observed, but sometimes forgotten in the myths of time, the discussions at the Constitutional Convention were not inspired primarily by political theory, but rather by political experience and pragmatism. In fact, the framers set out to achieve precisely that balance between open and efficient policy making that we have just considered. Firstly, they wanted a policy-making process that was free of the tyranny they had experienced under the British colonial regime. Although they did not want democratic policy making, with universal adult suffrage, regardless of sex or race, they did pursue open policy making through the notion of multiple centres of government with the power to make policy. On the other hand, although the framers had a minimal view of the need for governmental policy making, they nevertheless felt an urgent need to make the enactment and implementation of policy far more effective than was the case under the Articles of Confederation.

All those with even a passing acquaintance with the Constitution of 1787 know that the balance struck by the framers rested on three basic concepts: federalism, the separation of powers and a system of checks and balances. As a result, the power to make public policy in the United States was necessarily a fragmented one: federalism gave power to both the national government and the states' governments; the separation of powers gave independent authority to each of three co-equal institutions – the Congress, the Presidency and the Supreme Court; and the system of checks and balances, which obliged all of these institutions to co-operate in the making of most policies, created a veritable policy-making maze. For example, federalism was further complicated by giving the states control of the Senate; and the principle of the separation of powers was muddied by the injection of a Presidential veto over Congressional legislation and a variegated system of elections which meant that Representatives, Senators and the President would each represent and be answerable to different constituencies. Without listing here all the numerous complications built into the legislative system by the framers, one can readily identify the centrifugal dynamics of policy making in the United States which result from the constitutional arrangements, and the abundant opportunities it affords for conflict, delay and bland compromise – all enemies of efficient and effective policy, critics would assert. Furthermore, even where there has been sufficient co-operation between different institutions to devise satisfactory policy, the implementation of that policy is subject to yet a different configuration of interlocking jurisdictions which, if not in agreement, may derail the policy. Thus, to take but the most infamous of examples, southern states were long able to thwart the national policies on civil rights contained in the Fourteenth and Fifteenth Amendments to the Constitution.[4]

We may reasonably deduce from this that when the framers came to strike the balance between open and efficient policy making, they leaned toward the former:

> If making rational decisions requires us to develop a *method* – a series of steps – by which we can move towards certain goals rather than others, the structure of American government defeats this purpose. Fragmentation at all levels hinders the system's capacity to define problems, establish goals, and survey alternate policies comprehensively. This should not be surprising, since the founding fathers were more concerned with preventing tyranny than with establishing a smooth-running government machine.[5]

If we next ask why the framers were more concerned with preventing tyranny than creating efficient policy making, we find an answer that sheds considerable light on today's critique of the Constitution. For quite simply, they shared the common view of the eighteenth century of government as an essentially negative entity and national government, in particular, as having few positive responsibilities. And the Constitution of 1787 gave very few powers to the national government and these were a direct response to the most serious problems experienced under the Articles of Confederation.[6] Thus, the legislative power granted to Congress in Article I, Section 8 of the Constitution was both specific and very limited, something soon reinforced by the passage of the Tenth Amendment in 1791. In essence, the new federal government was empowered to ensure the defence of the country, to maintain order at home, to raise taxes for these purposes and to prevent the states from interfering with the free development of national commerce by imposing penalties on goods coming from other states in the union. These were and are, of course, very important policy functions, but they are essentially negative aspects of government and the break they represented with previous American governmental powers should not be exaggerated:

> The powers granted the new government reflected in part American experience with federalism under the British Empire and the Articles of Confederation, in part the Enlightenment belief in the negative state. The scope of federal authority was essentially that of the central governments under the old British Empire and under the Articles of Confederation. Experience had taught the statesmen of the revolutionary era that a central government could not function effectively without the right to tax and regulate commerce, and they now added these items to the grant of federal authority. Yet the federal government was still conceived of as having few other functions ...[7]

And if the governments of the individual states retained greater *rights* to legislate than the federal government, that does not mean that they actually used them in the positive pursuit of the public welfare, in the way that became increasingly common in the twentieth century.

In short, the demands upon governmental policy-making structures in 1787 were so few and relatively straightforward, that it was easier to live with a cumbersome policy-making process than it was to run the risk of a return to tyranny.

However, this should not be read as implying that the framers were not fully aware of the balance they were striking between open and efficient policy making. On the contrary, some of those who later campaigned most ardently for the ratification of the new Constitution were originally in favour of a much more co-ordinated and centralised policy-making process, at the expense of the openness

of the system. Thus, no less a constitutionalist than James Madison,
however much his position evolved later, originally proposed a
policy-making process in which the lower house of the legislature
would control both the upper house and the executive, since its
members would select the occupants of both the other institutions.
This was the scheme laid out in the so-called Virginia or Randolph
Plan, the authorship of which is usually attributed in great part to
Madison.[8] Moreover, this plan, which was the first working document of the Philadelphia Convention, also proposed to make the
states totally subservient to the federal government by empowering
the Congress 'to legislate in all cases to which the separate states
are incompetent, or in which the harmony of the United States may
be interrupted by the exercise of individual legislation ...'[9] As
Roche says, then, 'it should be reiterated that the Madison model
had no room either for the states or for ''the separation of powers'':
effectively *all* government power was vested in the national legislature.'[10] At one fell swoop, most of the structural problems of
policy incoherence would have been avoided, then as now. However,
other delegates, fearing that such arrangements might prove too
efficient for the political health of citizens and the smaller states,
were able to ensure the compromise that prevails largely unaltered
in formal terms to this day. This choice of legislative structures has
obvious implications for policy making: as John Lees wrote,

> The policy process, in Washington as in state and local government, is
> atomised and porous ... Government exists, in effect, not as a whole but
> as a collection of sub-governments who must try to obtain the maximum
> coordination possible in a system which establishes checks and balances
> but where the checks are more often visible and effective than the will
> and capacity to define policy goals or priorities and put them into
> effect.[11]

Or, as Duane Lockard paraphrased drily, the Constitution was
inspired by the sentiment that 'that government is best which has
the greatest difficult in doing anything.'[12]

However, for the next hundred years or so, the government was not
required to do a great deal more than the framers had envisaged.
True, the federal government, and especially the Supreme Court
under Chief Justice Marshall, ensured conditions under which
national commerce could flourish; and a line of thought from

Hamilton to McKinley, via Clay and Lincoln, urged federal government support for western expansion, the development of a transportation infrastructure and a centralised banking system. Nevertheless, there were few demands that the government intervene directly in the economy, other than to impose high protective tariffs, and little in the way of social legislation was urged. Between 1787 and the end of the nineteenth century, the ideologies of Jeffersonian Agrarianism, Jacksonian Liberalism and Social Darwinism successively and successfully militated against the development of the concept of positive government in the United States. Thus, in the last quarter of the nineteenth century, both Populist and socialist challenges to the prevailing minimalist vision of government were decisively rejected. Even at this late stage, William Graham Sumner, a leading disciple of Herbert Spencer, could proudly proclaim the conservative orthodoxy as follows: 'At bottom, there are two chief things with which government has to deal. They are, the property of men and the honour of women. These it has to defend against crime.'[13] As long as this negative concept of government prevailed, the policy-making process could function adequately since the less government tried to do, the less need there was to mobilise it. When legislation was required, however, the successive party systems which had evolved since 1787 were usually able to co-ordinate policy between the various institutions.

Thus, the real test of the constitutional framework of policy making did not come until there arose an irresistible demand that government should not merely protect society, but should also seek to change it. Positive activism on the part of the government was not at all what most of the framers had in mind when they designed the Constitution in such a way as to make legislation possible only when there was a broad consensus. For government activism required not simply much more frequent mobilisation of the policy-making process, it also required agreed solutions in policy areas that are usually characterised by ideological conflict.

Of course, positive activism did not replace laissez-faire overnight as the predominant public philosophy in the United States: rather it advanced in fits and starts from the late nineteenth century onwards. But it is clear that the first sustained period of activist policy making came during the Progressive Era, roughly from 1900–1920.[14] Due to a combination of gross political corruption, the abuse of corporate power and the dire living and working conditions of the mass of Americans, government at all levels pursued policies of reform which heralded a new faith in the beneficial power of public policy. And indeed, in partly vindicating this faith, the Progressive movement demonstrated that the constitutional system of policy making was capable of producing vigorous and, to a lesser extent, effective governmental action. The mechanisms of constitutional amendment were invoked to both alter political structures and to advance new policies: thus, the Seventeenth Amendment introduced the direct election of United States Senators, the Nineteenth Amendment enfranchised women and the Sixteenth Amendment permitted the introduction of income tax, with all the implications which that has for funding new public policies. Furthermore, whilst the states took the lead in enacting social legislation aimed at improving the living and working conditions of the toiling classes, the federal government also passed a series of remedial measures, ranging from the Pure Food and Drug Act of 1906 to the Warehouse Act of 1916. The latter, designed to raise the income of farmers, hinted at a new direction in government intervention in the economy, although in the Progressive Era, the main effort in this regard was the attempt to bring under regulatory control the giant corporations and monopolies that were a threat to both economic and political liberties. And here, the record of governmental policy making is not too impressive. To take but one example, President Wilson's attempt to actually break up the monopolies, through the Clayton Bill, faltered in the face of conservative opposition in Congress. As a result, Wilson lost interest in it and the Clayton Act of 1914 emerged as a more useful weapon against labour unions than the trusts, since the former were not exempted from the definition of a trust. Meanwhile, Wilson switched to the idea of dealing with corporate abuses through the medium of a federal regulatory commission. However, the Federal Trade Commission Act of 1914 was not only in part designed by businessmen, but the Commission itself was rendered largely ineffective through being staffed with friends of business. Thus, even sympathetic historians concede that 'twenty years after the enactment of the Wilsonian anti-trust legislation ... the trusts were as numerous and monopolies as powerful as ever.'[15] The history of governmental anti-trust activities under the Progressive Presidents demonstrated that as long as big business was firmly entrenched within Congress, no President, however strong his popular mandate, would succeed with his policies towards the monopolies. Here, then, was a classic instance of the way in which the separation of powers thwarted effective policy making.

Nevertheless, the Progressive Movement also had its significant successes in governmental policy making and indicated that the positive state did not lie outside the reach of the constitutional framework. This was confirmed during the New Deal in the 1930s. There was certainly no shortage of legislative–executive co-operation during the first administration of President Franklin D. Roosevelt. A veritable flood of legislation was enacted, much of it on the initiative of the executive branch and much of it breaking new ground in the traditions of American political economy. For example, the National Industrial Recovery Act of 1933 was based on the notion of government planning of the economy, and the Social Security Act of 1935 permanently established the responsibility of the federal government for the welfare of the aged and unemployed. However, it has also been recognised that the plethora of policies which emerged as a response to the worst-ever economic depression in American history, was often mutually contradictory in principle. As Jim Potter wrote of the legislation passed during Roosevelt's legendary first One Hundred Days in office,

> The measures abounded in contradictions, the actions of the right hand often being nullified by those of the left one. Any search for consistency will be in vain: all that can be found is a conviction that the Federal Government should be active together with a vague notion that policy ought to aim at helping the underdog.[16]

These contradictions partly account for the failure of the New Deal to produce full economic recovery, yet it is not clear that the policy-making process was a causal factor of these weaknesses. True, the Supreme Court did oppose and strike down some of the most important legislative elements of the New Deal; yet, by 1937, the Court had recognised and given its constitutional blessing to the new positive state and thus removed the judicial barrier erected by the framers to interventionist governmental policy making in socio-economic matters. In other words, in the crisis of the Great Depression, the three main branches of the federal government were eventually able to agree to a new concept of policy making. More-over, the states had conceded so much policy-making competence to the federal government that the principle of federalism would no longer constitute a serious block on many of the most important socio-economic issues.

However, there was a major flaw in the new policy-making process engendered by the New Deal: the changes had not been formally recognised in the constitutional framework. Roosevelt had exploited his own inimitable political skills to effect changed attitudes to public policy making and, of course, had operated during a desperate crisis. As Godfrey Hodgson pointed out, by failing to bring the Constitution into line with the new *de facto* realities of policy-making, Roosevelt bequeathed a difficult legacy to his successors, who would have to operate in normal political conditions and who would almost certainly not possess FDR's remarkable talents.[17] Yet the public would continue to look to the federal government and, in particular, Presidential leadership, to solve the nation's problems with effective policies.

In a real sense, then, since 1945, the United States government has had to work with a formal constitutional framework that has failed to keep pace with the policy demands and expectations of American society. Yet it is precisely in this same period that the development of the national positive state accelerated at an impressive speed:

> The central development in American domestic politics in the last quarter century has been the vast and virtually incomprehensible growth in the range and complexity of activities regulated by government, especially the federal government ... We need reminding that extensive federal regulation of such matters as racial and sexual discrimination, education, health care, water and air pollution, urban and consumer affairs, and national economic development, to name only a few, either did not exist or were in early developmental stages two short decades ago.[18]

Those hostile to these changes have turned to hyperbole to express their outrage at what they perceive as this betrayal of the values of the Founding Fathers. For example, one conservative wrote in 1980 that 'the size of government in the US today is authoritarian, and more so than any English king. In terms of the ideas of liberty in America in 1776, the alternative of George III is not very attractive. But compared to the indigenous colonial power that Washington has become, George III might be an improvement.'[19] Nevertheless, greatly centralised and expanded policy making is the reality of American government today, the Reagan administration notwithstanding.[20]

Thus, more than ever, it would seem, the constitutional system has been put under severe strain by the policy-making demands on the positive state. And in the remainder of this chapter, we will examine how well it has coped with the making of policy in an area in many ways typical of these new responsibilities – that of women's rights.

In one sense, the issue of women's rights is not new at all. But from the Seneca Falls Declaration in 1848 until the adoption of the Nineteenth Amendment in 1920, the main focus of attention was women's suffrage and, with this achieved, the issue receded from public debate until the 1960s. Since then, however, there has been considerable government action on issues of women's rights and analysis of these highlights the possibilities and advantages, as well as the limitations, of the fragmented American policy-making process. The major limitations are obvious: first, with so many institutions taking initiatives in this field without prior agreement or co-ordination, there is no coherent overall strategy to the various policies enacted. Indeed, in some cases, one institution has deliberately sought to undermine and counter the policy of another. Second, although progressive women's pressure groups have been able to influence the actions of certain parts of the governmental structure, they have failed to move others and have sometimes 'lost' these to opposing pressure groups. The outcome has not been a general governmental policy on women which is rational and internally coherent, but an assortment of policies which form the site of a continuing ever-shifting political and ideological struggle. In a unitary state, where the legislative and executive powers are effectively synonymous, as in the United Kingdom, it is possible for the government to throw its determining weight to one or other of the opposing groups. In the United States, however, the design of the Constitution makes this extremely difficult and unlikely, except where there is a very broad consensus: in which case, of course, there is actually little pressure on the policy-making process in the first place. Thus, as we shall see, a vital factor in determining how smoothly and effectively the policy-making process performs is the level of political contentiousness involved in any particular issue. And again, if this seems an obvious observation, it should be remembered that it is not the case to anything like the same extent in other political systems. For example, in the last decade in the United Kingdom, Mrs. Thatcher's government has been able to impose its will on a broad range of contentious issues, simply because it has had control of pretty much all the government institutions with policy-making powers. During the same period, President Reagan, with far greater electoral support than Mrs. Thatcher, was permitted to advance his similar agenda only in piecemeal fashion.

Thus, what the fragmented governmental structures of the Constitution yield is incremental policy-making: rather than fitting together to form a whole picture, like pieces of a jigsaw puzzle, various government actions are often ad hoc responses to particular problems, with little thought being given to how each action will mesh with the others in finding a solution to the broader problem. As Charles Jones put it:

> Whether or not one supports incrementalism as the way to make decisions, it does seem descriptive of what normally happens in this political system. Certainly it occurs more often than does the so-called comprehensive-rational approach in which the dominant values are identified, all proposals are studied for their effect, and the choice is made on the most rational bases possible.[21]

And if incrementalism is the reality in the United States, it is for a very good reason, as Fred Harris says: 'The incremental method is the most popular approach in government, largely because it stirs up the least opposition and is the easiest way to build majority coalitions for action.'[22] Here, then, we arrive at the most important of all the links between the constitutional framework and the nature and substance of policy making in the United States: fragmentation demands coalition building which, in turn, means compromise and incremental change of a non-radical kind.

However, if fragmentation makes decisive change difficult, it also entails at least one distinct advantage, namely, that the existence of multiple centres of power provides numerous points of entry into the policy-making process for groups whose political influence is too weak to sustain a frontal assault on the whole system. In particular, it affords disadvantaged groups some opportunity to coax a governmental response to their needs, even if the policy results are far from what is ideally required. Governmental action on women's rights in the last twenty-five years has revealed all of these characteristics of the fragmented policy-making process: different agencies taking policy initiatives independently of each other; different agencies opposing each other's policies; various pressure-groups exerting conflicting influence on different institutions; and incremental and non-radical policies which nevertheless constitute very important steps towards new social goals.

The first such major step towards establishing a policy on American women strongly reflected the development of the positive state. Without coming under strong pressure from any interest group, the executive branch of the federal government, partly in response to the findings of a public-oriented think-tank, sought to prompt new policies. The think-tank was the Ford Foundation, which, in 1957, published a study of women in the workplace, entitled *Womanpower*. The report recognised and encouraged the trend of women entering the workforce in increasing numbers, though it eschewed any radical or feminist ideas. The new Kennedy administration soon took up the policy challenge by establishing a Presidential Commission on the Status of Women. When it reported in 1963, the Commission made clear that it did not propose fundamental changes in the status of women by opposing the Equal Rights Amendment and by stressing that women's primary role would remain that of wife and mother. However, 'despite the failure to take a feminist position, the President's Commission on Women nevertheless constituted a major turning-point in the evolution of the modern women's movement. It was the first effort on the part of the Federal government to address the question of women in American society.'[23] Moreover, it did help to produce new policies aimed at ending discrimination against women in the workplace, most immediately the Equal Pay Act of 1963. The Act did not meet with strong opposition, partly because it attacked the most blatant of discriminations against women and partly because certain established pressure groups believed that it advanced their own self-interest: labour unions thought it would help prevent low-paid women workers from replacing male workers.[24] Its passage was also made easier because it was limited in scope, both in terms of the number of employees it covered and, more importantly, in its reach as far as the root causes of women's low wages were concerned, for as Jo Freeman put it, 'then, as now, equal pay was irrelevant without equal job opportunity.'[25] Furthermore, by mandating only equal pay for the same work, rather than for broadly comparable work or work of comparable worth, the Equal Pay Act was never going to put women on an economic par with men. And indeed, such have been the results: for example, in 1984, female college graduates earned $20,257 a year on average, whilst male college graduates averaged $31,487. In fact, male high school dropouts earned almost as much as women graduates, averaging $19,120.[26]

On the other hand, the United States government did manage to get equal pay legislation onto its statute books seven years before the United Kingdom and, as far as it was intended to go, it has worked tolerably well in improving women's wages. For example, in the first decade of its implementation, the Act was responsible for the recovery of some $84 million in back-pay alone.[27] The policy has also been supported at the state level, with most states passing similar legislation to the federal act, and by the executive branch of the federal government. What the Equal Pay Act suggests then, is that the policy-making process works as well in the United States as elsewhere when the policy is perceived as moderate and incremental: thus, the legislation was given a further moderate boost in the 1972 Education Amendments Act when the coverage of the equal pay policy was extended to administrative, executive and professional positions.

One of the principal features of incrementalism is, of course, that policy makers are never sure about how far their efforts will lead. It is rather like construction workers building the ground floor of a home, without the architects having decided whether it is to be a bungalow or an apartment block. And the Kennedy Commission on Women certainly had unforeseen consequences. In the first place, the Commission's Report spurred the creation of similar commissions in each of the fifty states. Then, in 1966, at the Third Annual Conference of these state commissions, the organisers prevented the submission of a formal motion calling for stronger government action on sex discrimination. In protest, the dissenters formed the National Organization of Women and a host of other new women's groups soon followed, thus creating what became known as the women's rights movement.[28] This was an historic development in that there now existed in Washington, D.C. a network of groups with the skills and resources to make persistent and wide-ranging demands upon the policy-making process. Yet such an important development was neither planned nor foreseen by government.

An even more remarkable policy-making surprise was the inclusion of a prohibition against sex discrimination in employment in Title VII of the Civil Rights Act of 1964. The Act was orginally devised as a means to combat race discrimination and, as usual with such efforts, southern members of Congress did their best to render the legislation useless. However, this time, in the emotional aftermath of President Kennedy's assassination, it seemed as if a strong bill would be forthcoming. Consequently, in a desperate attempt to scupper the bill through ridicule, Representative Howard K. Smith of Virginia introduced an amendment adding a prohibition against sex discrimination. The idea, almost unbelievable twenty years later, was that many members of the House would find the amendment so ludicrous and undesirable that they would rather vote down the whole bill than see it pass into law. And indeed, many liberal members opposed the provision at first because they shared Smith's view, if not his hope, that the amendment made the civil rights bill considerably more difficult to pass. But President Johnson let it be known that he wanted the amendment left in,[29] its supporters in the House worked hard for it and the Civil Rights Act of 1964 was passed with the 'joke' amendment included. Its status was not even taken seriously by the director of the Equal Employment Opportunity Commission, which had been created to enforce the provisions of the Act: he described it in derisory terms and called it a 'fluke'.[30]

In one sense, it was indeed a fluke, although it might be more profitably thought of as a graphic illustration of the almost infinitely manipulable nature of the legislative process in the United States. For advocates of rational policy making, it should rank as the nadir in modern times, for what is undoubtedly the major item of federal legislation on women's equality to date was enacted for reasons having little to do with women and without serious intention of doing anything to improve their condition. Thus, by the mid-1960s, the United States had not so much devised a public policy on women, as found itself in the possession of one. Consequently, the interpretation and implementation of the policy was riddled with even more imponderables than usual. The courts, for example, could hardly be expected to find much guidance as to Congressional intent by perusing the legislative history of the act! And how could the executive branch, in the form of the E.E.O.C., vigorously enforce a provision to which the legislature had given such little thought? It is hardly surprising if, in these circumstances, the Supreme Court has failed to review sex discrimination allegations with quite the same strict scrutiny that it has used in race discrimination cases;[31] or that E.E.O.C. enforcement of Title VII has left a lot to be desired. As the history of the Sears case demonstrates, neither judges, E.E.O.C. officials nor even feminist academics agree on the nature of the problem to be tackled by Title VII, never mind the appropriate means of enforcement.[32] At stake in the Sears case was the fundamental question of whether women fail to take up certain types of jobs, specifically here, high commission sales jobs, because employers discriminate against them or because women prefer to steer clear of such jobs because they possess different values and aspirations than men. In other words, it was a version of the same question which lies at the root of all discussion of sex discrimination policy, namely, to what extent there are differences between women and men that do not result from patriarchy and that should not, therefore, be the object of remedial policies. But Congress did not only fail to reach a conclusion on this, it failed to have even a full, serious discussion on the matter. Undoubtedly the separation of powers makes it easier for legislators to behave so irresponsibly, since the blame for bad policy can always be off-loaded onto those independent branches of government who are charged with its implementation. This option is not so readily available in political systems where the legislative and executive branches are inextricably linked.

Nevertheless, policy making on women's issues was transformed by these developments of the mid-1960s. The government had registered the need for new policies and the women's rights movement was able to identify problems, provide information on them and draft legislative proposals to deal with them. But if the women's movement can generally be said to have been quite successful in doing this, it is only because the movement has limited its legislative ambitions and has been willing to compromise on its values. In particular, women's rights activists appear to have understood the link between the strategic and ideological biases of the political system and have tailored their demands accordingly. Gelb and Palley assert that 'feminists in politics have conformed to both the scope and bias of the system',[33] taking a reformist and incrementalist approach to change and being willing to form coalitions where tactically advantageous. In one sense, Gelb and Palley argue, the women's rights movement has become rather like the policy-making process itself: 'though there is an absence of overall 'strategizing' and planning within the movement, it seems that the ad hoc nature of policy development is particularly well-suited to constraints determined by the structure of the political system, a system characterized itself by incrementalism and shifting policy concerns.'[34] Within the confines of such an approach, it can be said that the policy-making system has been able to respond to the demands placed upon it by changing socio-economic realities. The women's rights movement has been able to exploit the one great advantage of the American policy-making process, namely, the numerous access points which it makes available to organised groups. The fragmentation produced by the Constitution of 1787, which militates against comprehensive policy making, conversely enables groups to select between different institutions with policy-making powers: if one institution fails to respond adequately, another may be tried. So whereas in a unitary system, where there exists only one major channel for policy-making, those making policy demands are playing an all-or-nothing game, there is the possibility in the United States to turn a loss in one institution into a victory in another. For example, in the early part of this century, the organised women's movement abandoned a state-by-state approach to gaining the vote, which had produced only meagre results, and instead opted for a national movement aimed at securing the vote through constitutional amendment. More recently, when the Hyde Amendment, which cut off federal funds for abortions for indigent women, was passed by Congress, feminists could try to recoup their loss at the state level and, indeed, they achieved some important successes there.[35] Of course, as we shall see in our discussion of abortion policy, this is a sword that cuts both ways; and opposing groups have the same opportunities to modify their defeats at the expense of the victors.

Nevertheless, despite some setbacks, women have won important, if not necessarily outright, victories from all three branches of the federal government. Presidents have used the independent authority of the executive branch, such as Johnson's Executive Order 11375, issued in 1967, which prohibited sex discrimination by employers under federal contract and also led to the creation of the Federal Women's Program.[36] In other cases, the bureaucracy has been pressed into generally effective action to implement the legislative intentions of Congress. This was the case with the Department of Health, Education and Welfare regulations implementing

Title IX of the 1972 Education Amendments Act, which prohibited sex discrimination in most educational programmes receiving federal funds.[37] Although the legislation had passed with little difficulty, some at HEW were wary of forceful implementation of a policy that favoured a relatively new and untried 'client'. And the fact that draft regulations had to be re-submitted to Congress for approval prior to implementation, meant that Congressional opponents of the bill could yet seek to weaken its impact. It eventually took three years for HEW to implement the act. Anne Costain, who traced its history, has described all the difficulties of mobilising the legislative-bureaucratic policy-making processes:

> New interests like those pushing for an end to sexual discrimination in education must get legislation through Congress; block congressional efforts to amend or negate this legislation through subsequent bills; stimulate a skeptical, if not unfriendly, bureaucracy to act; and, in the case of educational policy, thwart congressional efforts to delay enforcement further through concurrent resolution rejecting agency regulations.[38]

From this example, one can see that the policy-making system can be made to respond on new policy issues, though it may do so only when skilful and well-resourced pressure groups sustain a vigorous lobbying effort.

Other major Congressional policies on women's rights include the Equal Credit Opportunity Act of 1974 and the Pregnancy Disability Act of 1978. The latter is particularly interesting from a policy-making perspective, since it was partly intended to negate a decision of the United States Supreme Court. In the case of General Electric v. Gilbert in 1976,[39] the Court had ruled that Title VII of the Civil Rights Act of 1964 was not infringed by employers who denied various employment benefits – such as seniority rights – to employees absent with pregnancy-related disabilities. A bill was introduced into Congress to correct this and, despite opposition from influential business interests, including the US Chamber of Commerce and the National Association of Manufacturers, it passed quite smoothly through the Senate. In the House, however, the women's rights movement had to pay the price of its coalition tactics, when one of the pro-life groups supporting the bill insisted on an amendment exempting elective abortions from compulsory medical coverage of the new law. After protracted resistance, the pro-choice groups accepted modified anti-abortion clauses in order to secure passage of the Act. Of course, for many, the anti-abortion amendment contradicted their broader policy goal of enabling women to choose to pursue a career on an equal footing with men. But it is precisely that kind of policy coherence which has to be sacrificed in order to secure incremental progress in the American policy-making system. Thus, 'the final bill, other than the anti-abortion language, does represent a sweeping victory for feminist forces.'[40]

In spite of its decision in the Gilbert case, the Supreme Court too has responded to the task of devising appropriate policies to promote a new status for American women: at least, in most cases. Acting largely through the due process and equal protection clauses of the Constitution, the Court has struck down a wide range of anachronisms in public policy that confined women to an inferior social and legal position. For example, in its first such case, Reed v. Reed, in 1971,[41] the Court decided that states could not give automatic preference to men over women as administrators of estates. And other decisions ended sex discrimination in jury selection, in benefits for the spouses of government employees and in the legal age for buying alcohol.[42] In the view of one authoritative commentator, Judge Ruth Bader Ginsberg, 'the gender classification decisions of the 1970s have a spectacular aspect.'[43]

These various judicial decisions, legislative enactments and executive measures constitute a range of policy action that goes some way in refuting the allegation that the policy-making structures of the Constitution of 1787 are incapable of responding to the policy responsibilities of the positive state in the late twentieth century. However, as the consideration of our final policy issue will demonstrate, the system can only go so far before it begins to descend into confusion and incoherence. We have seen that where the generation of new policies involves developments that are essentially uncontroversial, the policy-making process is capable of intelligent and meaningful response. When, however, as in the case of abortion, the policy issue engenders bitter policy antagonisms, the system proves too unco-ordinated to effect a policy resolution. Certainly at the time of writing, abortion policy in the United States is something of a shambles and there is little likelihood that things will improve in the near future.

The evolution of abortion policy in the United States over the last twenty years has brought into play all the major lines of fragmentation that the Founding Fathers built into the Constitution – federalism, the separation of powers and checks and balances. Prior to 1973, abortion had been the sole province of state policy makers and, as more liberal attitudes to abortion emerged in the 1960s, some states reformed their abortion laws to make the procedure more freely available. The result was that some American women, like those in New York and California, had the right to this most fundamental aspect of reproductive freedom, whilst others, in Texas, for example, did not, even where pregnancy had resulted from rape. It was hardly surprising, then, that in this age of positive national government there should be some attempt to devise a national abortion policy that would standardise rights and freedoms for all women in the United States. However, neither President nor Congress was eager to take this tack, partly out of respect for federalism and partly because it was becoming the kind of controversy that many elected politicians prefer to avoid: highly emotional, unsusceptible to compromise and capable of threatening the re-election prospects of any politician brave enough to take a firm stance.

Pro-choice activists turned to the Courts and in 1973, in the case of Roe v. Wade,[44] the Supreme Court duly established a new and national policy on abortion. The Court determined that women had a constitutional right to have an abortion which left legislatures with few regulatory powers: in effect, women were free to have an elective abortion up until the sixth month of pregnancy and a therapeutic abortion at any stage.[45] The Roe decision was clearly a sweeping policy innovation and the major victory to date of the women's movement: consequently, it set off the great abortion controversy that continues to this day and which has also brought with it considerable policy ambiguities and contradictions.

Congress, under great pressure from anti-abortion activists, passed the Hyde Amendment in 1976, cutting off Medicaid funds for abortions, whether medically necessary or not.[46] Four years later, in something of a retreat from its Roe decision, the Court upheld the constitutionality of the Hyde Amendment, whilst maintaining that the fundamental right to an abortion for all women was not thereby infringed.[47] However, constitutional logic aside, the Hyde Amendment created a massive anomaly in abortion policy by trying to prevent poor women from exercising their right, whilst doing nothing to hinder abortion for the better-off. On a matter of such basic concern to the psychological and physical health of women, and indeed to their families, this anomaly in abortion policy is nothing less than grotesque.

In the 1980s, the Court's abortion policy also came into confrontation with that of the executive branch, whose incumbent, Ronald Reagan, had sought and won the electoral support of anti-abortion sympathisers. Although the president gave considerable rhetorical backing to the anti-abortion movement, he failed to give a substantial legislative lead on the subject. On the other hand, he did use his power to nominate new Supreme Court justices to attempt the creation of a majority on the Court which is ready to reverse the Roe decision.[48]

In the meantime, many states and local governments have sought to undermine the Court's policy by hedging the right to an abortion with practical obstacles. For example, the state of Pennsylvania emulated the city of Akron, Ohio, in passing legislation that was designed to put great psychological pressure on women wanting abortions, by compelling their doctors to inform them that abortion is the taking of a human life. And the mayor of St. Louis simply banned all non-therapeutic abortions from being performed in the city's hospitals.

Quite obviously, the fragmentation of the policy-making structures in the United States has permitted partly contradictory policies to be adopted by different centres of power. And, even allowing for the understandably controversial nature of the abortion issue, it is an adverse comment on the American political system that it has been unable to produce a policy resolution whilst allowing debate to continue – as has been the case in the United Kingdom, for example. Thus, the 1988 Alton bill, seeking to amend Great Britain's 1967 Abortion Act by reducing the limit within which abortions were permitted, provoked both heated debate and a clear-cut resolution, which left all British women with the same legal rights.

The empirical evidence from the issue of women's rights is a mixed one with regard to the contemporary viability of the policy-making structures established by the Constitution of 1787. On the one hand, there have been important policy innovations and, even if these are viewed as far from ideal, they easily stand comparison with developments in other countries with different policy-making systems.

Furthermore, the fragmented nature of policy-making in the

United States has at least given women's rights activists several alternative arenas in which to advance their cause. In that sense, there is justification for a certain optimism about policy making in the United States. On the other hand, the innate tendency in the Constitution towards compromise and contradiction in policy making certainly makes satisfactory policy solutions more difficult to devise and implement; and this is particularly so when the policy problem is controversial and the solutions put forward numerous. Abortion is precisely the kind of fundamental policy issue in which contradiction and incoherence is least tolerable. This is not to suggest that a blanket ban on abortions would be preferable to the current situation, but simply that where compromise on policy is politically unavoidable, it is better that this should be incorporated within uniform laws for all women, as in Britain, rather than in multiple and unreconciled laws which leave women insecure and unequal in their fundamental constitutional rights.

As stated earlier, however, the structure of policy making is only one factor affecting policy outcomes in liberal democracies. More important are economic inequalities that produce severe imbalances of political power and ideologies that obscure some new lines of policy from view. Thus, the resolution of the abortion conflict lies ultimately in the realm of ideology rather than in any particular configuration of policy-making institutions. As it stands at the moment, the policy-making process in the United States is more open than in most other countries, but also, perhaps, less efficient than in some. The alternative would seem to be to allow unitary, centralised, party-based governments to impose their will, regardless of alternative viewpoints and policy options. If that is the choice, there seems to me to be little reason to move away from the policy-making values of the framers of the Constitution of 1787; for with its proven capacity for growth and change, it would appear as well equipped as any to facilitate present and future policy requirements. And those who seek radical changes in American policy face far greater obstacles than institutional arrangements.

NOTES

1 D. L. Robinson (ed.), *Reforming American Government: The Bicentennial Papers of the Committee on the Constitutional System*, Boulder, Westview, 1985.
2 C. E. Lindblom, *The Policy-Making Process*, Englewood Cliffs, Prentice-Hall, 2nd edn, 1980, p. 7.

3 M. Levin, 'Ask not what our presidents are "really like"; ask what we and our political institutions are like: a call for a politics of institutions, not men' in W. D. Burnham and M. W. Weinberg (eds), *American Politics and Public Policy*, Cambridge, MIT Press, 1978, p. 116.
4 And the same applies to attempts to desegregate Southern schools in the wake of the Supreme Court's decision in *Brown v. Board of Education* in 1954: see, for example, R. Wolters, *The Burden of Brown: Thirty Years of School Desegregation*, Knoxville, University of Tennessee Press, 1984.
5 I. Sharkansky and D. Van Meter, *Policy and Politics in American Government*, New York, McGraw-Hill, 1975, p. 330.
6 A. H. Kelly and W. A. Harbison, *The American Constitution: Its Origins and Development*, New York, Norton, 5th edn, 1976, especially ch. 4.
7 *Ibid.*, pp. 155–6.
8 J. P. Roche, 'The Founding Fathers: a reform caucus in action' in Gordon S. Wood (ed.), *The Confederation and the Constitution: The Critical Issues*, Washington, D.C., University Press of America. 1979, pp. 113–36.
9 'Debates in the Federal Convention of 1787 as reported by James Madison' in P. Smith, *The Constitution: A Documentary and Narrative History*, New York, Morrow Quill, 1980, pp. 96–8.
10 Roche, 'The Founding Fathers', p. 128.
11 J. Lees, *The Political System of the United States*, London, Faber and Faber, 3rd edn, 1983, p. 299.
12 D. Lockard, *The Perverted Priorities of American Politics*, New York, Macmillan, 2nd edn, 1976, p. 33.
13 William Graham Sumner, quoted in C. Rossiter, *Conservatism in America: the Thankless Persuasion*, New York, Random House, 2nd edn, rev., 1972, p. 138.
14 See, for example, A. S. Link and R. L. McCormick, *Progressivism*, Arlington Heights, Harlan Davidson, 1983.
15 S. E. Morison, H. S. Commager and W. E. Leuchtenberg, *The Growth of the American Republic*, London, OUP, 6th edn, 1969, p. 347. See also G. Kolko, *The Triumph of Conservatism: a Reinterpretation of American History, 1900–1916*, New York, The Free Press, 1963; and A. S. Link, *Woodrow Wilson and the Progressive Era, 1900–1917*, New York, Harper and Row, 1954.
16 J. Potter, *The American Economy Between the World Wars*, London, Macmillan, 1974, p. 124.
17 G. Hodgson, *All Things To All Men: The False Promise of the American Presidency from Franklin D. Roosevelt to Ronald Reagan*, New York, Touchstone, 1980, ch. 2.
18 S. C. Halpern, 'On the imperial judiciary and comparative institutional development and power in America', S. C. Halpern and C. M. Lamb, *Supreme Court Activism and Restraint*, Lexington, Lexington Books, 1982, pp. 221–47, 223.
19 J. T. Bennett and M. H. Johnson, *The Political Economy of Federal Government Growth: 1959–1978*, College Station, Texas A. and M. University Center for Education and Research in Free Enterprise, 1980, p. xi.
20 J. E. Chubb, 'Federalism and the bias for centralization', J. E. Chubb and P. E. Petersen (eds), *The New Direction in American Politics*, Washington, D.C., The Brookings Institution, 1985, pp. 273–306.
21 C. O. Jones, *An Introduction to the Study of Public Policy*, North Scituate, Duxbury Press, 2nd edn, 1977, p. 7.
22 F. R. Harris, *America's Democracy: The Ideal and the Reality*, Glenview, Scott, Foresman and Co., 2nd edn, 1983, p. 545.
23 C. N. Degler, *At Odds: Women and the Family in America from the Revolution to the Present*, New York, Oxford University Press, 1980, p. 442.
24 J. Freeman, *The Politics of Women's Liberation*, New York, Longman, 1975, p. 176.

25 *Ibid.*, p. 176.
26 'Women's status rises but pay lags behind', *International Herald Tribune*, 3 August 1987, p. 5.
27 Freeman, *Politics of Women's Liberation*, p. 177.
28 J. Gelb and M. L. Palley, *Women and Public Policies*, Princeton, Princeton University Press, 1982, ch. 2.
29 Degler, *At Odds*, p. 442.
30 Freeman, *Politics of Women's Liberation*, p. 54.
31 A. E. Freedman, 'Sex equality, sex differences and the Supreme Court', *Yale Law Journal*, 92, 1983, pp. 913–68; R. B. Ginsberg, 'The Burger Court's grappling with sex discrimination' in V. Blasi (ed.), *The Burger Court: The Counter-Revolution That Wasn't*, New Haven, Yale University Press, 1983, pp. 132–56.
32 R. Milkman, 'Women's history and the Sears case', *Feminist Studies*, 12, 1986, pp. 375–400.
33 Gelb and Palley, *Women and Public Policies*, pp. 4–5.
34 *Ibid.*, p. 38.
35 R. Tatalovich and B. W. Daynes, *The Politics of Abortion: A Study of Community Conflict in Public Policymaking*, New York, Praeger, 1981, p. 203.
36 I. Tinker (ed.), *Women in Washington: Advocates for Public Policy*, Beverley Hills, Sage, 1983, p. 11.
37 A. N. Costain, 'Eliminating sex discrimination in education: lobbying for implementation of Title IX' in M. L. Palley and M. B. Preston (eds), *Race, Sex and Policy Problems*, Lexington, Lexington Books, 1979, pp. 3–11.
38 *Ibid.*, p. 4.
39 429 US 125.
40 Gelb and Palley, *Women and Public Policies*, p. 165.
41 404 US 71.
42 Respectively, *Taylor v. Louisianna*, 419 US 522 (1975); *Frontiero v. Richardson*, 411 US 677 (1973); and *Craig v. Boren*, 429 US 190 (1976).
43 Blasi, *The Burger Court*, p. 151.
44 410 US 113.
45 There are many books and articles dealing with the abortion issue and the Supreme Court's role in it, but among the most useful are K. Luker, *Abortion and the Politics of Motherhood*, Berkeley, University of California Press, 1984; N. Ford, 'The evolution of a Constitutional right to an abortion', *Journal of Legal Medicine*, 4, 1983, pp. 271–322; P. J. Conover and V. Gray, *Feminism and the New Right: Conflict over the American Family*, New York, Praeger, 1983; and Tatlovich and Daynes, *Politics of Abortion*.
46 There were exceptions to the ban on the use of Medicaid funds, but even these varied from year to year, since the Amendment had to be passed each year and, therefore, renegotiated. In all its forms, the Hyde Amendment exempted abortions where the mother's life would otherwise be endangered: K. A. Petersen, 'The public funding of abortion services: comparative developments in the United States and Australia', *International and Comparative Law Quarterly*, 33, 1984, pp. 158–80.
47 *Harris v. McCrae*, 48 US 297.
48 To date, President Reagan nominated Sandra Day O'Connor, Antonin Scalia, Robert Bork, Douglas Ginsburg and Anthony Kennedy, all of whom are considered to be critical of the Roe decision.